Vera
Lex

Journal of the International Natural Law Society

New Series Volume 6, Numbers 1&2　　　　　Winter 2005

CONTRIBUTORS
Address all submissions and correspondence to The Editor, VERA LEX, Pace University, Department of Philosophy & Religious Studies, 1 Pace Plaza, New York, NY 10038. Please send two copies of the paper submitted. Include adequate margins, double space everything (text, notes, works cited, quotations). Use U.S. spelling and punctuation style, (e.g. periods inside quotation marks; "double quotes" for opening and closing quotations). The University of Chicago Manual of Style, 13th Edition, is to be consulted regarding matters of style. Notes are to be numbered consecutively (in Arabic numerals) and placed at the bottom of the page.

SUBSCRIBERS
VERA LEX is published annually by Pace University Press, 41 Park Row, Room 1510, New York, NY 10038. Subscription price: $40. Please send all subscription inquiries to: PaceUP@services.pace.edu

INDEXING AND ABSTRACTING
VERA LEX is indexed in *Philosopher's Index*.
Copyright © 2005 by Pace University Press. Permission is required to reprint an article or part of an article.

VERA LEX, the journal of the International Natural Law Society, was established to communicate and dialogue on the subject of natural law and natural right, to introduce natural law philosophy into the mainstream of contemporary thought, and to strengthen the current revived interest in the discussion of morals and law and advance its historical research.

Why do we use a shell (*Nautilus pomplilus Linnaeus*) to symbolize *vera lex*? The logarithmic spiraling and overlapping chambers of the shell are endless. They suggest a patterned development and evolution that, by its radial and circular design, never comes to an end. This means that the shell is at once specific and real, while its form, like law, is abstract and ideal.

The pattern of a shell is, like good law, uniform, regular and reliable. It can therefore be anticipated and known. The pattern of a shell is balanced, like justice. *Una iustitia*.

A shell is a biological being. Like law, it has life and dynamic. It grows. (There is an average of thirty growth lines per chamber, one for every day in the lunar cycle, suggesting that a new chamber is put down each lunar month and a new growth line each day, thus recording two different natural rhythms, lunar and solar.)

The shell is a universal and common object known to everyone. A shell is not soft tissue easily destroyed. And yet, like liberty, it is fragile in certain respects if stepped on with an iron boot. It has to be guarded with vigilance or it is crushed.

In every shell lives a nautilus. If the shell is law, the nautilus (snail) is a person—it is alive—person and law. Their destinies, like person and law, are interdependent.

Vera Lex

leges innumerae, una iustitia

CONTENTS

NEW SERIES VOLUME 6, NUMBERS 1 & 2   WINTER 2005

Editor's Note

This issue of *Vera Lex* celebrates two twenty-fifth anniversaries: the International Natural Law Society (founded in 1979) published the inaugural issue of *Vera Lex* in 1980 and, in the same year, John Finnis's now classic *Natural Law and Natural Rights* was first in print. Both events served to reintroduce natural law theory to a philosophical and legal community beleaguered by positivism and dizzied by the Saint Vitus dance of postmodern dilettantes.

When Virginia Black founded the Natural Law Society, she did so to provide a contemporary voice for a venerable tradition in philosophy and legal theory that at that time received little serious attention from academic philosophers and legal scholars. When John Finnis published his seminal work in natural law he did so, presumably, to address contemporary concerns that many thought were anomalous within traditional natural law theory.

Twenty-five years later the natural law tradition has regained prestige and prominence both inside and outside the academy; *Vera Lex* (Virginia Black) and, more so, John Finnis are responsible for this successful revival. It is fitting (even prescient) that the last issue of *Vera Lex* under Professor Black's editorship (vol. XV, 1995; 89 - 92) published a talk by John Finnis, "The Foundations of Human Rights," given at the Law School of the University of Navarra in Pamplona, Spain.

Praise and gratitude go to Professor Peter Widulski for bringing together under one cover today's leading scholars on natural law and expert commentators on the work of Professor John Finnis. Peter's editorial skills made my work that much easier and making deadline that much more certain.

As editor, I am greatly pleased with this valuable collection of essays and certain they will go far in advancing scholarship in natural law theory.

RLC
NYC
Summer 2005

PREFACE

In *Natural Law and Natural Rights* (1980), John Finnis did for the tradition of natural law theory what his great teacher, H.L.A. Hart, had done twenty years earlier in *The Concept of Law* for the tradition of legal positivism. He revitalized a classic tradition of thought about law, morality, and their relations by recovering and developing its greatest insights, answering its leading critics, and proposing revisions where thinkers in the tradition had gone astray.

In the course of his project, Finnis made important contributions to contemporary debates about practical reason, justice and the common good, authority, obligation, rights, and the problem of legal injustice. It is fair to say that the field of jurisprudence has not been the same since. At every turn, writers in the discipline find it necessary to grapple with Finnis's defense of natural law and criticisms of competing doctrines. As the eminent Scottish legal philosopher Neil MacCormick described Finnis's achievement, a "theory which more than one generation of thinkers had dismissed as an ancient and exploded fallacy kept alive only as the theological dogmatics of an authoritarian church was rescued from a whole complex of misunderstandings and misrepresentations." Finnis provided, according to MacCormick, "a thoroughly challenging account of law, fully capable of standing up to the theories which were regarded as having refuted and superseded it, while taking into account and accepting into its own setting some of the main insights and discoveries of these theories."

To mark the twenty-fifth anniversary of the publication of *Natural Law and Natural Rights*, *Vera Lex* has brought together essays by a group of distinguished scholars from the disciplines of law, philosophy, and political science. Each essayist addresses one of the themes central to Finnis's work, often engaging that work but always striving, in the spirit of Finnis's book, to make a new and original contribution. These are essays that will repay careful reading and intense reflection.

GUEST EDITORIAL

John Finnis is the preeminent exponent of natural law theory in our time. Educated at Oxford University under the renowned philosopher of law, H.L.A. Hart, Professor Finnis has, in his teaching and through numerous publications, utilized the insights of his great teacher and of analytic philosophy in articulating a theory of natural law that preserves the essential conclusions of the great tradition of natural law theory, while responding to modern insights and criticisms. *Vera Lex* is honored and delighted to dedicate this issue to the work of Professor Finnis. We are particularly happy to submit to the public this special issue of *Vera Lex* in the year marking the twenty-fifth anniversary of the publication of Professor Finnis's great foundational work, *Natural Law and Natural Rights*. At the time this book was published in 1980, many in the scholarly community dismissed natural law as a question-begging theory or as a sectarian doctrine of no relevance to scholarly or public debate. But the publication of *Natural Law and Natural Rights*, with its superb philosophical rigor and penetrating insight, changed the jurisprudential landscape dramatically. Its teachings continue to inform debate to this day and no doubt will do so for generations to come.

This volume contains articles by seven outstanding scholars who have written extensively in the field of natural law. Their essays demonstrate the fruitful revitalization of natural law inquiry that has been stimulated and nourished by Professor Finnis's work. The papers that follow range over a number of key matters that Finnis has addressed in his long and productive scholarly career. Among other issues, they discuss Finnis's critique of legal positivism (the principal competitor of natural law theory), the foundations of Finnis's theory of natural law as grounded in basic goods (but yet non-consequentialist), Finnis's interpretation of thinkers such as Thomas Aquinas and Aristotle, his writings on marriage and sexual ethics, and the application of his natural law theory to disputed moral questions involving moral absolutes and medical ethics (including end-of-life issues), and the extent to which a moral agent bears responsibility for effects that are arguably not intended by the agent.

Professor Joseph Boyle, a long-time collaborator with Professor Finnis and Professor Germain Grisez in articulating and advancing natural law theory, particularly honors us with his contribution to this volume.

In their work, Finnis, Grisez, and Boyle have developed and defended a sophisticated theoretical account that grounds natural law in the recognition of certain basic and distinct intrinsic goods upon which they articulate and explore a theory of human choice and action. Among other intellectual confrontations, this theory of the good and of practical reasonableness sets itself against consequentialism – an ethical theory premised on the view that ethical choice can be consistently determined by comparing and summing the variety of goods at stake in moments of decision. In *Natural Law and Natural Rights*, Finnis argues that consequentialism fails, in large part, because there are many situations in which the incommensurability of goods renders purported consequentialist solutions useless.

In his essay in this volume, Professor Boyle explores some of the issues involved in these foundational disputes and addresses a possible question as to whether the natural law theory articulated by him in conjunction with Finnis and Grisez, in opposing consequentialism, must somehow devolve into a deontological theory. In the elementary university education of students on philosophical matters (particularly in light of the popular theory of John Rawls), the paradigmatic example usually put forward of an ethical theory opposed to the utilitarian consequentialism set forth by the likes of Bentham and J.S. Mill is the ethical theory of the great eighteenth century German philosopher Immanuel Kant. Kant argued that true and binding ethical rules issue exclusively as categorical imperatives arising from the concept of the freedom of rational beings— a freedom and rationality that transcends any particular instantiation in the material world in which humans find themselves and which imperatives, accordingly, are not informed by the complex of relationships that constitutes the human good in any particular world. Kant argues, for example, that there are situations in which moral choice is determined by respect for others as rational beings even when it would seem that the good would be better served by a contrary choice.

This Kantian alternative to an ethical theory grounded in the good has come to be referred to as a paradigmatic example of a "deontological" theory. Because, like Kantian theory, the ethical theory of Finnis, Grisez, and Boyle opposes consequentialism and acknowledges situations in which there are moral constraints on the pursuit of certain goods, this theory might be interpreted as a theory in which such constraints must be understood as deontological in character. While acknowledging that in the writings he has co-authored with Finnis and Grisez, their view has sometimes been stated in ways that might be construed as deontological, Professor Boyle argues that the constraints in question are in fact grounded in the good. He argues that "excluding non-rational motivations from choices among incommensurably good options generates constraints that look deontological but in fact are rational requirements of pursuing the good." Thus, in Professor Boyle's view, the natural law theory he shares with Finnis is not deontological but a non-consequentialist teleological theory.

Readers unfamiliar with *Natural Law and Natural Rights* and wishing to understand how Professor Finnis's natural law theory sets itself against the theory of legal positivism will benefit from reading the essay in this volume by Michael Baur. The first third of Baur's paper sets forth some of the basic premises of Finnis's theory and provides a brief but very useful account of some of the basic concepts Finnis deploys in his argument against positivism. Baur gives a nice exposition of Finnis's concepts of (a) the focal meaning of law and (b) the internal point of view, the latter being a concept that Finnis adopts from his teacher, the positivist H.L.A. Hart, but which Finnis develops in ways that undermine a positivist account of law. In his paper, Baur defends Finnis against a recent attack by Matthew H. Kramer, in which Kramer argues that legal positivism can successfully account for the focal meaning of law while rejecting the conclusions favorable to natural law that Finnis draws from this concept. Baur argues that Kramer's attack fails because Kramer fails to appreciate the implications of both the focal meaning of law and of the internal point of view. Baur's paper thus provides the reader with an instructive account of how these concepts are contested in the intellectual battle between natural law and positivism.

The writings of the great medieval theologian and philosopher Thomas Aquinas have continued to exert fruitful influence on writers on natural law in our time. In the course of his manifold arguments in Natural Law and Natural Rights, Professor Finnis addresses several important theses of Aquinas relating to natural law that have been subject to commentary and debate over the centuries. And in 1998, Finnis published an influential book devoted to the interpretation of Aquinas's philosophy. In his essay in the present volume, Stephen Brock provides an

interpretation of an important passage in Aquinas that has been the subject of much debate among scholars, including Finnis. The passage
includes Aquinas's statement that (in Brock's translation) "all those
things to which man has natural inclination, reason naturally apprehends
as good." Brock takes issue with many commentators (among whom he
includes Finnis) for assuming that the natural inclinations referred to by
Aquinas are pre-rational. He argues instead that that the inclinations
Aquinas has in mind are rational—that they are not spontaneous but
formed by the intellect's understanding of human goods. As such, they
are movements of man's rational appetite and inclinations of the will, not
of mere sensual desire. Among the interesting points Brock makes in the
course of his argument, the reader should pay particular attention to
Brock's comments on the famous argument by David Hume on the
is/ought fallacy, an argument that has had particular importance for
Professor Finnis in his articulation of natural law theory.

Natural law, as a theory of human action and decision, addresses the
problems of difficult moral choice with which all individuals at one time
or another are confronted. Natural law theory seeks to identify the fundamental principles governing practical reason and to consider how and
to what extent such principles can and should be used in determining
moral action. In the intellectual inquiry exploring the existence and
application of fundamental principles and the related concept of the
responsibility of moral actors, resort has often been made to the crucible
of morally vexatious situaion – both real and hypothetical – in which the
validity and scope of moral principles is tested. A typical kind of example is a situation in which one is confronted with a course of action that
would bring about a good (such as saving the lives of one or more people) but which can only be effected through the choice of means that
inevitably result in harm (such as the deaths of one or more other individuals). The Catholic tradition, upon which Professor Finnis draws,
includes a long history exploring such issues and utilizing analytical distinctions between, for example, what an actor intends as opposed to
"side-effects" of carrying out the intention that are, arguably, to some
degree unintended. Modern philosophers, both Catholic and non-
Catholic, have taken possession of these distinctions, subjected them to
scrutiny, and fruitfully extended the debate.

In his paper, Christian Brugger, taking as his point of departure Aquinas's theory as analyzed by Professor Finnis, provides another contribution to this debate. He explores the meaning of intention and argues that the intention of a moral agent must be understood as an internal act separable from the physical behavior, objectively viewed, that carries it out. Brugger elucidates this by application to a much-discussed example of a morally vexatious situation in which performing a craniotomy on a fetus is necessary to save the life of a pregnant woman. Brugger argues that such a procedure is morally permissible because and provided the physician's end is to save the mother's life and the physician intends as a means the narrowing of the fetus's skull and not the death of the fetus. The objection often made to this proposed solution is that, viewed objectively, the inevitable death of the fetus must be understood to be a crucial part of the physician's intention. Relying on his analysis of intention and related concepts, Brugger attempts a thoughtful analytical refutation of this objection. Whatever one may ultimately conclude about Brugger's thesis, his paper constitutes a thoughtful and significant contribution to the debate.

As the above discussion shows, natural law theory throughout its history and as advanced by Professor Finnis has not addressed only issues of high abstraction. It has vigorously attempted to provide principles of action that can guide moral choice in difficult situations, including troubling issues relating to medical care. In this context, Finnis and natural law theory in general have addressed difficult moral issues relating to medical care at the end of life. To that end the reader will benefit from a paper by Daniel Sulmasy, who holds an M.D., a doctorate in philosophy, and a chair in Ethics at St. Vincent's Hospital in Manhattan, and is Professor of Medicine and Director of the Bioethics Institute of New York Medical College. Sulmasy provides an extensive historical survey of some of the basic moral principles developed by Catholic scholars grounded in the natural law tradition that have been—and continue to be—deployed to instruct decisions relating to medical care in general and to care at the end of life in particular. He focuses especially on the principle of double effect and the distinction between ordinary and extraordinary medical care (the O/E distinction).

Professor Finnis's work has accepted and relied in certain important ways on the principle of double effect, and Sulmasy's survey shows that this principle has an important and acknowledged role to play in many situations, including certain situations involving care at the end of life. But Sulmasy argues that other end-of-life questions, relating to when it is appropriate to forgo life-sustaining intervention, are better analyzed in accordance with the O/E distinction. He thinks that Finnis (if he reads certain of his statements correctly) may be read to imply that the O/E distinction has no application independent of construal in light of the principle of double effect. Sulmasy argues that the O/E distinction has a much older pedigree in Catholic moral analysis than the principle of double effect and that, among other differences, it is grounded in analysis relating to moral impossibility and not to means and side effects and so is not reducible to double effect reasoning. Sulmasy explores several case situations that he thinks show the significantly different moral conclusions that would arise from analysis pursuant to the O/E distinction as opposed to analysis pursuant to the principle of double effect. He concludes that analysis pursuant to the O/E distinction is preferable in these situations. Grounded as it is in extensive scholarship and thoughtful analysis, Sulmasy's paper merits careful consideration by the reader interested in an important issue in medical ethics.

Kevin Flannery takes as the point of interest for his paper, an argument made by Professor Finnis in his McGivney lectures (published in 1999 under the title, *Moral Absolutes*) that Aristotle upholds the proposition that there are certain moral absolutes. Flannery notes that in the context of Finnis's discussion in these lectures, Finnis mentions, but does not elaborate on, the concept of force discussed by Aristole – a concept that might be understood to attenuate or defeat the moral obligation to refrain from actions otherwise absolutely forbidden. In a masterful scholarly presentation, Flannery pursues this issue and takes the reader through a close textual reading of the pertinent passages in Aristotle's works that explore the meaning of force and of the classical commentators that address Aristotle's use of this and related concepts. Flannery's analysis leads the reader through several interesting and important considerations, exploring, among other things, the meaning of voluntariness and the applicability of the principle of double effect. As Flannery notes, the matters he addresses have a bearing on some of the most difficult problems in the theory of human action.

An especially important part of Professor Finnis's work has been devoted to a proper understanding of the nature of marriage and of the ways in which sexual acts contribute to marriage. Based on such understanding, Finnis defends the traditional position that only within marriage can sexual acts be morally right. Contributor Patrick Lee, who has written extensively on such matters, provides the reader with a review of Finnis's position according to which, in Lee's words, "marriage is the community formed by a man and a woman who publicly consent to share their lives, in a type of relationship oriented toward begetting, nurturing, and educating of children together." Lee argues that Finnis's position is correct and that only within marriage can sexual acts (provided they are reproductive in kind) constitute genuine good and realize a bodily union of the partners. In the second part of his paper, Lee defends Finnis's view against objections (1) that this view would imply that vaginal intercourse of sterile married couples is necessarily immoral, and (2) that non-marital sexual acts can sometimes realize a common good for, and express a personal communion of, the participants. Central to Lee's response to these objections is his explication of the meaning of "sexual acts of a reproductive kind" and of such acts as intrinsically good within marriage, even if they cannot result in procreation.

FEATURED ARTICLES

BEING REASONABLE IN CHOOSING AMONG INCOMMENSURABLE GOODS
Joseph Boyle

INTRODUCTION[1]

Some philosophers believe that there are moral constraints on the pursuit of the good, that is, constraints a moral person would recognize on his or her doing what he or she judges good, or in cases of competition among good alternatives, what he or she judges better or best. Some of these philosophers believe that at least some such constraints are deontological in the sense that they have no justification in the good. Although one might wonder how it is that the judgments justified in such deontological approaches come to have motivational force, I will not discuss these views here.

I want instead to consider a view according to which there are moral constraints on the actions we have reason to do that are justified precisely by the rationality involved in having a reason to act, which I take to be the rationality of pursuing the good. Very roughly, the idea is as follows: the good practically relevant to human action is what presents itself as to be done and pursued. As Aquinas famously put it: *bonum faciendum est et prosequendum et malum vitandum est.*[2] Thus understood, the good enjoins promotion when some good is understood to be available to be realized by human action, and the good enjoins protection or defense when some good is under threat that can be forestalled by human action. When applied in respect to bads or evils, the idea of the good as what is to be done and pursued becomes a recommendation of avoidance or opposition. The view to be considered, therefore, is whether these ideas

---

[1] An earlier version of this paper was presented to the Ethics Workshop of the Department of Philosophy of the University of Toronto, April 15, 2005. I thank the participants for their helpful comments and criticisms.

[2] *Summa Theologiae*, 1-2, q. 94, a. 2. This standard form of citation indicates the relevant passage in all scholarly editions and translations of this work.

of pursuit, promotion, protection and their near cognates can underwrite constraints on action. This is what I shall mean by ethical teleology, namely, a view based on the idea that states of affairs instantiating intrinsic goods are what confer value, and that moral constraints are the implications of the pursuit of that value. (I believe that morality arises when choices must be made about pursuing value, but that is a further thought than teleology.)

Consequentialist ethical theories are clearly teleological in the sense I have specified. But it is not evident that teleological ethics must be consequentialist. Aristotelian virtue ethics and Thomistic natural law certainly appear both teleological and non-consequentialist. The ethical writings of John Finnis are perhaps the best known contemporary example of a teleological moral theory that is non-consequentialist. This paper explores the structure of the moral theory that has emerged in his authored and co-authored writings.

I have defined teleology as the moral approach in which constraints on the pursuit of what people have reason to do arise from precisely the directiveness the good provides towards actions in which it is instantiated or caused. How the very good that underlies reasons for action can be the ground for restraints on acting is one of the central questions for teleological theory.

Before addressing this question, however, the idea of teleology can be further clarified by contrasting it with a similar sounding, but quite different view, namely, that the good does more than simply direct us towards its promotion and protection. On this distinct view, the basis in the good itself for constraints on action would not be the very directiveness of good—its to-be-doneness—towards actions in which it is pursued, promoted or protected, but something else, perhaps, for example, the special status or dignity of the agent or beneficiary as a rational creatue.

These two moral approaches may appear more similar than they in fact are because some actions taken to promote, protect or refuse to damage an instance of good are reasonably described in deontological-sounding terms. For example, choosing not to take an action that destroys an instance of a good shows respect for that good. But the respect involved in this choice plainly is an aspect of the directiveness of the good: what is to be done and pursued in respect to a good when facing a choice to destroy it or not is to refrain from that destructive action. Destroying something is inimical to pursuit, promotion, or protection of it. The contrasting view sees the ground of this kind of respect in something about the good that calls for a kind of respect or concern for the good that is not grounded in the directiveness, or "to-be-doneness" of the good,[3] and for that reason might be considered a deontology of the good.

It is not my aim to refute this deontological view here (although it is unclear how the notion of the good, practically understood, could provide a ground for moral norms except by its unquestioned role in practical reason, namely underwriting reasons for action). Rather, I wish to explore the idea that the good, just as what gives us reason to act, provides a basis for morality. More starkly, this is the idea that the good as what is to be pursued can itself generate constraints on that pursuit. I will further explore this notion of ethical teleology in the first section below.

My analysis of the structure of a non-consequentialist teleology involves a second supposition, namely, that there is enough incommensurability in the value or goodness of options for choice that comparative value judgments that one option is decisively better than others are not generally available-at least not so generally as to settle most tough moral issues. I will spell that out in the second section. If it is possible to be rational or irrational in choosing among incommensurably good options, then promoting the good rationally can constrain some choices to pursue the good. In the third section of this paper I will argue that this possibility is real. In the final section I will suggest how excluding non-rational motivations from choices among incommensurably good options generates constraints that look deontological but in fact are rational requirements of pursuing the good.

THE NOTION OF TELEOLOGY

To begin this exploration, I will consider a way in which a straightforward development of the idea of pursuing the good justifies a sort of constraint on some possible actions. This development is the application of the mandate of promoting the good to situations in which there is com-

---

[3] By distinguishing teleological ethics from a deontology of the good, I propose a teleological interpretation of the position I hold along with John Finnis and Germain Grisez. We have sometimes stated our view so as to seem to embrace the deontological understanding of respecting the good. See John Finnis, Joseph Boyle and Germain Grisez, *Nuclear Deterrence, Morality and Realism* (Oxford: Oxford University Press, 1987), pp. 282-83.

petition among possibilities promising good, and consequently a need for comparative judgments of goodness. This development is closely related to consequentialist moral theories and seems either a constituent of or closely connected to essential elements of such theories.

Consequentialist rules and judgments justified in this way begin with a recommendation to promote the good—the requirement implicit in the good as a practical concept. They proceed to specify this recommendation to cases where there is competition between good prospects. In virtue of the logic of comparison, they conclude with a recommendation to choose the prospect promising more or most good, or less or least evil. Thus construed, consequentialism relies on the logic of the good, or of what we have reason to do, expanded by the logic of comparison, to what is better or best, and concluding with the recommendation of what we have most reason to do. These consequentialist norms, in other words, recommend the greater good or the lesser evil.

Whenever the options to which such consequentialist norms are to be applied can be considered in terms of everything about them that contributes to their desirability, and whenever all those desirability characteristics can be ranked and compared in terms of their desirability, then the determination of greater good generates a norm completely vindicated by applying the logic of comparison to the idea of the good.

The recommendation provided by such a norm includes a *kind* of constraint on acting for the good, namely, on choosing the lesser good, however favored that action might be. Perhaps the rationality underlying such straightforward consequentialist rules will be thought to generate more than simply a *recommendation*. For when a person's deliberation shows that one option is the thing he or she has most reason to do—in the strong sense specified above—the motivation for the other options is thereby removed. The option supported by the best reason has desirability characteristics that better promise whatever of the good the desirability characteristics of the other options promise.

Consequently, a form of consequentialism that exploits as its basic ideas only the idea of the good and its extension to comparatives requires an explanation as to why it remains possible to be motivated to choose what one recognizes to be a lesser good, as seems to happen in weak-willed actions, when one judges that there is a greater good, but chooses contrary to it.

The preceding paragraphs proceed on the assumption that the action for which there is a best reason—the action that promises the greater good—must contain everything that makes the other options desirable and then some further desirability than they possess. This is not to say that the desirability characteristics of the options must be identical, but only that there must be something in the desirability characteristics of the better that taken as a whole beats, value-wise, everything promised by those of the worse. This is a strong and narrow construal of "greater good," as suggested by the fact that expressions such as, "action supported by the best reason," "the best thing to do," and "the greater good" do not usually refer to an action whose desirability characteristics taken together contain all of what is good in all the desirability characteristics of the alternatives.

However, since my purpose in introducing this idea of the greater good is to articulate an obvious way in which rational constraints on action can emerge from pursuing the good, the strong, narrow conception is legitimate. One such constraint is that provided by the form of consequentialism I specified. In the comparative contexts addressed by this approach, only considerations taking into account all the desirability characteristics of the options involved are sufficient rationally to constrain the promotion of a lesser good. For if the lesser good had a desirability characteristic not better found in the (otherwise) better option, the former's claims for promotion would remain unsilenced. There would be nothing irrational—nothing that violated the implication of pursuing the good or of the meaning of comparatives—for a person to choose an option on the basis of such an unsilenced desirability characteristic.

I recognize that most versions of consequentialism assume a conception of the greater good that is weaker and broader than the one I specified. Similarly, there are consequentialist views according to which the determination of what there is most reason to do includes some limitation either on the desirability characteristics considered, or on the way they are considered. For example, the impartial perspective of moral concern characteristic of utilitarian theories seems to introduce just such a limitation: the desirability of options that are worse from the impartial perspective can remain after the relevant comparisons and perspective are taken. The norms justified within such forms of consequentialism do not emerge simply from the requirements of promoting the good as they do when options containing strictly commensurable goods are compared. The justification for taking a deliberative point of view on options other than that in which the acting person finds them desirable in various ways does not appear to be based simply or immediately on the good and the meaning of comparative terms. The same is true if desirability characteristics are sorted and excluded from comparative consideration, or if the standard for regarding options as commensurable in value is not strict.

My purpose here is not to contest the justification for various forms of consequentialism. I am exploring how teleologically based but non-consequentialist moral constraints arise from the good. In particular, I am exploring how there might be non-consequentialist constraints on pursuing the good which emerge from its logic in a way analogous to that in which the recommendation of the strictly greater good emerges from that logic. Such constraints would remain thoroughly teleological in their justification, even though non-consequentialist, and even if the ethical content of the constraints turned out to be similar to that of deontologically based constraints.

This prospect might appear unpromising. To consider an analogous case: how could the lure of the delectable, just as such, constrain my pursuit of the delectable? You might tell me that too many *hors d'oeuvres* will spoil my appetite, but that seems just the constraint generated by the comparative judgment of delectability. In other words, the relevant delectability does not contain a ground for constraining itself other than by what promises greater delectability; the balance of delectabilities promised by the various goals settles the matter, and that is promoting delectability, constraining only an inadequate response to it. So, if that extra snack promotes delectability (including its effect on one's capacity to enjoy the coming meal), there is no delectability-based objection to it. Analogously, the good seems incapable of providing constraints on its own pursuit—other, of course, than those required precisely by its own more adequate pursuit, and that seems fully captured in the logic of the greater good.

In spite of this, I will argue that the good—taken as the object of our interest in acting—can constrain actions justified, or at least favored, because they pursue it in some way. This claim supposes the broadly teleological conception of morality already suggested: that the right depends on the good and that the good is what is to be done and pursued. This can be spelled out a bit further.

It is accurate, if somewhat rough, to say that the motivation for any human action includes a direction towards certain states of affairs which human beings value. *Bringing down this child's fever* or *preventing that person from being harmed* are examples of valued states of affairs the consideration and desiring of which can motivate a person's action and rationalize it for others' understanding.

These valued states of affairs have several important features, suggested by my examples: one element in the state of affairs is at least one beneficiary, someone benefited in some way by whatever value is present in the state of affairs. Of course, humans can also be elements of these states of affairs in other ways, for example, the goal of *my triumphing over him* includes two people, but only one, myself, as the beneficiary. This reference to a beneficiary can remain in the motivational background, especially when the motivating states of affairs are embedded within complex, larger projects: Grant's goal in the winter of 1863 of *getting his army south of Vicksburg on the east side of the Mississippi* does not indicate the exact benefit or the beneficiaries of this goal, but both are fairly obvious and plainly motivationally essential.

Another aspect of valued states of affairs is that they motivate insofar as they are understood as future states of affairs that can be realized in or by action as concrete, datable events. We are sometimes motivated to bring about a completely new state of affairs, but motivation to preserve or protect an already existing entity involves considering and desiring a future state of affairs: *the entity's continuing to exist at some future time* or perhaps *my bringing it about that the entity continues to exist at that time*.

The future reference of motivations, and the concreteness of the goals that motivate action are both plainly compatible with considerable vagueness. The goals we seek motivate us because we anticipate a future in which they can play a valued part, but that does not require precise dating. Still, we anticipate these goals as elements of a valued future, and so necessarily as concrete states of affairs: getting the army back across the river is vague but the state of affairs that instantiates it is not. The details of such states of affairs distinct from the elements and relationships that render them valuable can remain unsettled as we project and refine our goals.

The good-making features or desirability characteristics of states of affairs are not concrete but are intelligible features that can be instantiated in an indefinite number of possible actions. These features or characteristics, which can be called goods, are properties or relationships in virtue of which agents are interested in the states of affairs in which they instantiate these properties or relationships by or in acting. Those states of affairs, of course, are individual events. And it is the instantiation of goods that realizes the good, and so we are interested in creating the concrete events that can instantiate the good.

Since interest in realizing what is good—that is, a state of affairs or goal having a desirability characteristic—is so apparently basic in motivating human actions, specifically moral judgments must have *some* connection to the good. At the very least moral judgments must be capable of motivating action, and of doing so successfully in the face of sometimes strong motivations to act immorally. For this reason teleological approaches to ethics have a powerful, initial consideration in their favor, for they regard moral obligation as a function of the good as a basic category of practical knowledge and motivation. I believe that this function is specified by the need to settle conflicts or competition among the goals in which we are interested.

This much of teleology as an ethical theory can be stated independently of a theory of the good. But to determine what is involved in rationally pursuing the good, some aspects of the nature of the good must be considered. I will say something about the conception of the good at work in what follows.

It is a sort of objective list view of intrinsic goods, like that stated by Aquinas, with a perfectionist criterion for membership on the list.[4] The items on the list I think correct—items such as survival, health, skillful performance, and decent relations with others—are the most general categories within which are gathered the non-instrumental desirability characteristics human beings seek as elements of their full being or perfection.

On this theory of the good, it is possible that something not good but nevertheless desired can be regarded as if it were a good—we can project a favored, desired, future in which some desire not connected with a good

---

[4] See St. Thomas Aquinas, *Summa Theologiae* 1-2, q. 94, a.2; Finnis, Boyle and Grisez, *Nuclear Deterrence*, pp. 277-281: John Finnis, *Natural Law and Natural Rights* (Oxford: Oxford University Press, 1980), pp. 85-90.

is satisfied or in which some strictly hedonistic satisfaction is fulfilled, but continue to accept that that agreeable future is not really good. Such apparent goods do, however, present themselves as having the thin desirability characteristic I just suggested. So, they can enter into the comparative judgments of value we seek in deliberating.

THE VALUE INCOMMENSURABILITY OF OPTIONS FOR CHOICE

The notion of value incommensurability I have in mind obtains when two or more valued items are compared and the result of the comparison is that it is not true that one is better than the others and also not true that all are equal in goodness. The valued items that are important for my exploration of non-consequentialist but teleological constraints on action are options for action.

Such options arise when there is a conflict of desire sufficient to provoke reflection as a basis for settling the conflict. That reflection or deliberation involves formulating the objects of desire as competing options and then considering their merits—including their relative merits—as desirable or good. The consideration of the relative merits of the goodness of options involves comparing the goodness of the options. That involves considering the value of each desirability characteristic and the adequacy of its projected instantiation in the options. For desirability characteristics can specify a covering value differently, and they can be differently instantiated in different states of affairs. Both dimensions of the value of each of these characteristics must be considered and given weight if the deliberation is to cover all that is good about the set of possibilities. Thus, the comparison of options having health as a desirability characteristic must attend to the different ways the different expected results will instantiate health. And when comparing the goodness of options including health and knowledge as desirability characteristics one must consider the different ways these characteristics might specify some common covering value, or fit more or less well with some established goal controlling the deliberation.

There are three possible outcomes of this process of comparing the goodness of any two such options: either one is found to be better than the other; or one to be as good as the other; or one is judged neither better than nor as good as the other.

In the first case, the requirement of rationality, as already suggested, is obvious: one will, at least if rational, choose what there is the best reason to do. Indeed, as suggested above, even this proviso is not needed if there is nothing of desirability that has not been adequately addressed by the comparison. For to judge that one option is strictly better than the other, is to judge that it embodies desirability characteristics better than the other, or that it has more or better of what makes both options desirable. In the light of that judgment any reason for choosing the lesser good would be a better reason for choosing the better option.

This strong and narrow idea of the commensurability of the comparative goodness of the value of options does not require that one ordinarily make close cardinal rankings of the values involved. What is required is simply that one be able to make judgments such as that some healthy action is less healthy than another, and that as between friendship and success in scholarship the former is more valuable. Successful comparisons of these sorts do not imply the existence of an articulated metric for all options, or even for a given set of options. But the relevant comparison of options leading to the judgment that one is better does seem to involve the ability to arrive at an ordinal ranking of the overall value of the options ranked. And that arrival must determine the judgment and subsequent decision, not be established by the decision.

In the second possible outcome of this stage of deliberation—the possibility of equal value exhibited in Buridan's example of the hungry ass deciding between two equally good and equally accessible bales of hay—the reasons for the options do not settle the choice. In that case, given that settling it is important, some arbitrary procedure such as flipping a coin or going for the option one thinks of next, or perhaps going for the one with which one is least uncomfortable (supposing that this could function without being a desirability characteristic already considered) seems to be the requirement of promoting the good. The directive is simply: "do not fail to do *something* good when the options are equally good."

On the assumption that morality is somehow a function of what is good, no moral issue can arise in these cases once all the values have been considered. For everything about the value of the options has been *ex hypothesi* considered in the judgment that the options are equally good. How could the result of a coin flip be subject to moral assessment if the flip is to settle which of equally valuable options to pursue, on the assumption that morality arises from those values?

The third possible outcome of the comparison of the values of options is the judgment that they are incommensurable. Here the imperatives of the good that settled the cases where one option is better or where the options are equally good simply do not apply. The choice between incommensurable options is not determined by the full comparative assessment of the goods underlying desirability of the options. The response to the value in the options revealed in this outcome of deliberation is to endorse one of them—to overcome the block to action caused by the conflict of motivations by choosing that one of the options will prevail, that its goods will be realized instead of those of the other option.[5]

Although that endorsement is not determined by the goods involved in the options, it remains possible that a choice responding to the goodness of one of a set of incommensurably good options will not be as reasonable as the choice of the alternative. To assume that this is impossible is to assume that any form of rationality that is practically relevant will necessarily commensurate goods. That will be question begging in the absence of a considerable argument. For there is no a priori reason to suppose that the choices in which one endorses one incommensurable option cannot be governed by rational norms, and that these norms can be based on the good as long as they do not commensurate the options in terms of value.

This possibility is exhibited by the case of a choice between a moral and an immoral option, where there is both incommensurability and goods based rational considerations favoring the moral option. There is incommensurability because the immoral option has its irreducible attractions, which remain after comparison with the moral option. Goods-based rational considerations are in play because the moral option serves goods, e.g. "I'll be wasting time, hurting myself, letting down the team, etc., if I

---

[5] This kind of selection, namely, a selection from among incommensurably desirable options in response to deliberation, is a free choice; as responsive to deliberation it is a volition, a choice; and as responsive to incommensurables it is free, since determination of the choice by reasons, often named psychological determinism, is ruled out by the incommensurability. The necessary link between free choices and incommensurable options is not meant to establish the existence of either one. Further argumentation for the existence of one of them is required.

do the immoral act." Moreover, the norms prescribing the morally good act, once recognized, cannot be violated without failing to serve the goods of practical reasonableness and conscientiousness. These and the other goods served directly by morally good choices just insofar as they are morally good do not themselves provide the ultimate criterion for right action. That as we shall see below arises from excluding non-rational factors from inappropriately skewing the pursuit of intelligible good. But choosing in accord with this form of practical rationality is itself humanly desirable.

In short, there is reason to choose the moral option as such, but this is not a reason that necessarily removes the attractions of the immoral option, because, although connected to a good or goods, the justification of the moral norm is not grounded in commensurating considerations.

We saw above that in the case of equality of value there is no value in one option that is not in the other, and so interest in the good implies that one be chosen, it matters not which. Factors not rationalized by their connection to the good—for example, the results of a coin flip or likings not measured in comparison of values—reasonably settle which of equally valuable options to choose. In such cases there are no differences in intelligible value, and the otherwise non-rational procedure allows the agent to get on with action.

Where the options are not equal but incommensurate in value, the goods involved promise quite different futures, not intelligibly identical futures. So, it can make a great deal of difference if the agent chooses one or the other. Those incommensurable values continue, as it were, to have a voice of their own. If the voice of an option that includes a justified moral demand, that prescription is serious even though it does not overcome the desirability of other options. The fact that choosing the morally worse option is not choosing an option that is not worse goods-wise does not imply that there are no rational considerations favoring it. Consequently, an agent's using any particular non-rational factor to settle the choice might fail in promoting the good—that is, fail to promote it intelligently recognizing the condition of incommensurability.[6]

---

[6] See Joseph Raz, *The Morality of Freedom* (Oxford: Oxford University Press, 1987), pp. 225-335, for the source of some of a development of these ideas, and for other arguments concerning the differences between rough equality and incommensurability.

For example, a person with authority to hire a company to carry out a public project faces a choice between a new company whose track record is unproved but whose bid is well crafted and sensible, and an established group which does steady but expensive and unspectacular work. Suppose that the deliberation about these alternatives leads to the judgment that their values are incommensurable. But suppose also that the authority has relatives in the latter group, and, therefore, tilts towards giving the contract to the latter group. Even if explicitly noticed in deliberation, this might not be a factor making commensurably better the option of giving the contract to the group employing relatives. It is even possible that this tilt is not reflected in the deliberation at all, but is simply a liking of the one option. In this case, it seems that these partial feelings of the authority could settle the matter, even though the merits of the options were judged incommensurable. It is appropriate to question whether these admittedly partial feelings are inconsistent with the demands of promoting the good.

This example is not introduced to establish the existence of incommensurability, but to indicate a juncture in deliberation at which the possibility of teleological but non-consequentialist constraints on action can emerge, namely, whenever there are options that are incommensurably valuable and where the distinctive rational appeal of the options includes matters of moral concern that would be compelling except for motivations not connected with the goods at stake.

More generally, I am not trying to establish here that some options are incommensurable in value or that value incommensurability is pervasive.[7] Consequently, the present relevance of the theory of the good outlined at the end of the previous section is that this theory provides an

---

[7] For the sort of reasoning I would endorse in support of the existence of significant value incommensurability, see Joseph Raz, "Incommensurability and Agency,"in R. Chang, editor, *Incommensurability, Incomparability and Practical Reason* (Harvard, 1998), 1109-1128, and John Finnis, "Commensuration and Public Reason," *Ibid.*, 215-233. Finnis shows that the presence of an established, definite goal of the kind that controls technical reasoning is needed to commensurate values, and that when the horizon of the goods at stake in a choice is wider than in cases dominated by an established goal, commensurability fails and free choice is called for. The papers in Chang's collection taken as a whole suggest the complexity of the debate about the commensurability or incommensurabilty of values.

intelligible value framework within which incommensurable options are possible. This theory of the good plainly allows for incommensurability. The general categories in which the basic human goods are listed are understood to be categories of intrinsic good, irreducible to one another in their goodness, value or desirability. Their common goodness is just that that each in its irreducible way specifies the desirability of some desirable states of affairs. In no more robust sense do goods in these different categories indicate a common property that just is their value or goodness. Obviously, this conception makes it difficult to see how there is a common covering value for choices where the goods at issue are in different categories. Moreover, instances of the same good could be incommensurable in value as the vastly differing ways to realize the goods of life, knowledge and friendship suggest. Still, this account of the good will likely rise or fall with one's judgment about the existence of incommensurable values.

The supposition of incommensurability introduced here is meant to indicate a possible world in which there are non-consequentialist but teleological constraints on action. I suspect that there are no such constraints whenever options are strictly commensurable in value. When options are commensurable, the strictly better option is recommended by the good, and either of equally valuable options is similarly recommended. There seems no room in such cases for further constraints based on the good.

For example, consider a constraint on inflicting harm on an innocent person. If that were an option that arose because of a need to save many lives and if it were true that saving those other lives were simply better, the person facing that choice would have no reason to refrain from inflicting the harm. If there were such a constraint in the conditions specified, it would not be based on the pursuit of the good; the implications of that are clear enough. So, any other constraint must be deontological, and its ability to motivate explained. Similarly, if deliberation showed these options to be equal in value it would not matter as far as value is concerned which one was chosen.

But if these options are not strictly commensurable, if there is something desirable about not inflicting the harm on the innocent that is not captured by saving the lives of the many, then there could be a constraint on inflicting the harm, and that might be goods based since harming a person is damaging her good.

The idea then is this: if there are, and whenever there are, incommensurably valuable options, the choice among them might be guided by constraints that are based on the pursuit of the good. Those constraints will generated in different ways than those that emerge when options are commensurable.   This makes the exploration on the supposition of incommensurability interesting. Of course, this will be purely academic if there are no incommensurably valuable options or very few.

RATIONAL AND IRRATIONAL RESPONSES TO
INCOMMENSURABLE OPTIONS

The examples in the previous section suggest that when a person faces a choice between incommensurably good options, he or she may have a motivational tilt towards or away from one or more of the options that are judged incommensurable in value. If there are such motivational factors, and if they can affect choice among incommensurables, their assessment can constrain the choice. If that assessment is based on the pursuit of the good, then there are non-consequentialist but teleological constraints on choices.

Such motivating factors exist because of the individuality of human actions. Actions are singulars, and the projection of possible actions and their purposes in deliberation includes a vague and more or less schematic, but nevertheless *imagined* representation of a goal, and of the individual performances to be undertaken to achieve the goal. Sometimes the goal and the performance are identical, since some performances themselves instantiate the desirability characteristics sought in the action.

Goals, therefore, are not abstract states of affairs but are concrete realities in which goods are instantiated. So, goals have two aspects: the reasons for pursuing them—their desirability characteristics—and their concrete individuality. The motivational response to the individuality of actions and goals is distinct from the interest grounded in the knowledge of desirability characteristics.[8]   One may have a good reason to do something which one finds abhorrent, or to do something to which one finds oneself simply indifferent. Of course, felt abhorrence or indifference

8 See Germain Grisez, Joseph Boyle and John Finnis, "Practical Principles, Moral Truth and Ultimate Ends," *American Journal of Jurisprudence*, 32, (1987), 104-105.

might be fed back into the deliberation as factors counting against doing something, but that is not always what happens. Sometimes we have good reason to do something and just don't like the idea.

The existence of motivations that are not reducible to those responsive to the recognition of desirability characteristics is suggested by the fact that non-human animals and small children are motivated to act, and there is no need to suppose they are responding to knowledge of a property such as a desirability characteristic. Indeed, in much of adult human behavior, the motivation seems sub-rational in just this way—swatting a fly that buzzes at one's head, or shifting one's position as one becomes slightly aware of discomfort. Events such as these can quickly lead to deliberate action, in which getting comfortable or rid of a distracting bug become articulated as goals. But the initial motivations are often not a matter of focal attention, and not rationally articulated.

The idea here is similar to the medieval distinction between sensory appetite and rational appetite. There are motivations responsive to the recognition of properties and motivations responsive to aspects of actual or imagined individuals. These aspects can be conceptualized but motivate independently of that.

If these motivations always tracked the rational requirements of the good, then their role in motivating choices among incommensurably valuable options would not require rational assessment. But there is no reason to think that the feelings we have towards a concrete goal will generally be lined up with the good we wish to pursue by acting for that goal or for competing goals. For example, depressingly arduous work is called for to complete a project of great importance. When weighed into the mix of factors relevant to the decision to carry on, this consideration turns out to be unimportant. And yet imagining carrying on still evokes these feelings; and it could factor in a choice to give the project up.

Moreover, there are several reasons to think that we should not suppose that there is a kind of pre-established harmony between sensory motivations, such as feelings, and our assessments based on the good. The motives in question are those we share with non-human animals and small children. These motivations respond to information and to imagined possibilities connected with the goods we share with these others. Goods such as survival, rest, health, are common, and sensory motivation is closely connected to these concerns. But other human goods are somewhat removed from these concerns; for example goods such as knowledge, skillful performance, or living autonomously with others, have analogues in the interests of non-human animals, but are distinctive. Feelings about goals instantiating these goods surely are shaped by the survival and other vital interests we share with other animals, and this allows that the direction of the feelings and the goods need not coincide.

Similarly, there is a disconnect between the range of beneficiaries registered in sensory motivation and that made possible in considerations based on human goods. The circle of beneficiaries to which sensory motives point are simply ourselves and those near and dear, for example, the survival group. Human goods are capable of benefiting anyone.

Plainly, motivations of this kind can motivate choices among incommensurably valuable options because one can endorse one of the options in part because of such motivations. This can involve making the relevant feeling into another reason, or, perhaps better, a quasi-reason, for or against the option in question, even if one is firm in judging that the reason does not contain a proper desirability characteristic. This is the apparent good I spoke of at the end of section I. This form of motivation can also help settle the matter as deliberation progresses by inclining one's attention towards the grounds for the emotionally favored option and towards overlooking the merits of the more obnoxious option.

In short, there are motivations that are distinct from those based on recognition of desirability characteristics. These motivations function with some independence of motivations based on one's judgments about what is good. That allows that the choices motivated by these independent motivations are not choices in accord with the pursuit of the good. The constraints on acting for the good, therefore, are those that emerge by considering the ways such motivations are not integrated with the good and excluding them.

CONSTRAINTS EMERGING FROM BEING RATIONAL IN RESPONSE TO INCOMMENSURABLE OPTIONS

In this section I will consider just two constraints that emerge in excluding the influence of inappropriate motivations operating independently of values. The first of these addresses the limitation of beneficiaries which sensory motivation naturally involves. The second of these is exclusion of actions involving the intention to damage or destroy an instance of a human good for the sake of more favored yet incommensurably valuable instances of the same or other goods.

It is important that there are other constraints than these, which taken together give moral life its basic shape. For example, destroying instances of goods out of anger or hostility damages goods for no humanly perfective reason, but only for the satisfaction of these desires. Similarly, organizing one's life in a disciplined rational way so as to pursue some goods effectively is a requirement of pursuing the good, at least to the extent it rejects idleness and dabbling or self-indulgence that make an organized and successful life possible.[9]

The first constraint is the Golden Rule. Our sympathies for others appear to be naturally limited to those with whom we identify in some way. That natural limitation of our sympathies can affect choices among incommensurably good options, by favoring an option in which beneficiaries of goods are limited in ways not connected to the goods themselves. The imaginative strategies connected with the Golden Rule can expose and rule out these limitations, by expanding our limited sympathies. In effect, as much as possible, the intelligible goods themselves, as human goods realized by definite actions that are limited in effect, should settle the question of who is to gain the benefits or suffer the burdens of the actions to realize them. Merely natural attraction to some or indifference or hostility to others should not be allowed to settle choices concerned with who is to share the benefits of action or bear its burdens when the human goods at stake would settle them otherwise.

Some goods include within themselves a limitation on who can benefit from actions. Presumably some good human relationships can involve only a single other person or a small group. One cannot be a friend or a partner to everyone. But sometimes it is not the character of

---

[9] Finnis, Grisez and I have stated eight general forms in which non-rational factors capable of skewing the pursuit of the good when choices are called for are identified and excluded as unreasonable. We call them "modes of responsibility"; the two constraints considered here are two of them. See *Nuclear Deterrence* 284-287. In *Natural Law and Natural Rights*, pp. 100-133, Finnis lists a set of requirements of practical reasonableness. This list overlaps considerably with the various formulations of the modes of responsibility. The emphasis is different: Finnis's account emphasizes the goodness of these basic moral requirements; presentations of the modes emphasize their emergence from the rational exclusion of arbitrary limits on the pursuit of good in choices.

the good itself that limits those who can share it, but rather the inevitable limitations of human power and capacity. For example, a physician can only have so many patients, even though her skills and the relationship of a patient to a physician are not inherently exclusive.

The goods we instantiate in and by our actions are intelligible human goods. They are desirable as elements in a valued, or at least favored, future in which we anticipate somehow enjoying or participating in them. But we can recognize that the basic human goods, as intelligible, are good for other humans. The self-referring aspect of goods as the ground of reason-based motivation does not, therefore, prevent motivation towards goals that more directly benefit others, as when physicians act for patients' health. That interest in helping other humans is itself a human good, the agent's flourishing or welfare just as a social being.

Consequently, when deliberating about choices concerning the distribution of burdens and benefits of human actions, the sort of fairness that results from applying the Golden Rule is a requirement for promoting the good. Actions that unfairly burden some damage their goods, which is contrary to promoting the good. And actions that arbitrarily limit benefits to a favored group prevent the good from being realized where it could be. The idea here is not that the application of Golden Rule strategies promotes the good by inevitably leading to *more* beneficiaries and so to *more* actual instantiations of good. That would suggest considerations of fairness pursue the good only by the logic of the greater good, and the supposition in place is that of incommensurably valuable options. The idea, rather, is that feelings which limit considerations based on the good do not appropriately serve among the factors by which one settles a choice among incommensurably valuable options. That might but might not lead to more instances of goods or fewer of harms. If this is correct the logic of pursuing the good is not exhausted by its application to contexts in which desirability characteristics are commensurated.

A warfare example exhibits the reasoning of the last few paragraphs. In World War II, the Allies often bombed submarine pens in occupied France and in Northern Germany. The purpose of these raids was, let us suppose for the sake of the example, simply to destroy the sub-pens and not to terrorize the civilian population. Certainly that assumption is credible in respect to the ports in France. The Allies were not interested in terrorizing the French. But suppose they were not seeking to terrorize the

German inhabitants of the North Sea and Baltic ports. Still these civilians were the enemy, innocent or not, and the hostility or at least indifference towards them led to differential care being taken in avoiding collateral damage. The rules for targeting were a lot less stringent over Germany than over France. A more even-handed policy seems required by the Golden Rule: the populations were not different in the relevant respects and the relevant goods being pursued, most notably a just end to the war, were not pursued as well as they might have been.

This application of the Golden Rule suggests a meaning of "proportionate" and "disproportionate" relevant to this and many cases, namely, that causing harm as a side effect is disproportionate if it is unfair to impose it on those who must suffer it. And in the same way, violating any more specific duty to avoid inflicting such harm would render them disproportionate. This sense of proportionate and disproportionate does not assume that the goods involved are commensurate, only that considering the matter in ways that do not include partial feelings will lead to a rejection of the disproportionate.[10]

The second constraint to be considered is that of destroying an instance of a good for the sake of some goal that appears overwhelmingly important. Sometimes motivations operating independently of the desirability characteristics an agent understands may favor options in which an instance of a good is destroyed or damaged. Sometimes those motivations favor options supported by merely apparent goods, such as satisfying a desire for revenge. But sometimes these motivations favor options backed by genuine goods: an instance of basic human good is to be destroyed because doing that serves another genuine, but more favored though not commensurably better, good.

This is the case of doing something harmful or bad for the sake of a genuinely good end, an end that would be imperative if it were available otherwise than by damaging a person's basic good. An example would be the prohibition against killing an innocent person for the sake of great good, for example, saving many lives.

Often cases like this are considered to be cases where there is a plausible deontological constraint against the judgment of the greater good.

---

[10] For the bombing example, see John Finnis, Joseph Boyle and Germain Grisez, *Nuclear Deterrence, Morality and Realism* (OUP, 1987), p. 264; for the generalization concerning the meaning of "proportionate," and its cognates, see 261-67, 270-72.

But I am discussing this case on the supposition that it is a case representing a choice among incommensurably valuable options. There is, on this assumption, something of value about inflicting the harm that is not found in allowing the many to die—perhaps that killing sets different precedents than not saving, or that the many to be saved are not the agent's responsibility, or simply that the value of one human life, either to the person who will be killed or to the agent is simply incommensurable in goodness to another life. If some such considerations are not present, and if the issue were simply a matter of the number of lives lost by either choice, then the recommendation of the greater good would seem to prevail. My supposition of incommensurability is, therefore, in place. If my examples appear to founder on the question of whether the options are incommensurable in value, then perhaps examples more apparently incommensurable in value might be created and used.

Inflicting the harm on the innocent is so far forth not pursuing the good; it is precisely destroying an instance of good, a person's life. Since the option for the sake of which one inflicts this harm is good in virtue of desirability characteristics that are, *ex hypothesi* incommensurate with those supporting doing this, a reason based on the goods involved is lacking. In this situation, one is acting against an instance of the good for the sake of fostering other instances of good. But the goods involved are not commensurable, so the only thing that might favor the option including the destruction of good cannot justify it, and the preference for that option must be based only on the feelings favoring it. In this situation, pursuing the good just is incompatible with destroying instances of it. And doing that when there is no good justifying it is arbitrary in terms of the good.

It may be objected, however, that damaging and destroying instances of goods is unavoidable. In the case at hand, pursuit of the good excludes harming the innocent, but saving the lives to be saved by doing that is also pursuing the good. So refusing to inflict harm is also refusing to pursue the good involved in saving these lives. One's decision not to inflict the harm causes this state of affairs, at least in the morally relevant counterfactual sense that had one chosen otherwise, the goods not saved would have been saved.

But the agent's relationship to these two outcomes is ordinarily different. In the first case the harm is intentionally inflicted; in the second the harm, though voluntariliy brought about by the agent's decision not to kill the innocent person is ordinarily not intentionally brought about, but is a side effect of the choice not to kill the one person. I say "ordinarily" here because it is possible that the agent in my example could hate one of those to be saved and refuse to save them for that reason alone, making use of the existence of an accepted limit on killing innocents as a socially acceptable explanation. In this case the intentional action is not saving so as to contribute to the death of the hated person, and the side effect of that decision, that the innocent is not killed, is a side effect the agent might or might not regard as a bonus. I am not discussing this sort of case.

Of course, many people dispute the ethical significance of the distinction between what a person intends in acting and what a person accepts as a side effect of his or her intentional action. But there is a reason, compatible with the account I am developing, for attributing ethical significance to this distinction. The difference lies in the fact that it is always within one's power to choose to do something or not, even if doing that sometimes is very unpalatable. But in the case of accepting the harmful side effects of intentional actions, there will inevitably be some of them no matter what one chooses to do or not to do. At the very least, whenever we choose one intentional action when faced with options, we leave unrealized the goods that choosing the other option would instantiate.[11]

And in very many actions, including most of those that provide the fodder for double effect casuistry, intentionally promoting a good also has some bad side effects. Deflection cases illustrate this perspicuously: you turn a threat away from some—so far forth protecting good—with the anticipated result that it will fall onto others and harm them. As the variety of such cases suggests, there are moral norms applicable for determining which side effects falling on which people are morally acceptable. But one constraint that makes no sense is altogether to avoid causing harmful side effects. That is an impossibility, and cannot be required by the good or anything else.

---

[11] For more on this, see my "Medical Ethics and Double Effect: The Case of Terminal Sedation," *Theoretical Medicine and Bioethics* 25 (2004), 56-57; in "Who is Entitled to Double Effect?" *Journal of Medicine and Philosophy* 16 (1991), 475-491, I criticize other attempts to give the intended/foreseen distinction and argue for my view of its justification. For the earliest statement of this view that I know about, see *Nuclear Deterrence*, p. 292.

So, in the double effect cases, the directiveness of the good excludes destroying an instance of good even for a good cause. And the side effect of sticking with that conclusion is not necessarily excluded on the same ground, since some bad side effects are usually unavoidable.

The responsibility-limiting character of the inevitability of causing some bad side effects in choosing implies that the absolute character of the norm prohibiting choices precisely to damage or destroy instances of basic human goods cannot be reasonably extended to voluntarily accepting side effects. That, of course, does not mean that it is permissible to do what has those side effects, only that if they are wrong-making aspects of the action, it will not be in virtue of the sort of reasoning that can exclude precisely choosing against a good.

Double effect cases are usually seen as paradigmatically deontological. And by this point in my paper, its deontological flavor is unmistakable. Aside from the moral absolutism in the second of these constraints, in both of them the focus of moral concern appears to have moved away from state of affairs and into the choosing and the practical reasoning of the moral agent: in the Golden Rule cases to the imaginative exercise of exposing the unreasonable limits of affection; and in the double effect cases of taking as morally decisive a difference in modalities of willing.

The specifically moral is, therefore, a function of what is valuable, but is not identical with creating valuable states of affairs. Morality deals with the way we choose to pursue the good. This means that moral goodness is the specific goodness of willing rightly when there are competitors for our personal allegiance. That goodness is incommensurable with that of the goods of immoral options.

Still, the criterion of willing rightly is the pursuit of good unfettered by non-rational motivation that is not integrated with the pursuit of the good. The prescriptions generated by reason acting to exclude these motivations are not simply the requirements of the good of practical reasonableness, seeking as it were to dominate other goods. The considerations emerging from the rational assessment and rejection of such motivations address precisely the requirements of reasonably pursuing the good when faced by incommensurable options.

There plainly found is a shift in emphasis here from goods-based practical reasoning using the logic of comparison. This shift moves moral judgment to the neighborhood of the concern with the moral agent that is found in older, virtue oriented relatives of ethical teleology, such as Aristotle's moral theory. But I think the shift arises not because something else has displaced the instantiating of human goods as the point of human action, but because the incommensurability of the value of options significantly changes the shape of thinking about what is required in pursuing the good. I suggest that concern for the good just plays out differently if and when(ever) the goods at stake in a choice are incommensurable.

IN DEFENSE OF FINNIS ON NATURAL LAW LEGAL THEORY
Michael Baur

INTRODUCTION

The term "natural law" is spoken in many ways, but two of the most common ways in which the term is used have to do with "natural law" as a *legal* theory (henceforth NLLT) on the one hand, and "natural law" as a *moral* theory (henceforth NLMT) on the other hand. According to Michael S. Moore, a NLMT is a moral theory which holds that "there are objective moral truths"; by contrast, a NLLT is a legal theory which holds that "the truth of any legal proposition necessarily depends, at least in part, on the truth of some corresponding moral proposition(s)."[1] Philip Soper characterizes the distinction between NLMT and NLLT, and the relationship between them, somewhat differently. For Soper, a NLMT is a moral theory which holds "that moral principles are objectively valid and discoverable by reason"; by contrast, a NLLT is a legal theory which rejects the legal positivist's claim that "no necessary connection exists between law and morality"; the natural law legal theorist "denies that a sharp separation between these concepts [the concept of law and the concept of morality] is possible."[2] Notice already the subtle difference between Moore and Soper. While Moore characterizes NLLT in terms of a dependence-relation between the truth of legal propositions and the truth of moral propositions, Soper characterizes NLLT in terms of the alleged non-separability of legal and moral concepts.[3] According to

---

[1] Michael S. Moore, "Law as a Functional Kind," in *Natural Law Theory: Contemporary Essays*, edited by Robert P. George (Oxford: The Clarendon Press, 1994), pp. 189-190.

[2] Philip Soper, "Some Natural Confusions about Natural Law," 90 *Mich. L. Rev.* 2393, 2394-2395 (1992).

[3] Jules Coleman expresses positivism's "separability thesis" as follows: "The separability thesis is the claim that there is no necessary connection between law and morality. That claim does express a tenet of positivism." See Jules Coleman, *The Practice of Principle: In Defence of a Pragmatic Approach to Legal Theory* (Oxford: Oxford University Press, 2001), p. 104, n. 4. But note also that some theorists who consider themselves legal positivists have denied the "separability thesis," and thus have held that the truth of legal positivism does not, strictly speaking, depend on the truth of the separability thesis. For an example of this, see the work of Joseph Raz, who argues in favor of

NLLT as characterized by Moore, no legal proposition can be true if it is not somehow dependent on a true moral proposition or propositions; thus for Moore, one cannot be a natural law legal theorist if one is not also a natural law moral theorist. For Moore, both the natural law moral theorist and the natural law legal theorist are necessarily committed to the truth of at least some moral propositions. By contrast, Soper's characterization of NLLT allows him to hold that one can be a natural law legal theorist without necessarily being a natural law moral theorist. As Soper contends, "one might concede a connection between law and morality yet deny that the morality with which law is connected is that endorsed by the natural law moral theorist."[4]

These brief introductory observations should make clear that the grounds of the distinction between NLMT and NLLT, and the nature of the conceptual relation between the two, are far from clear and obvious. Even amongst those who regard themselves as committed "natural law" theorists in *both* senses of the term, there is widespread disagreement on what it is that constitutes a NLMT or a NLLT, and on how the relationship between NLMT and NLLT is to be characterized. My aim in this paper is not to address the rather complex and multifarious issues appurtenant to the nature of NLMT and NLLT and the relationship between them. My aim is simply to give a brief account of Finnis's NLLT, primarily as it is presented in *Natural Law and Natural Rights* (henceforth *NLNR*), and then defend Finnis's NLLT against the recent legal positivist criticism made by Matthew H. Kramer.

FINNIS ON NATURAL LAW LEGAL THEORY

Just as one can—as we have done above—distinguish between NLLT and NLMT, so too one can distinguish *within* NLLT itself between two important issues in legal theory or the philosophy of law. One issue (which we might call the "nature of law" issue) has to do with the grounds

---

legal positivism, but against the "separability thesis." Raz writes: "The separability thesis is ... implausible.... It is very likely that there is some necessary connection between law and morality, that every legal system in force has some moral merit or does some moral good even if it is also the cause of a great deal of moral evil." Joseph Raz, *Ethics in the Public Domain* (Oxford: The Clarendon Press, 1994), p. 211.

4 Soper, *op. cit.*, at 2395.

and nature of legality or legal validity: what is it that makes a rule or directive legally valid, or a genuine instance of law? The other issue (which we might call the "moral obligation" issue) has to do with the (alleged) moral obligation to obey the law: assuming that a particular rule or directive is legally valid (or a genuine instance of law), does there exist (and why does there exist) a moral obligation to obey it? Not surprisingly, some natural law legal theorists have claimed that "laws necessarily obligate to be laws."[5] Along these lines, Michael Moore—claiming an Augustinian heritage for his view—has argued that "the justness of a norm is *necessary* to its status as law,"[6] so that unjust norms or norms that fail to obligate morally are not even valid as law.[7] But one can contest this claim; one can hold that a particular rule or directive may be valid as law, even if it is unjust or does not obligate morally. This, indeed, is the position presented by Finnis in *NLNR*, and Finnis argues that he can hold this position while still remaining a natural law legal theorist.

Finnis famously challenges what has become a relatively common interpretation of the medieval (and Thomistic) principle that "an unjust law is not a law [*lex injusta non est lex*]." According to Finnis, Thomas Aquinas and the tradition to which Aquinas belonged never propounded the unqualified statement that an unjust law is not a law at all. Indeed it is quite easy to see that such a statement—if taken literally or without qualification—is "pure nonsense" or "flatly self-contradictory";[8] after all, one cannot coherently assert that the very same thing (in this case, unjust law) is both a law and not a law at the same time and in the same respect. So how does Finnis interpret this famous medieval principle, and how does this interpretation square with Finnis's understanding of his own contribution to NLLT?

---

5 Moore, *op. cit.*, at 224.

6 *Ibid.* at 198.

7 *Ibid.* at 224. But notice that one can draw a further distinction here, namely a distinction between the justness of a law and the capacity of that law to command obedience from a moral point of view. A law—considered on its own terms or considered in isolation—may be relatively just but it may nevertheless fail to obligate (or it may fail to command obedience from a moral point of view) because of some further relevant moral consideration(s).

8 John Finnis, *Natural Law and Natural Rights* (Oxford: The Clarendon Press, 1980), p. 364. Henceforth this text shall be indicated by the abbreviation *NLNR*.

For Finnis, the medieval principle that "an unjust law is not a law" is not to be taken literally but is best understood as a formula meant to dramatize an important point about the relationship between legal validity and moral validity. The point is that unjust or iniquitous laws do not count as law in the 'central' or 'focal' sense of the term, even though they may be genuine laws and may possess genuine legal validity. On Finnis's reading, Thomas Aquinas and the tradition to which he belonged made use of the principle in order to illustrate the point that unjust laws can indeed count as valid laws, but only in a secondary, derivative, or marginal sense. Thus for Finnis, the medieval tradition's adherence to the principle that "unjust laws are not laws" actually demonstrates the tradition's fundamental agreement with what has come to be identified as a central claim of legal positivism, namely that the existence of law is one thing, and its moral merit (or justness or moral worthiness) is quite another thing. Understood properly, the principle that "an unjust law is not a law" is consistent with the claim that morally iniquitous rules and directives actually can and do exist as perfectly valid laws:

> Far from 'denying legal validity to iniquitous rules', the tradition explicitly (by speaking of 'unjust *laws*') accords to iniquitous rules legal validity, whether on the ground or in the sense that these rules are accepted in the courts as guides to judicial decision, or on the ground and in the sense that, in the judgment of the speaker, they satisfy the criteria of validity laid down by constitutional or other legal rules.[9]

In addition to offering what some may consider to be an idiosyncratic interpretation of the famous medieval principle ("an unjust law is not a law"), Finnis also claims in *NLNR* that the principle—as interpreted by him—is fundamentally correct from a jurisprudential point of view. Thus Finnis can agree with the legal positivist claim that: "The identification of the existence and content of law does not require resort to any moral argument."[10] But by interpreting and endorsing the medieval principle in this way, has Finnis conceded too much to the legal positivist, and has he

[9] *Ibid.* at 365.

[10] See John Finnis, "The Truth in Legal Positivism," in *The Autonomy of Law: Essays on Legal Positivism*, edited by Robert P. George (Oxford: The Clarendon Press, 1996), p. 204.

undermined his own claim to be contributing to a genuinely "natural law" version of legal theory?[11]   It will not be possible here to present a full defense of what is required for a genuinely "natural law" version of legal theory; nor will it be possible here to present a complete justification of Finnis's own claims on behalf of NLLT. My aim is simply to defend Finnis against the positivist critique made by Matthew H. Kramer. And in order to present this defense, it will be necessary first to say a few more words about Finnis's NLLT.

Crucial to Finnis's attempt at presenting a defensible NLLT is his distinction between what he calls the 'focal' or 'central' meaning of the concept of law, and secondary, peripheral, marginal, or derivative meanings. By drawing this distinction, Finnis argues, we can "differentiate the mature from the undeveloped in human affairs, the sophisticated from the primitive, the flourishing from the corrupt, the fine specimen from the deviant case...."[12] And just as—following Aristotle—we can observe that there are 'central' and 'peripheral' cases of what we call 'friendship',[13] so too we can observe that there are 'central' and 'peripheral' cases of what we call 'law'. Thus to concede to the legal positivist that there may exist legally valid rules which are nevertheless morally unjust or iniquitous is not to concede that legal positivism is the correct view of the very nature of law. For while instances of unjust law are indeed genuine instances of law, it must be remembered that they represent the merely 'peripheral' or 'marginal' cases of law. They do not adequately represent what it is that constitutes law in its essential core. As Finnis puts it, they represent "watered down versions of the central cases" of law.[14] So while such peripheral, marginal, or watered-down versions of law certainly are instances of law, they are instances of law only because they instantiate—to an imperfect and lesser degree—the traits or principles that characterize the central cases of law and which properly belong

[11] Some thinkers believe that Finnis has, indeed, conceded too much to the legal positivist. See Philip Soper, "Legal Theory and the Problem of Definition," 50 *U. Chi. L. Rev.* 1170 (1983). See also Seow Hon Tan, "Validity and Obligation in Natural Law Theory: Does Finnis Come Too Close to Positivism?" 15 *Regent U. L. Rev.* 195 (2002).

[12] Finnis, *NLNR*, pp. 10-11.

[13] See Aristotle, *Nicomachean Ethics*, Book VIII, Chapters 3-4.

[14] Finnis, *op. cit.*, at 11.

to the very nature of law. Giving an account of the nature of law on the basis of these merely peripheral cases would be quite like explaining the nature of friendship by reference to the entirely mercenary interactions of two business partners (whose friendship is merely a friendship of utility, as Aristotle would call it).[15]   For Finnis, it is the central cases that provide the correct standard or point of reference for apprehending the true nature of law, and thus (derivatively) for explaining any watered-down or diluted or deviant instantiation of law as well.

Now in addition to insisting on the crucial distinction between the 'focal' and 'peripheral' meanings of the concept of law, Finnis also emphasizes the importance of the "internal point of view" for an understanding of law. Following a ground-breaking insight of the legal positivist H.L.A. Hart,[16] Finnis holds that any feasible account of the nature of law must take into consideration the concerns and evaluations of those who have an "internal point of view" with respect to the law, that is, those who do not merely "record and predict behavior conforming to rules," but rather who "*use* the rules as standards for the appraisal of their own and others' behaviour."[17]   But going beyond Hart and his positivist followers, Finnis also argues that taking account of this "internal point of view," and doing so with respect to law's central cases, should lead the legal theorist to realize that an adequate understanding of the law cannot prescind from a concern for answering the real practical and moral questions that the legal actors themselves regard as important and seek to answer when they participate in the making and the following of law in its central cases. For Finnis, the legal theorist concerned with identifying the central cases and the focal meaning of the law will have to be concerned about discerning the truth of practical, moral propositions, since the "theorist cannot identify the central case of that practical viewpoint which he uses to identify the central case of his subject-matter, unless he decides what the requirements of practical reasonableness really are...."[18]   So for Finnis, a viable NLLT will recognize that the law in its central cases seeks to arrive at cor-

---

15 Aristotle, *op. cit.*

16 See especially H.L.A. Hart, *The Concept of Law* (Oxford: The Clarendon Press, 1992), pp. 86-88.

17 Finis, *op. cit.*, at 12.

18 *Ibid.* at 16.

rect answers to real moral and practical problems, and so the natural law legal theorist will also have to be concerned—as the legal participants themselves are concerned—with arriving at correct answers to real moral and practical problems. In short, for Finnis, a viable NLLT must be linked to a NLMT:

> A sound theory of natural law is one that explicitly ... undertakes a critique of practical viewpoints, in order to distinguish the practically unreasonable from the practically reasonable, and thus to differentiate the really important from that which is unimportant or is important only by its opposition to or unreasonable exploitation of the really important. A theory of natural law claims to be able to identify conditions and principles of practical right-mindedness, of good and proper order among men and in individual conduct.[19]

Now with his account of 'central' cases and the 'focal' meaning of law, and his emphasis on the 'internal point of view', Finnis can credibly claim that law—when properly understood—is necessarily a moral concept, or a concept pregnant with moral meaning. This is because the law for Finnis represents a solution to a genuine practical and moral problem, namely the problem of coordinating the various ways in which individuals within a complete community can intelligently and harmoniously pursue the various goods at which they aim, and in so doing realize not only their own individual goods but also the common good of the community. Finnis acknowledges that there can be many senses attached to the 'common good,' but the sense that is of most concern to a NLLT is the sense of the common good as "a set of conditions which enables the members of a community to attain for themselves reasonable objectives, or to realize reasonably for themselves the value(s), for the sake of which they have reason to collaborate with each other (positively and/or negatively) in a community."[20]   Now according to Finnis, a community's coordination problems can be solved, and its common good realized, in only one of two ways: either all members of the community reach unanimous agreement on the commitments, orientations, projects, methods, and pri-

---

[19] *Ibid.* at 18.
[20] *Ibid.* at 155.

orities that the community ought to adopt in securing its common good, or else the members of the community establish a proper authority in whom will be vested the rightful power and means for solving the community's coordination problems on its behalf. Since unanimity is "far beyond the bounds of practical possibility,"[21] Finnis argues, the only practicable and reasonable solution to a community's coordination problems will be the establishment of a valid authority; and in the case of a complete community, this means a valid legal authority and legal regime. Because law "shapes, supports, and furthers patterns of co-ordination,"[22] it enables a complete (legal) community to achieve the common good for itself. With this, Finnis can credibly claim to be proffering a genuinely "natural law"version of legal theory; for on Finnis's account, law—when understood in its focal sense and from an internal point of view—is necessarily bound up with a moral concern for the common good. Not surprisingly, Finnis's formal definition of the law—while lacking the quotable pithiness of Aquinas's more famous definition[23]—emphasizes the essential connection between lawfulness and a moral concern for the common good. For Finnis, the law consists in:

> … rules made, in accordance with regulative legal rules, by a determinate and effective authority (itself identified and, standardly, constituted as an institution by legal rules) for a 'complete' community, and buttressed by sanctions in accordance with the rule-guided stipulations of adjudicative institutions, this ensemble of rules and institutions being directed to reasonably resolving any of the community's co-ordination problems (and to ratifying, tolerating, regulating, or overriding co-ordination solutions from any other institutions or sources of norms) for the common good of that community, according to a manner and form itself adapted to that common good by features of specificity, minimization of arbitrariness, and maintenance of a quality of reciprocity between the subjects of the

---

[21] *Ibid.* at 233.

[22] *Ibid.* at 267.

[23] See Thomas Aquinas, *Summa Theologica*, I-II, Q. 90, a. 4: "Law is nothing other than an ordinance of reason for the common good, made by the one who has care of the community, and promulgated."

law both amongst themselves and in their relations with the lawful authorities.[24]

In addition to asserting a necessary conceptual connection between morality and law (understood in its focal sense), Finnis also argues that there is a generic and presumptive (though defeasible) moral obligation to obey the law. The reason why there is such a moral obligation is that the law provides the best means for solving a complete community's coordination problems and achieving the common good for that community; and since the achievement of the community's common good is morally obligatory, the maintenance of the best or only means for achieving that common good is also morally obligatory.[25] Of course, Finnis also holds that there can be unjust laws which fail to live up to the nature of law (in its focal sense) and thus which fail to obligate. Thus the generic moral obligation to obey the law is presumptive but defeasible. But law understood in its focal meaning and from an internal point of view bears a necessary connection to a moral good, which is the community's common good. Furthermore, Finnis argues that even unjust laws may continue to obligate—in spite of their unjustness—since a refusal to obey the law may bring the law into contempt, and thereby destroy the moral good that is lawfulness itself.[26]

KRAMER ON NATURAL LAW LEGAL THEORY
In the face of the NLLT that Finnis presents, the legal positivist Matthew H. Kramer denies that law is a moral concept or a concept pregnant with moral meaning, and—in consequence of this—denies that there is a generic and presumptive (even if defeasible) moral obligation to obey the law. While acknowledging with Finnis that legal discourse is necessarily normative, Kramer argues that the normativity of legal discourse need not be tied to any moral concerns or to any concerns for the com-

[24] Finnis, *op. cit.*, at 276-277.

[25] For a helpful account of Finnis's reasoning about the generic and presumptive moral obligation to obey the law, see S. Aiyar, "The Problem of Law's Authority: John Finnis and Joseph Raz on Legal Obligation," 19 *Law and Philosophy* 465 (2000).

[26] Finnis, *op. cit.*, at 361-362. Thomas Aquinas makes a similar point in the *Summa Theologica*, I-II, Q. 96, a. 4.

munity's common good, but may be linked instead only to the prudential, self-interested, and perhaps entirely nefarious concerns of the legal officials themselves. In making this claim, Kramer is careful to point out that—on his account—a norm need not be a moral norm and need not be followed for moral reasons. "A norm is any general directive that lays down a standard with which conformity is required and against which people's conduct can be assessed."[27]   Understood in this way, a legal regime may enforce norms and the citizens may adhere to such norms for entirely self-interested and prudential (perhaps even nefarious) purposes. Thus for Kramer, the use of normative language in legal discourse may or may not have anything to do with any concern for the common good or the demands of practical reasonableness or morality. While there may be a connection between legal requirements and practical reasonableness (or morality) in a benevolent legal regime, such a connection is merely contingent and does not pertain to the very essence of law, even when law is understood in its focal sense. Kramer writes:

> To be sure, no one should doubt that benevolent legal regimes are characterized by such a function [social coordination for the sake of the common good]. But in certain other *full-fledged* legal systems, the paramount function resides in the sustainment of the officials' oppressive dominance and the pursuit of their sundry flagitious objectives.... The internal perspective of the officials is oriented toward the accomplishment of that function and is thus entirely prudential in its tenor. Yet, in connection with that very function, there will be strong reasons for those officials to endow their regime with the essential characteristics of law.... When the evil officials act on those reasons, their regime in all its monstrousness is a straightforward instance (a *central* case) of legal governance.[28]

What is crucial here is Kramer's claim that a legal regime whose only purpose is to reinforce the power of self-interested and perhaps even deeply wicked officials can and should be regarded as a 'central case' of a legal regime, or a 'full-fledged' instance of law in its focal sense; and

[27] Matthew H. Kramer, *In Defense of Legal Positivism: Law Without Trimmings* (Oxford: Oxford University Press, 1999), p. 80.

[28] *Ibid.* at 237-238.

correspondingly, that benevolent legal regimes (regimes aimed at solving social coordination problems for the sake of a common good) have no unique claim to be 'central cases' or to exemplify law in its 'focal' sense. Thus from Kramer's point of view, Finnis is wrong to hold that the concept of law in its focal sense is a concept pregnant with moral meaning, and equally wrong to hold that there is a generic and presumptive moral obligation to obey the law as such.

Now as Kramer points out, a response by Finnis that simply re-asserts the 'true' meaning of the concept of law in its focal sense, or that defends the 'central' purpose of law as promotive of the common good, would be unhelpful and question-begging.[29]   For the very thing at issue between Kramer as a legal positivist and Finnis as a natural law legal theorist is the meaning of the concept of law in its focal sense and whether this meaning is necessarily pregnant with moral significance. For Kramer, law in the focal sense of the term may or may not have anything to do with morality, and the features that necessarily belong to law in its focal sense (or to central cases of law) are features that pertain only to the (1) generality and (2) durability of the norms contained within a putative system of law, and the (3) regularity or consistency with which those norms are enforced.[30]

Now is there any way to rebut Kramer on Finnis's behalf without begging the very questions through which Kramer poses his challenge to NLLT? At first glance, it might seem possible to rebut Kramer by arguing that the generality, durability, and regular enforcement of legal norms—three features which Kramer admits are intrinsic to the nature of law in its focal sense—point to the necessarily (even if implicitly) moral purpose or function of the law. After all, one might ask, why must the norms of a legal regime be general and durable, and enforced with regularity or consistency, if not for the moral purposes of furthering the common good, securing fairness, and respecting the dignity of persons who are subject to the law? In the face of such a natural law rejoinder, Kramer is quite willing to acknowledge that the sustenance of these aspects of the rule of law (generality, durability, and regularity) *might* be motivated—

[29] *Ibid.* at 238.
[30] *Ibid.* at 95-96.

especially in a benevolent legal regime—by moral concerns.   But, Kramer insists, such moral concern or purposiveness is not an *intrinsic* feature of law in its focal sense; and in an evil legal regime, officials might insist for entirely self-interested and nefarious reasons that legal norms be general, durable, and consistently enforced.   In other words, Kramer argues that moral purposiveness is only an accidental and not an essential feature of law in its focal sense. Most crucially, Kramer insists that a thoroughly evil legal regime, so long as it sufficiently exhibits the features of generality, durability, and regularity of enforcement (even if these features are maintained solely in order to serve the self-interested, unjust, and nefarious aims of the legal officials themselves) will qualify (just as much as a benevolent legal regime displaying the same three features) as *a central case of law* and will represent *law in its focal sense*. Indeed, Kramer goes so far as to argue that a Mafia-like criminal syndicate "that exerts a comprehensive reign over the populace of some territory via norms that are general and durable and regularly applied . . . should be designated as a legal regime" in the focal sense of the term.[31] The question of whether a particular regime should or should not be designated as a 'legal' regime in the focal sense of the term depends entirely on the degree of generality, durability, and regularity of enforcement displayed in the regime's directives, and not on the regime's moral worthiness, or even its approximation to moral worthiness or its claim to moral worthiness.

Now in furthering his case for legal positivism, Kramer explains that the regularity which necessarily belongs to a legal regime's enforcement of its norms should not be misunderstood as implying any sort of moral purpose (such as concern for fairness or respect for the citizens' capacity for self-determination). For Kramer, the regularity that is an integral and defining feature of what constitutes a 'legal system' in the focal sense might be sustained by legal officials solely for the self-interested, entirely nefarious purpose of reinforcing the citizens' incentives to obey. The purpose of such evil legal officials might be:

> ... to make clear that violations of applicable legal require-
> ments will indeed trigger punishments and that punishments

---

[31] *Ibid.* at 97.

are not inflicted on anyone who abstains from such violations. In emphasizing the connection between the breaching of duties and the incurring of penalties, the officials need not be motivated by a desire to establish that their rulings are fair. They may simply want to sustain people's incentives for conformity with the law's evil demands.... If people presume that they will often undergo penalties notwithstanding the lawfulness of their conduct, or if they presume that they will often escape penalties notwithstanding the unlawfulness of their conduct, then a crucial motivation for their adherence to the terms of wicked laws will have been undercut.[32]

Explaining this point further, Kramer argues:

If a legal system is known to depart frequently from the terms of its own norms by punishing lawful conduct or by conniving at unlawfulness, then citizens' incentives for compliance with the norms will greatly diminish. Hence, given that wicked rulers will doubtless want their malevolent laws to operate effectively, they will have good grounds for insisting that the laws be enforced in accordance with the terms thereof. A policy of strict enforcement is what best sustains incentives for obedience. Thus law's continuousness [or durability] helps to ensure its regularity-which means one distinctive feature of law ... helps to ensure the existence of another indispensable feature.[33]

Kramer also acknowledges that legal officials sometimes announce and explain their legal decisions in language that seems to carry with it a justificatory (and thus implicitly moral) meaning. But once again, Kramer argues that the apparently justificatory language use by legal officials need not imply anything about *moral* justifications. Even in legal systems where publicly accessible explanations are rather common, there is nothing about such explanations that requires us to attribute any moral significance to them. Such explanations may be nothing more than another means (like the regularity of the enforcement of norms) by which

---

[32] *Ibid.* at 90-91.
[33] *Ibid.* at 96.

purely self-interested and evil legal officials seek to maintain their own power:

> Thus, faced with the task of providing strong inducements for people to behave in accordance with the prevailing legal norms, the officials who administer those norms in a malevolent regime are well advised to explain their decisions by reference to citizens' legal duties. Highlighting the correlations between nonfulfillment-of-duty and subjection-to-punishment is the means of promoting a pattern of incentives that will secure the efficacious functioning of a scheme of imperatives.[34]

It is at this point in his defense of legal positivism that a certain ambiguity enters into Kramer's account. The ambiguity has to do with the question of whether publicly accessible explanation (even granting *arguendo* that such explanation has no moral meaning or purpose) is a necessary or only contingent feature of law in its focal sense. Kramer is not entirely clear on the matter. On the one hand, he argues that legal officials would be "well advised to explain their decisions by reference to citizens' legal duties," thus suggesting that publicly accessible explanation is only a contingent feature of law in its focal sense. On the other hand, Kramer raises the possibility that such explanation by officials (again, where the explanation need not imply any essential connection to morality) might be a necessary and defining feature of law in its focal sense:

> ... even if we allow that publicly accessible explanations of official decisions are an integral feature of anything that counts as a full-fledged legal system, we should recognize that explanations need not be present as moral explanations. Both the actual purpose and the avowed purpose of the explanations can consist in the reinforcement of incentives for submission to evil dictates, rather than in the ascription of fairness to the decisions that apply those dictates.[35]

[34] *Ibid.* at 91.
[35] *Ibid.*

Here we can see Kramer wavering between two different propositions:

> *Proposition A:* "Publicly accessible explanations are not an integral feature of what counts as a legal system in the focal sense of the term."

> *Proposition B:* "Publicly accessible explanations are an integral feature of what counts as a legal system in the focal sense of the term, but the *actual* and *avowed* purpose of such explanations may have nothing to do with morality, and may pertain only to the reinforcement of incentives for the citizens' ongoing submission to the evil and self-serving dictates of the legal officials themselves."

In assessing the feasibility of the two possible propositions that Kramer might be endorsing here, it is important to keep in mind that the crucial question is not whether law in *any* sense of the term must involve publicly accessible explanations. The crucial question is whether law in its *focal* or *full-fledged* sense must involve publicly accessible explanations. And in what follows, I would to like to show that Kramer's position (whether it be represented by Proposition A or Proposition B) is not a feasible position regarding law in its *focal* sense.

If Kramer is taken to be asserting Proposition A, then his position is that a legal system which sufficiently displays the three integral features of law (generality, durability, and regularity in enforcement), but in which legal officials offer no publicly accessible explanation whatsoever for their directives, qualifies as a 'full-fledged' legal system or a legal system in the focal sense of the term. Such a legal system would be one in which the citizens are given no reasons whatsoever for complying with the directives of legal officials. Now of course, it is quite possible (and even likely) that citizens living under such a system would try to come up with reasons of their own (even if such reasons pertained only to their own entirely selfish interests) for complying with the directives of the system's legal officials. But it is also conceptually possible—on Kramer's account, if Kramer is taken to be asserting Proposition A—that citizens living under such a system might fail in their attempts to come up with reasons of their own for continued compliance. Even if the citizens are living under a system of social control where the norms of the system are general, durable, and consistently applied (thus qualifying the system as a full-fledged legal system on Kramer's account), the citizens may nevertheless fail in their attempts to come up with reasons for their compliance. They may simply comply for no reason at all, and there is nothing in Kramer's account of law in its focal sense (assuming that Kramer is affirming Proposition A) to rule out this conceptual possibility. Indeed, the citizens living under such a system may not even seek to come up with reasons for their own compliance. They may simply comply without having any reasons and without even caring about having reasons. In such a case, the citizens' continued compliance in the face of the officials' unexplained norms would not differ in any theoretically significant respects from the continued compliance of a group of zombies that are subjected to (unexplained) directives which are general, durable, and applied with regularity. On Kramer's account (if he is asserting Proposition A), it would seem that a system of directives applied to a group of zombies (provided only that the norms implied by such directives were sufficiently general, durable, and consistently applied) would qualify as a legal system *in the focal sense*. Just as no explanation is needed on the part of the legal officials, so too—and correlatively—no understanding would be needed on the part of those who comply with the directives of such legal officials. On Kramer's account (if it includes Proposition A), a system of general, durable, and regularly applied norms that happened to elicit the continued compliance of a group of zombies (who comply, but not for any reason) would qualify as law *in its focal sense*.

Now if Kramer is asserting Proposition A, he might seek to defend his account against this *reductio ad absurdum* by adding an important further requirement to his notion of law in its focal sense. In order to distinguish the sort of compliance at work in a legal system from the reason-less compliance of a group of zombies, Kramer might acknowledge that law-abiding citizens—unlike zombies—at the very least *see themselves as having a reason or reasons* for complying with the directives of the legal system (no matter what the specific content of such reasons might be). But once Kramer allows this further requirement—as I believe he would have to, in order to present a credible account of what law is, *in its focal sense*—he would have already conceded enough to undermine his own position. For when citizens see themselves as having a reason or reasons for compliance with the directives of a legal system, they inevitably see those reasons (no matter what the specific content of those reasons might be) as *good reasons*, all things considered. Of course, the citizens may be wrong in thinking that the reasons they have for continued compliance really are *good* reasons, all things considered. From the point of view of objective moral standards (assuming that there are objective moral standards), the citizens' reasons might be altogether bad or misdirected. But insofar as the citizens see themselves as having reasons for continued compliance, and insofar as their seeing themselves as having reasons is actually the cause or ground of their continued compliance (i.e., insofar as they actually *act on those reasons* and comply), it must be the case that the citizens see themselves as having *good* reasons, all things considered.[36]   For if the citizens did not see themselves as having such *good* reasons, then their having of reasons (whatever those reasons might be) would not be the cause or ground of the citizens' continued compliance with the law (i.e., they would not *act on those reasons* and would not choose to comply). The only kinds of reasons that can serve as the cause or ground of the citizens' acting to comply with the law, are reasons that the citizens apprehend as *good* reasons, all things considered.

Now if this appeal to reasons (which the citizens take to be *good* reasons, all things considered) is the only way in which Kramer can endorse Proposition A and nevertheless present a credible account of law *in its focal sense* (one which distinguishes credibly between the compliance of zombies and the compliance of citizens under the law), then Kramer—I believe—must concede the relevant point here to Finnis as natural law legal theorist. For once again, the crucial point is not that the citizens actually *do* have (objectively, morally) good reasons for continuing to comply with the law. The crucial point is only that the citizens *see themselves* as having good reasons for doing so (no matter how mistaken they may be). But even this is enough to undercut Kramer's alternative legal

---

[36] Given the limited scope of this paper, I am unable here to present any extended justification of this claim. But for now, let it suffice to say that in making this claim, I take myself to be doing nothing other than endorsing two central Aristotelian claims: (a) all distinctively human actions are undertaken for the sake of achieving some good or some perceived good (*Nicomachean Ethics*, Book I, Chapter 1); and (b) the conclusion of a practical syllogism is not just a statement about what is 'good', but consists in some human action, and—conversely—all actions that are distinctively human (i.e., undertaken voluntarily and with reason) are the conclusions of practical syllogisms (*Nicomachean Ethics*, Book VIII, Chapters 1-3).

positivist' account. For even the *apparent* or *perceived* goodness of reasons held by citizens is enough to establish a crucial conceptual link between the citizens' ongoing *compliance* with the legal system (and thus its ongoing durability or continuousness) and the apparent or perceived *goodness* of what the legal system does. And as Kramer himself acknowledges, if a legal system's *being perceived* or *appearing* to be good is crucial to its being a legal system, then the concept of a legal system cannot—after all—be entirely separated from concepts that are pregnant with moral meaning.[37]

If I am correct here about the conceptual implications of Proposition A (and assuming that Kramer's positivistic account includes Proposition A), then the citizens' ongoing compliance with legal directives (and thus the durability of the legal norms under which they live) must be connected to their seeing themselves as *having reasons* for such compliance; and their seeing themselves as having reasons for such compliance amounts to their seeing themselves as having *good* reasons for compliance; and finally, their seeing themselves as having *good* reasons for compliance inevitably links their compliance (and with it, the durability and very existence of the law *as* law in its focal sense) with a concern for making correct judgments about what is good. Thus against Kramer's positivistic account (assuming that this account includes Proposition A), the concept of law cannot be separated from the concept of the good or the perceived good. On my analysis here, the fundamental problem with Kramer's account is that his impoverished understanding of 'norms' allows him to think of norms simply as directives which are externally

---

[37] Kramer makes this point in his analysis of Lon Fuller's jurisprudence. See Kramer, *op. cit.*, at 66: "Hence, if officials adhere to Fuller's principles solely for the sake of appearing to take account of citizens' interests, their pattern of conduct will lend support to the characterization of those principles as morally pregnant.... To clarify this point, let us return briefly to the example of the smoker who renounces his habit. Suppose that a person X has decided to act upon the proposition 'I ought to stop smoking'. If his only reason for abandoning the habit of smoking is the enhancement of his reputation by appearing to show solicitude for the interests of others, then his decision—though purely prudential—is a testament to the moral significance of the proposition on which he acts. In such circumstances, we are not justified in inferring (from the purely prudential character of his conduct) that the proposition 'I ought to stop smoking' has no intrinsic moral force. Indeed, if the only credible prudential ground for desisting from smoking were the desire for plaudits that has motivated X, we could safely conclude that the aforementioned proposition does partake of an inherent moral worthiness."

applied to citizens so that the citizens' compliance is no longer meaning-fully distinguishable from the compliance of reason-less zombies. And with his impoverished understanding of 'norms,' Kramer essentially abandons the 'internal point of view' regarding law-abiding citizens and regarding the reasons that they *see themselves as having* for ongoing compliance with the law.

Now in light of the foregoing analysis, it might seem that Kramer's 'legal positivist' account may fare better if it is understood as incorporat-ing Proposition B instead of Proposition A. But further analysis reveals that Kramer's version of legal positivism remains infirm, even if under-stood as incorporating Proposition B. Recall that the main problem with Kramer's version of legal positivism (understood as incorporating Proposition A) was that it abandoned a genuinely 'internal point of view' regarding law-abiding citizens and regarding their reasons for complying with the law. Proposition B may seem to allow Kramer to overcome this problem, since Proposition B includes the claim that "publicly accessible explanations are an integral feature of what counts as a legal system in the focal sense of the term." If Kramer can acknowledge that the giving of publicly accessible explanations by legal officials is an integral feature of law, then it seems that he should also be able to take the next step and acknowledge that the citizens *having of reasons* for compliance is also an integral feature of law (after all, the giving of explanations by legal offi-cials seems quite naturally to imply the citizens' having of reasons for compliance, or at least to imply the *desirability* of this having of reasons). But Kramer explicitly refuses to take this further step (perhaps because he realizes that the further proposition about the citizens' having of reasons would lead him quite ineluctably to a positivism-adverse proposition about the citizens' having of reasons which they take to be *good* reasons).

Kramer's rejection of this further step is indicated by what is contained in the latter portion of Proposition B. While asserting that publicly acces-sible explanations by legal officials is a necessary feature of law, Proposition B also asserts that the *avowed purpose* of these explanations may pertain only to the reinforcement of incentives for the citizens' ongo-ing submission to the dictates of legal officials. Thus on Kramer's account (understood as incorporating Proposition B), the content of the publicly accessible explanation(s) required of legal officials may refer only to the reinforcement of incentives for the citizens' ongoing compliance with the legal officials' directives. In other words, the content of the explanation(s) given by legal officials might run as follows: "The reason why we officials enforce the norms of the prevailing (legal) system is to reinforce the incentives that you citizens will have for complying with these norms." But what is the legal officials' explanation for reinforcing the incentives that citizens will have for ongoing compliance? On Kramer's account (understood as incorporating Proposition B), the legal officials may give no explanation for their reinforcing of the incentives that citizens will have for compliance, other than the 'explanation' that such reinforcement will allow the officials themselves to remain in power and succeed in enforcing the norms that they happen to enforce. Thus on Kramer's account (understood as incorporating Proposition B), the publicly accessible explanation(s) required of legal officials can be entirely circular. The content of the explanation(s) required of legal officials can conceivably run as follows: "The reason why we officials enforce the norms of the prevailing (legal) system is to reinforce the incentives that you citizens will have for complying, so that we can succeed in enforcing the norms that we enforce." But to say that the publicly accessible explanations required of legal officials can be entirely circular is to say that they can fail at being explanations at all. After all, an apparent explanation that explains nothing, but only re-asserts the very fact to be explained, is not really an explanation, even if it is presented nominally or linguistically in the form of a real explanation. So on Kramer's account (understood as incorporating Proposition B), the publicly accessible explanations required of legal officials might not be explanations at all; nominally they might appear to be explanations, but they may fail to explain anything at all. And so the critique presented earlier regarding Proposition A (according to which no explanations are required of legal officials) is a critique that applies equally well with regard to Proposition B (according to which no *real* explanations are required of legal officials).

CONCLUSION

What I hope to have shown in this paper is that Kramer's legal positivist account of law in its focal or full-fledged sense—through which he seeks to undermine Finnis's natural law account—is ultimately not credible. It does not follow, however, that I have succeeded in presenting a complete defense of Finnis's natural law legal theory. After all, some legal theorists have remained legal positivists (and have continued to challenge Finnis's 'natural law' conclusions), even while accepting the claim that (implicit or explicit) explanations by legal officials (and even explanations that are justificatory or moral in their tenor) are an essential ingredient of law in its focal sense. Indeed, this is the sort of claim that Joseph Raz endorses as part of his own version of legal positivism. However, it is this sort of claim that also leads Raz to reject the "separability thesis" of traditional legal positivism.[38]   And as least one commentator has argued, it is Raz's acceptance of this claim (regarding explanations or justifications by legal officials) that ultimately destroys his legal positivism 'from within'.[39]   But we can leave any discussion of Raz's legal positivism for another occasion. In this paper, my limited aim has simply been to show that Kramer's particular version of legal positivism cannot be proffered—as Kramer seeks to do—as a credible alternative to Finnis's natural law theory.

[38] See note 3 above.

[39] See Jeffrey D. Goldsworthy, "The Self-Destruction of Legal Positivism," 10 *Oxford J. Legal Studies* 449 (1990). Indeed, it seems that Kramer is so intent on rejecting this claim (regarding the necessity of explanations or justifications by legal officials) precisely because he agrees with Goldsworthy that any acceptance of this claim is ultimately fatal to legal positivism. See Kramer, *op. cit.*, at 79.

NATURAL INCLINATION AND THE INTELLIGIBILITY OF THE GOOD IN THOMISTIC NATURAL LAW
Stephen L. Brock

Size is not always a gauge of significance. The issue that I propose to address here centers on a single clause from the *Summa theologiae*. But it goes nearly to the heart of St. Thomas's teaching on natural law. It concerns the way in which Thomas thinks the human mind comes to understand good and evil. The specific question raised by the clause is the role played in this process by what Thomas calls "natural inclination." This question leads to an even more basic one: what it is, for Thomas, that constitutes a truly intellectual grasp of the good.

The paper is set up as follows. First I present the text and survey the principal ways in which recent interpreters, including John Finnis, have handled it (section I). Then I argue for the reading of it that I find most satisfactory, considering particularly its context in the *Summa* (section II). From here I move to the more basic question. Drawing upon passages from various works, I try to bring out a number of fundamental and, I think, insufficiently noticed elements in Thomas's account of the understanding of the good; these bear directly upon on how that understanding is related to "inclination," and also to "nature" (III and IV). Finally, I draw some conclusions about the practical significance of Thomas's way of associating the precepts of natural law with natural inclinations (V). At various places there will emerge points of comparison, and sometimes of contrast, with Finnis's interpretation of Thomas on natural law.

I THE TEXT AND ITS INTERPRETATIONS
The article in which our clause appears is I-II, q. 94, a. 2. The clause is the central portion of the following sentence.

> Since good has the *ratio* of end, and bad the *ratio* of the contrary, hence it is that *all those things to which man has natural inclination, reason naturally apprehends as good*, and consequently as to be pursued by action; and their contraries as bad, and to be avoided.[1]

[1] Translations throughout this paper are mine. For the most part I leave *ratio* untranslated.

In the vast literature produced over the past few decades on natural law in St. Thomas, this article of the *Summa* has received a great deal of attention. Interpreters often feel a need to offer some explanation for the passage that I have singled out. It is not surprising. Thomas simply lays it down that the objects of natural human inclination are things that reason naturally apprehends as good. One may well wonder why this is so, and here he does not say. The variety of answers that have been offered is astonishing. Here is a brief sketch of what I think are the most prominent positions on the question.

On some readings, what Thomas has in mind in the passage is what he elsewhere speaks of as judgment "by connaturality" or "through inclination." Reason's grasp of an object of natural inclination as good would be an act moved directly by the inclination itself. It is not that reason consciously reflects upon the inclination and then goes on to judge its object good. Rather, the very presence of the inclination casts a kind of light upon the object, and reason spontaneously judges the object in this light. The most famous proponent of this view, Jacques Maritain, holds that such judgments do not even involve rational formulation or conceptualization.[2]

This seems to be a minority position. More interpreters take Thomas to be talking about a kind of knowledge that is more properly rational, involving some conscious reflection and conceptualization. Still, on some accounts, the connection between knowledge and inclination remains very tight. Reason's natural grasp of human goods, though not knowledge "through" inclination, would consist simply in the apprehension "of" natural inclinations and of their objects.[3] Knowing an object of natural inclination as good would be nothing other than knowing it to be such an object.

---

[2] Jacques Maritain, *Man and the State* (Chicago: University of Chicago Press, 1951), 92; "On Knowledge through Connaturality," *The Review of Metaphysics* 4.4 (June 1951): 473-481 (esp. 477-480); "Du savoir moral," *Revue Thomiste* 82 (1982): 533-549. See also Yves R. Simon, *Practical Knowledge* (New York: Fordham University Press, 1991), 33.

[3] For example, Paul-M. van Overbeke, O.P., "La loi naturelle et le droit naturel selon S. Thomas," *Revue Thomiste* 57 (1957): 65 ff.; Leo Elders, "Nature as the Basis of Moral Actions," *Jacques Maritain Center, Thomistic Institute*, 2001, http://www.nd.edu/Departments/Maritain/ti01/elders.htm, section III, ¶1 & ¶3; John C. Cahalan, "Natural Obligation: How Rationally Known Truth Determines Ethical Good and Evil," *The Thomist* 66 (2002): 126.

Others, however, judge it necessary to assign a somewhat less immediate role to natural inclination in the formation of reason's apprehension
of the human good. Here there is an even greater insistence on the rationality of the apprehension. The thought would be more or less as follows.
That something is the object of natural inclination only means that desire
for it naturally exists. But truly rational knowledge that something is
good, genuine understanding of its goodness does not consist in merely
registering the existence of desire for it, even desire that exists naturally.
Rather, such knowledge serves to make the desire itself intelligible. It
shows the desire to be "right" or to "make sense." It consists in seeing the
object as something intrinsically desirable, "fit" to be desired. In other
words, the mere "fact" of being desired does not show a thing to be *truly*
good. Surely, in our passage, Thomas is speaking about apprehending
things as true human goods. Seeing them as objects of natural inclination
cannot suffice for this. It must only be some kind of preliminary.

What else is required? For some, what is needed is reason's penetra-
tion to the root source of the natural inclinations, which is human nature.
To understand something as a true human good is to see it as an end
toward which man is aimed by nature, a purpose of his being human.[4] For
others, the decisive factor in practical reason's natural apprehension of a
human reality as a true human good is not the determination of its relation to human nature. It is rather the sheer understanding of the good in
general—the basis of the first precept of natural law—and the consideration of the reality in light of it. The latter view is the one initially proposed
by Germain Grisez and subsequently adopted by John Finnis.[5]

Finnis and Grisez do however still acknowledge a preliminary role for
natural inclinations in the genesis of practical reason's natural understanding of human goods. Experience of the inclinations would be what

[4] See Douglas Flippen, "Natural Law and Natural Inclinations," *The New Scholasticism*
60.3 (Summer 1986): 290-1, 306.

[5] To cite only the initial works: Germain Grisez, "The First Principle of Practical
Reason: a Commentary on the *Summa theologiae*, I-II Question 94, a. 2," *Natural Law
Forum* 10 (1965): 168-201; John Finnis, *Natural Law and Natural Rights* (Oxford:
Clarendon Law Series, 1980), esp. 33-36.

provides the data in which the goods are first grasped. They point us to the goods, though they are not the criteria by which we judge them good.[6] Now, despite the serious differences among the positions so far considered, there is one assumption that they all share. I have presented them so summarily because what really interests me here is this assumption. It is that the natural inclinations in question are pre-rational. That is, they would exist independently of reason's apprehension of their objects as good, and the apprehension would somehow follow on them.[7] The differences that I have signaled only regard how it follows.

The assumption is seldom even stated explicitly. However, in Finnis's recent book on Thomas, there is a very interesting and well documented set of observations which I think show him to be uneasy with some of its implications.[8] He is clearly worried about what sort of inclination it is that Thomas could have in mind in our passage. As he explains in considerable detail, there are several types of human inclination that are in some sense "natural" for Thomas, and that cannot possibly fit the bill.

In any case, the assumption that the inclinations are pre-rational has not in fact gone entirely unremarked in the literature, or unchallenged. I am referring to the interpretation offered by Lawrence Dewan in two very important articles.[9] It seems to me that Dewan's work in this area has received far too little attention. Elsewhere I have expressed my adherence

[6] See Grisez, "The First Principle of Practical Reason," 357-358; Finnis, *Natural Law and Natural Rights*, 34, 402. A similar line, giving a somewhat stronger role to the inclinations, is found in Martin Rhonheimer, *Natural Law and Practical Reason: A Thomist View of Moral Autonomy* (New York: Fordham University Press, 2000); see my review in *The Thomist* 66.2 (April 2002): 311-315.

[7] In her recent *Nature as Reason. A Thomistic Theory of the Natural Law* (Grand Rapids: Eerdmans, 2005), Jean Porter dwells at some length on the role of the natural inclinations. Her account is complex, but I think it is clear that she too treats them as prior to reason's grasp of their objects as good; see 68-82, 116-39 (esp. 127), 189-90. Of the positions that I have sketched, perhaps the closest to hers would be that of Flippen.

[8] John Finnis, *Aquinas. Moral, Political, and Legal Theory* (New York: Oxford University Press, 1998), 92-93.

[9] Lawrence Dewan, O.P., "Jacques Maritain and the Philosophy of Co-operation," in M. Gourgues and G.-D. Mailhiot (ed.), *Alterité. Vivre ensemble différents* (Montréal and Paris: Bellarmin/Cerf, 1986), 109-117; "St. Thomas, Our Natural Lights, and the Moral Order," *Angelicum* 67 (1990): 285-307 [originally published in *Maritain Studies/Études maritainiennes* 2 (1986): 59-92]. Also quite pertinent is his "The Real Distinction between Intellect and Will," *Angelicum* 57 (1980): 557-593.

to his view and added a few considerations regarding Thomas's intention in I-II, q. 94, a. 2.[10] What I want to do here is to confirm the position and develop it a little further.

II THE INCLINATIONS AS RESULTS OF
THE UNDERSTANDING

My basic thesis, then, is that not only the apprehension that Thomas is talking about in our passage, but also the inclination, is rational. Reason's natural understanding of human goods does not follow the natural inclinations to them. The inclinations follow the understanding. I think this is a much more plausible reading of our passage, for several reasons. (These partly overlap with the observations by Finnis that I mentioned a moment ago.)

First, this reading explains easily why Thomas can simply lay it down, as though obvious, that reason naturally apprehends as good all the things to which man is naturally inclined. If he were talking non-rational inclinations, inclinations that do not follow from reason's own apprehension, it would be a very dubious assertion. There are many non-rational inclinations existing in us by nature whose objects do not become known to us except after much investigation, if at all—certainly not "naturally." Think of some strictly physiological inclination, such as the natural tendency for our brain synapses to fire. Their firing is certainly a good thing. But it is hardly something that we are naturally aware of. Thomas did not even know that brains have synapses. If, however, he is talking about inclinations that follow upon the natural apprehension of their objects as good, his assertion is self-evident.

Another point is the caliber of the inclinations that he must be talking about. They are right inclinations. Their objects are true human goods. Otherwise they could hardly correspond to precepts of natural law.[11] But Thomas is quite explicit about the fact that sometimes the non-rational

---

[10] Stephen L. Brock, *The Legal Character of Natural Law according to St. Thomas Aquinas*, Ph.D. dissertation (University of Toronto, 1988), 143-166.

[11] See I-II, q. 93, a. 6: he speaks generally of "inclination to what is consonant with the eternal law."

inclinations existing naturally in a human being are not right.[12] This is particularly clear in the case of the sensitive appetite.[13] Unreasoned feeling may be right or wrong. The rectitude of a person's feeling is guaranteed only when it is directed by (right) reason. In the very article to which our passage belongs, Thomas says that "the inclinations of the parts of human nature, such as the concupiscible and irascible appetites, pertain to natural law insofar as they are regulated by reason."[14]

Should we see the inclinations as contained in man's very essence, prior even to his physical dispositions and feelings? Thomas does teach that the elements of a subject's essence—its substantial form and matter—are already a sort of inclination (I, q. 59, a. 2). And no doubt he thinks such inclination always right. However, as he explains in the same place, its range is rather limited. It is only toward what is included within the subject's own substantial being.[15] Any inclinations toward objects that extend outside the subject's being must be distinct from its essence. Many of the objects of inclination mentioned in I-II, q. 94, a. 2 are clearly not included in man's substantial being.

If the inclinations are neither physical dispositions, nor spontaneous feelings, nor elements of man's very essence, then in Thomas's conception of human nature, only one possibility remains. They must be movements of man's rational appetite, inclinations of the human will. But if so, they must be inclinations that derive from reason's apprehension of their objects as good. The will is not moved toward anything except what reason—practical reason—apprehends as good and desirable.[16]

---

[12] See Finnis, *Aquinas*, 93, n. 150. He also points out that Thomas must be talking about inclinations that everyone has. This too suggests that they cannot be natural bodily or sensitive inclinations, since these vary among individuals; see I-II, q. 51, a. 1, near the end of the corpus.

[13] See especially I-II, q. 71, a. 2, ad 3; I-II, q. 78, a. 3. Also I, q. 81, a. 3, ad 1 & ad 2; I-II, q. 91, a. 6; I-II, q. 94, a. 4; *In VI Eth.*, lect. xi, §1278; *In XII Meta.* lect. vii, §2522; *De malo* q. 16, a. 2.

[14] I-II, q. 94, a. 2, ad 2. See I-II, q. 94, a. 4, ad 3.

[15] Compare Anthony Lisska, *Aquinas's Theory of Natural Law. An Analytical Reconstruction* (Oxford: Oxford University Press, 1996), 96-100.

[16] I-II, q. 9, a. 1, ad 2. Compare Clifford G. Kossel, S.J., "Natural Law and Human Law (Ia IIae qq. 90-97)," in Stephen J. Pope, ed. *The Ethics of Aquinas* (Washington, D.C.: Georgetown University Press, 2002), 174.

I think this is the correct view. If we suppose that Thomas is speaking of inclinations of the will in the corpus of I-II, q. 94, a. 2, none of the aforementioned difficulties arises.

First, these inclinations cannot exist in such a way that any of their objects, or the goodness thereof, escape reason's apprehension. This is obvious, since the inclinations of the will always follow upon such apprehension.

Thomas also teaches that the will's natural inclinations are always right—just as intellect's natural understanding is always true.[17] This in fact is why they are always right. In voluntary matters, he says, even if the rectitude of reasoning about the things that are for an end depends on the rectitude of the appetite of the end, nevertheless the rectitude of the appetite of the end itself depends upon the right apprehension of the end, which is through reason.[18] Here we are surely talking about the right apprehension of the end.[19] "Good has the *ratio* of end."

Finally, the natural inclinations of the will are by no means limited to the goods contained in a man's substantial being. In fact they extend to the whole range of goods cited in I-II, q. 94, a. 2. They include "universally all the things that befit the willing subject according to his nature." And so, "man naturally wants not only the object of the will [the good in general], but also other things that befit other powers, such as knowledge of the true, which suits the intellect; and to be and to live, and other such things as regard natural continuance."[20]

Besides skirting the various difficulties, taking the inclinations to be rational rather than pre-rational also gives our passage a much clearer connection with the truly fundamental article on natural law in the *Summa*, the one concerned with its very existence: I-II, q. 91, a. 2.

Thomas begins the corpus of this article by observing that all creatures

---

[17] I, q. 60, a. 1, ad 3; see I, q. 17, a. 3, ad 2.

[18] I-II, q. 19, a. 3, ad 2; I-II, q. 58, a. 5, ad 1.

[19] Even as regards the last end considered merely formally or abstractly—*beatitudo in communi*—the desire of it depends on the apprehension of it; see I-II, q. 5, a. 8, c. & ad 1; I-II, q. 10, a. 2.

[20] I-II, q. 10, a. 1. I use "natural continuance" to translate *naturalem consistentiam*. An indication of what this covers is found in I-II, q. 60, a. 5, where he speaks of the "*bonum ... ad consistentiam humanae vitae pertinens in individuo vel in specie, sicut sunt delectabilia ciborum et venereorum.*"

have their natural inclinations from some impression of the eternal law of divine providence. He then argues that the rational creature is subject to providence in a higher way than the rest, since he himself "becomes a sharer in providence, providing for himself and others." This in turn shows that he shares in "the eternal reason (*ratio*) through which he has natural inclination toward due act and end."(Note the "through which.") Man partakes in the *ratio*, the intelligible conception that is the very source of natural inclination in him. Thomas goes on to trace this share in the eternal reason to the light of man's own natural reason, "by which we discern what good is and what evil is."

Moreover, the article's second objection and reply refer explicitly to the will. The objection argues that there is no natural law in man, because the ordination of human acts to their end is not through "nature," but through reason and will. The objector is taking 'nature' in the sense of something "pre-rational." But Thomas's reply makes no appeal to anything in us that is "natural" in this sense. Instead, he simply reminds us that reason and will themselves have a natural dimension. "All reasoning derives from principles naturally known, and all appetite of things that are for the end derive from the natural appetite of the last end. And so likewise, the first direction of our acts toward the end must come about through a natural law." Thus, to adopt the usual reading of the 94, 2 clause is to slip back into the wrong sense of 'natural.' The inclinations that it is referring to are natural effects of reason and will, i.e., of the principles by which man acts *humanly*.[21] They are inclinations of man *as man*.[22]

There is, however, at least one obvious objection to this reading of the 94,2 clause. This is that the conclusion which Thomas draws from it is that "the order of the precepts of natural law is according to the order of the natural inclinations." He then uses this rule to lay out the order of the precepts. So it may seem that the inclinations are prior to the apprehension, not its result.

I shall discuss Thomas's rationale for the order that he assigns to inclinations and precepts in the final section. But to answer this objection, I think it suffices to draw a distinction.

---

[21] I-II, q. 1, a. 1. It is no accident, I think, that earlier in the corpus of I-II, q. 94, a. 2, Thomas remarks that *qui dicit hominem, dicit rationale.*

[22] Very pertinent here is III, q. 19, a. 2.

Earlier in the article, we are told that the very first precept of natural law, "good is to be done and pursued, and bad avoided," is "founded upon the *ratio* of good." But we should note that the precept is not simply identical with the *ratio* of good, any more than the absolutely first principle of reasoning, the principle of non-contradiction, is simply identical with the *ratio* of being. One thing is the very discernment of what good is, and another is the judgment that it is to be pursued through action. And likewise, I believe, while the other precepts of natural law present the objects of man's natural inclinations as things "to be done and pursued," they are founded upon the prior apprehension of the objects simply as good. Thus, what Thomas says is that "all those things for which man has a natural inclination, reason naturally apprehends as good, and *consequently* as things to be pursued by action."

In other words, *both* the inclinations and the precepts follow upon the understanding of the objects as good. And if anything, the inclinations follow even more immediately than do the precepts. For the inclinations require nothing but the consideration of the objects as good, desirable. But the precepts require a consideration of the objects not only as good, but also as matters of action, doable or pursuable.

Some might call these distinctions hairsplitting. I would rather call them metaphysics. It seems to me that this reading of our text has deep roots in Thomas's philosophy of the good. What I want to focus on here are certain elements of his account of the good's intelligibility.

III UNDERSTANDING DESIRE

Picking up on a point mentioned earlier, I think that Finnis and others are quite right in holding that for Thomas, the properly intellectual apprehension of something as good does not consist in merely registering a desire for it. There is a passage in his commentary on the *Metaphysics* where he is very clear about this.[23]

He is discussing Aristotle's argument that the first, highest cause of things must be a final cause—a desirable, a good—and that, as the first desirable, it must be an *intelligible* good. Thomas observes that not everything *we* find desirable is an intelligible good. He points to the inconti-

[23] *In XII Meta.*, lect. vii, §2522.

nent person. "According to reason, he is moved by the intelligible good. But according to the concupiscible power, he is moved by something pleasant to the senses, which seems good, although it is not good unqualifiedly (*simpliciter*) but only in a way (*secundum quid*)." Further on Thomas indicates how different these two ways of "seeming good" are:

> what is desired according to concupiscence seems good because it is desired. For concupiscence perverts the judgment of reason, such that what is pleasant seems good to it. But what is desired with intellectual appetite is desired because it seems good in itself (*secundum se*).

That which is unqualifiedly good, then, is an intelligible good; and it is not something that seems good to reason merely because it is already desired. It seems good, desirable, in itself. Things that are good in themselves are what Thomas elsewhere calls *bona honesta*. These, he says, "have in themselves that whence they are desired."[24] They are genuine origins of desire. Neither reason's judgment that they are good, nor the will's resulting desire of them, supposes any prior appetitive response such as pleasure.[25] To be sure, the *bona honesta* are pleasant. But the pleasure of them presupposes the judgment that they are good.[26]

So it certainly is not a judgment "through inclination." In fact, pleasure need not even accompany it. There is pleasure only when what is judged good is also judged to be present.[27] If we tend to think that judgments of good and bad must always be associated with pleasure and pain, perhaps it is because we do not always distinguish sufficiently between intellect and sense. Thomas brings out the relevant difference in his commentary on *De anima* III.7 (at 431a8-16).

Aristotle says that when what is sensed is pleasant or painful, the sensitive soul, "as it were affirming or denying," pursues or shuns it. Pleasure and pain, he explains, are "the operation of the sensitive mean

---

[24] I, q. 5, a. 6, ad 2.

[25] Even as regards goods to which sense-appetite also extends, is it true in every case that we experience sense-desires for them before we understand their goodness? For instance, can a child not understand the good of *coniunctio maris et feminae* before he feels any urge toward it himself?

[26] See I-II, q. 4, a. 2, ad 2.

[27] I, q. 20, a. 1.

with respect to the good or bad as such." Thomas remarks that although making an affirmation or a negation is proper to intellect, the sense makes something like it when it apprehends something as pleasant or painful.[28] A little further on, turning to the intellectual soul, Aristotle says simply that when it affirms or denies an object as good or bad, it pursues or shuns. Thomas picks up on the fact that this time there is no mention of pleasure or pain. In Aristotle's account of the sensitive part, Thomas says,

> desire or shunning did not follow at once from the grasp of that which is good or bad, as here with intellect; but pleasure and pain followed, and then from this, desire and shunning. The reason for this is that just as sense does not grasp universal good, so too the appetite of the sensitive part is not moved by universal good or bad, but by a certain determinate good which is pleasant to sense, and by a certain determinate bad which is painful to sense. But in the intellective part there is the grasp of universal good and bad; whence too, the appetite of the intellective part is moved immediately by the apprehended good or bad.[29]

Intellect grasps "universal good and bad," the *ratio boni* and the *ratio mali*. It discerns "what good is, and what bad is." It can move desire and shunning by simply applying the concepts of good and bad. Neither the judgment, nor even the desire or shunning that the judgment moves, presupposes any prior appetitive response such as pleasure or pain.[30]

What may make all of this difficult to understand (besides our tendency to confuse intellect and sense) is that the *ratio* of good does after all contain a reference to appetite. To be good is to be desirable. So in order to grasp "what a good is" and to move desire, intellect must also grasp "what desire is." This might lead us back to thinking that its grasp of the good does somehow depend upon some sort of primordial experi-

---

[28] *In III De Anima*, lect. xii, §767.

[29] *Ibid.*, §771.

[30] In fact, even at the level of the senses, Thomas posits an apprehension of "suitable or harmful" prior to the response of pleasure or pain (*In III De Anima*, lect. xii, §769; I-II, q. 9, a. 1, ad 2). If pleasure or pain must follow, I take it that this is because what sense apprehends, it apprehends as somehow present. But universal apprehension of something abstracts from its presence or absence. It bears absolutely on "what the thing is."

ence of inclination or appetite.³¹ And this could only be pre-rational appetite, sense-appetite.

But Thomas is very clear that the experience of sense-appetite does not provide the basis for grasping the *ratio boni*. This is a point that Dewan has brought out especially forcefully.³² In order to grasp the good, what intellect must understand is its own appetite, intellectual appetite. This is why, before it grasps the good, it must grasp *itself*.

"First," Thomas says,

> intellect apprehends just a being (*ipsum ens*); second, it appre-
> hends itself understanding (*apprehendit se intelligere*) a being;
> and third, it apprehends itself desiring (*apprehendit se
> appetere*) a being. Whence, although the good is in things,
> there comes first the *ratio* of a being; second the *ratio* of a true
> [which is in the mind]; and third the *ratio* of a good.³³

This talk of intellect apprehending "itself" desiring is striking. In a way, of course, it is only shorthand for the *person* apprehending himself desiring. But it is the person *qua* intellectual apprehending this; and, it is the person apprehending himself desiring *qua* intellectual.

So the appetitive act relative to which intellect knows "what a good is"—the desire essentially associated with the *ratio boni*—is something intellectual. It is the operation of the will. Yet this cannot mean that in order to know the *ratio boni*, one must first "experience" the will's oper-ation, as though there were already an operation of the will there to be experienced. For again, the will does not operate except through intellect. It bears on "universal" good and bad. There is no such thing as operation about universal objects that does not involve intellect.

But knowing the will's operation does not require that it already "be there." In general, even though it is true that what is known is always somehow "in act," it need not always be in act in itself. It suffices that its proper causes or principles be in act. This is how we can know some

---

³¹ Cf. Rafael T. Caldera, *Le jugement par inclination chez saint Thomas d'Aquin* (Paris: J. Vrin, 1980), 34; Fulvio Di Blasi, *Dio e la Legge Naturale. Una rilettura di Tommaso d'Aquino* (Pisa: ETS, 1999), 185-6.

³² "Jacques Maritain and the Philosophy of Co-operation," 114-115; "St. Thomas, Our Natural Lights, and the Moral Order," 293-297.

³³ I, q. 16, a. 4, ad 2.

future events: by discerning them in their present causes. As for the acts of the will, the cause in which the intellect knows them is itself. Thomas says that the intellect knows the act of the will, not just once it has its own existence, but insofar as it already "exists in" the intellect, "as the principled is in the principle, in which there is a notion of the principled."34

This is how intellect *first* knows the act of the will. This act *must* be known before it occurs, because its occurrence is caused by the practical intellect of the one who has it.35 Practical intellect causes its effects by ordering or directing to them. It *always* pre-conceives them. It knows them, not as already existing, but as fit or due to exist.36 This is how it knows, and causes, the will's desire for something: by judging the thing "good," i.e., fit to desire, *conveniens ad appetendum*.37

Perhaps we can even say that when Thomas speaks of intellect apprehending "itself" desiring, he is speaking in the way in which he elsewhere speaks of practical intellect as "moving"; viz., as *directing to* movement.38 Then it would truly be intellect knowing itself (though also knowing the movement of the will as what it is directing toward). In any case, we should not overlook the fact that prior to its knowledge of itself as practical, intellect knows itself absolutely, as "understanding 'a being'." Thus it can grasp "a true." As Dewan says, "The intellect, in conceiving 'the true', already knows itself as terminus of the «movement» from being to the soul; its natural «next thought» is of the «movement» from the soul to being."39

I think we might also say that in knowing the true, the mind already knows itself as principle of a certain "ordering" of the soul's operation. For the very acts of affirming and denying are a sort of ordering, though one that terminates "in the soul itself." They are intellect ordering its own thoughts, applying conceptions to its consideration of things, or remov-

34 I, q. 87, a. 4, ad 3.

35 I-II, q. 9, a. 1, ad 2

36 See I-II, q. 93, a. 2, ad 3.

37 I-II, q. 19, a. 1, ad 1.

38 I, q. 79, a. 11, ad 1. Thomas also speaks of *synderesis* as "inclining": I, q. 79, a. 12, obj. 2 & *Sed contra*.

39 "St. Thomas, Our Natural Lights, and the Moral Order," 294-295.

ing them, as it sees fit.[40] Knowing itself as a "soul-orderer," it can go on to conceive itself ordering the soul with respect to things "outside," directing appetite. Aristotle's comparison of appetitive acts to affirmations and denials would then be no mere afterthought. It might even be the most natural way to think of them.

At any rate the comparison is not confined to acts of sense-appetite. In his account of the principles of good choice in *Nicomachean Ethics* VI.2, Aristotle remarks that "what affirmation and denial are in intellect, pursuit and avoidance are in appetite" (1139a21). Thomas's comment ties the comparison to the very possibility of "intelligent desire."

> Intellect in judging has two acts, namely affirmation, by which it assents to the true, and negation, by which it dissents from the false. To these two there respond proportionally two [acts] in the appetitive power, namely pursuit, by which the appetite tends to a good and adheres to it, and shunning, by which it draws back from a bad and dissents from it. And accordingly, intellect and appetite can be conformed, insofar as what intellect affirms to be good, appetite pursues, and what intellect denies being good, appetite shuns.[41]

IV UNDERSTANDING DESIRABILITY

So although 'good' means desirable, grasping it need not be a function of pre-rational desire. Still, it must be a function of *something*. To understand a thing is to know its nature. There is such a thing as the nature of desirability, the "what good is" that the natural light of reason enables the rational creature to discern.[42] And there is more involved in it than what the merely abstract notion of desire—of "movement from the soul to things"—expresses. For not every possible object of such movement is something that even *seems* to have the "nature of the good."

This was the point of the passage from the *Metaphysics* commentary. What seems to have the nature of the good is what seems to be good "in itself" or to "have in itself that whence it is desired." It is what seems *honestum*. But being pleasant to the senses also makes a thing seem to be a possible object of desire (indeed it makes it able to move the will), and

---

40 See I, q. 16, a. 2.

41 *In VI Eth.*, lect. ii, §1128 [809].

42 I-II, q. 91, a. 2.

yet it does not, by itself, make the thing seem *honestum*. It only makes it similar in a certain effect: pleasure.

The merely "pleasant good," Thomas says, is "good" only in a qualified, derivative *sense*. The unqualified sense is that of the "good in itself," the *honestum*. This is the *primary* sense, the one *first* understood, to which all others refer.[43] And the "that whence it is desired" which the *honestum* has in itself, whatever this is, will be what goodness or desirability primarily consists in.

In other words, from the very start, understanding "a good" means not only grasping a certain relation to desire, but also grasping the *principle* of this relation, that which the relation is a function of.[44] It is just as with "a true." In part, 'true' signifies a certain relation to intellect. A true thought is one to which intellect "tends"[45] or which is acceptable to it. But 'true' also signifies the basis of this relation. There is something "in" the thought that makes it acceptable: its conformity to what it is about. This is what its acceptability is a function of, and what its truth consists in. I think a brief look at what Thomas thinks desirability or goodness consists in can shed further light on his use of natural inclinations in I-II, q. 94, a. 2.

We have already heard him saying that first the mind grasps a *being*, then it grasps itself understanding a *being*, and then it grasps itself desiring a *being*. So 'a good' always means at least: a being. It also means something relative to the soul: an *understood* being. But there is something else as well that it also means (in the primary sense), something pertaining to the good thing in relation to itself. Thomas explains this in the corpus of I, q. 16, a. 4. "A good," he says, is not quite as "close" (in intelligibility) to "a being" as "a true" is. "The true regards being absolutely and immediately. But the *ratio* of good follows on being insofar as it is somehow *perfect*; for thus is it desirable."[46]

43 I, q. 5, a. 6, ad 3. The *bonum delectabile* seems to coincide with what Thomas calls the *bonum apparens*, the "specious good"; see I-II, q. 19, a. 1, ad 1, alongside the following texts: I, q. 5, a. 6, ad 2; I, q. 63, a. 1, ad 4; *In III Eth.*, lect. x, §495 & *passim*.

44 John I. Jenkins, "Good and the Object of Natural Inclination in St. Thomas Aquinas," *Medieval Philosophy and Theology* 3 (1993): 62-96, holds that while the real nature of the good is something more than merely being desired, our first and natural apprehension of it is only as what is desired.

45 I, q. 16, a. 1.

46 See I, q. 5, a. 1.

What goodness consists in is perfection.[47] It is so in the good thing, and it is also so in the mind's initial grasp of it. Thomas is arguing that good comes after true *in ratione*, in intelligibility. He says this means that it enters the mind later.[48] Its *ratio* supposes and includes the *ratio* of perfect. (Presumably the *ratio* of "a bad" includes that of "a defective.")

What is "a perfect"? It is something "from which nothing is absent according to the mode of its perfection."[49] This is not circular. Thomas is presenting perfection as something related to a *measure*, that which sets a "mode."[50] Elsewhere he calls perfection "fullness of being."[51] The fullness of a container is measured by its capacity, which is determined by its inner shape (its inner peri*meter*). What Thomas identifies as the measure of a being's fulfillment is "what it is," its nature; this is determined by its *form*.[52] And so, "for each thing, that is good which befits it according to its form, and bad, that which departs from the order of its form."[53] Moreover, "every existence and every good is *considered* through some form."[54]

A sign of how basic the *ratio* of "perfect" is for the *ratio* of "desirable" is that desire is understood, from the start, as movement from what is "in the soul" to what is "in reality"; i.e., from a thing's "being known" to its simply "being." If grasping goodness presupposes grasping truth, it is not only because the desire to which goodness is relative is intellectual, but also because grasping desirability involves comparing the two modes. Merely "being known" is a "ghostly" way of being—insubstantial, unfulfilling. It is not "being *in act*."[55]

---

[47] Cf. *In IX Eth.*, lect. xi, §1904.

[48] See I, q. 16, a. 4, ad 2.

[49] I, q. 4, a. 1; I, q. 5, a. 5.

[50] See I, q. 5, a. 5, obj. 1 & c.; I-II, q. 85, a. 4. Also *In III Sententiarum*, d. 34, q. 1, a. 3, c.; d. 34, q. 2, a. 1, qc. 3, c.

[51] I-II, q. 18, aa. 1 & 2.

[52] I, q. 5, a. 5.

[53] I-II, q. 18, a. 5. Other pertinent texts: I, q. 21, a. 1, ad 3; I, q. 49, a. 1; I-II, q. 71, aa. 1 & 2.

[54] I-II, q. 85, a. 4.

[55] See I, q. 18, a. 4, ad 3.

Nor is it *active*. "Heat *in the mind* does not heat," Thomas says, "but *in the fire*."⁵⁶ Thomas finds the notion of "perfect" closely associated with that of active power. A being is perfect, mature, when it can effect its like.⁵⁷ This makes sense, since likeness is "communication in form."⁵⁸ The being is "full" when its form can "overflow." Thus grasping active power entails grasping form; and the *ratio* of good, or of final cause, pre-supposes the *rationes* of formal and agent cause.⁵⁹

We should notice that the thought is not at all that goodness is "implied" in perfection, as though "derivable" from it by some kind of conceptual analysis. It is the *ratio* of the perfect that is included in the *ratio* of the good, not vice-versa. To say otherwise would be to fall into the "is-ought fallacy" that Hume exposed, and that Finnis and Grisez are so wary of.⁶⁰ The *ratio* of "a good" adds something new to those of "a being," "the nature of a being," and "the fullness of a being according to its nature." It adds the relation to desire, the final causality.

However, this novelty definitely has the status of an *addition*, an "out-growth." The *ratio* of the perfect is the matrix in which it is begotten (and apart from which it corrupts). In relation to Hume, this is very important. For even though what Hume exposed is a genuine fallacy, the larger argu-ment that he was engaged in is itself nothing short of sophistry. What he showed was that the notion of "according to nature" does not contain the notion of "good." But what he actually needed was the sophistical infer-ence from this, which he leaves tacit, that the notion of "good" does not contain the notion of "according to nature." For it is really only this infer-ence that provides grounds for his main thesis, which is that the notion of "good" has no rational or intelligible basis at all—that it is a mere func-

---

⁵⁶ *De ver.*, q. 22, a. 12; see I-II, q. 5, a. 6, ad 2.

⁵⁷ I, q. 5, a. 4.

⁵⁸ I, q. 4, a. 3.

⁵⁹ I, q. 5, a. 4.

⁶⁰ See, for example, Finnis, *Natural Law and Natural Rights*, 33-49; *Aquinas*, 90; Germain Grisez, Joseph Boyle, & John Finnis, "Practical Principles, Moral Truth, and Ultimate Ends," *American Journal of Jurisprudence* 32 (1987): 127.

tion of sentiment or feeling.[61] Of course Finnis and Grisez reject this thesis. They *say* that reason grasps "intelligible" good. Yet they give every appearance of accepting that tacit inference.[62] Its effect, I believe, is just what Hume wanted: to eviscerate the intelligibility of the good.

On the other hand, I think that Finnis and Grisez are right to maintain that our original apprehension of the good is practical, not speculative.[63] For we should not lose sight of precisely how it is that grasping "the nature of a being" is needed for grasping what a good or a final cause is. It is needed as a principle for grasping perfection, "fullness of being." But the mind need not yet be seeing "the nature of a being" as itself an *effect* of goodness. That is, it need not be judging that a thing's perfection is what the thing is *aimed* at by nature, the *purpose* of its being what it is.[64] One thing is to see what human perfection is, and that this is desirable; quite another is to judge that human kind *exists* for its sake (rather than, say, by chance). This judgment is speculative. It uses the notion of the good to *explain* man's existence. It involves coming to see nature itself as the work of a mind. But the first thing our mind apprehends as an effect of goodness, the effect tied to its initial grasp of "what a good is," is its own desire. As we saw, it first apprehends this in a practical way. Eventually it may come to see this too as involving the influence of a higher mind.

[61] See David Hume, *A Treatise of Human Nature*, ed. L. A. Selby-Bigge (Oxford: Oxford University Press, 1888), Book III, Part I, Section i, esp. 469-70, and Section ii, 470-476. It is interesting to note that for Thomas, even the mere *bonum delectabile*, to the extent that it retains something of the *ratio boni* and is capable of moving the intellectual appetite, also retains some appearance of being "according to nature"; see I-II, q. 6, a. 4, ad 3.

[62] Finnis says, "the *underived* first principles of practical reasonableness . . . make no reference at all to human nature, but only to human good"; *Natural Law and Natural Rights*, 36. He seems to qualify this somewhat in *Aquinas*; here he remarks on the close association between the notions of "good" and "perfection" (91), and he suggests that the practical knowledge of the first practical principles does "amount to an understanding however informal," of human nature (92). However, what he seems to mean is that this understanding of human nature would be a *result* of the practical knowledge, not a principle of it. Thus, he says that "the epistemic source of the first practical principles is not human nature or a prior, theoretical understanding of human nature.... Rather, the epistemic relationship is the reverse..." (91).

[63] See Finnis, *Natural Law and Natural Rights*, 33-4; *Aquinas*, 89.

[64] See above, at n. 4.

We might ask: why does the mind find the perfect fit to desire, and the defective fit to shun? Here I believe we reach a sheer beginning, something immediate. We might as well ask: why does the mind find acceptable the proposition that states the case as it is, and unacceptable the ones that do not? It is just the nature of mind.

V UNDERSTANDING HUMAN GOODS

Returning now to I-II, q. 94, a. 2, we may be struck by how concerned this article is with the order in which the human mind understands things. In fact the order of intelligibles given in I, q. 16, a. 4—being, true, good— shows up here. Before giving the first precept of natural law, which is founded on the *ratio* of good—this being the first, most common notion in *practical* reason—Thomas gives what is absolutely first and common to all reasoning whatsoever, namely the *ratio* of being, together with the principle founded upon it. And his formulation of this principle points to the true: "affirming and denying do not go together."

It is from this high, quite "metaphysical" vantage-point that he goes on to contemplate the order in the precepts of natural law. The first one rests on the good taken absolutely or universally. The others rest upon certain particular goods, the ones we are familiar with: "those to which man has natural inclination." As we saw, the order among these precepts is said to be "according to the order of natural inclinations."

Now, if I was right in arguing that both the inclinations and the precepts flow from the natural understanding of human goods, then one might wonder why Thomas even mentions the inclinations. Why does he not say simply that the order of the precepts is according to that of the understanding of human goods? I would suggest two reasons, interrelated.

First, bringing in the inclinations is a way of recalling the fundamental account in I-II, q. 91, a. 2, where the existence of natural law, although proper to man, was explained within the setting of the common subjection of all creatures to the eternal law, from whose impression all have their natural inclinations. This underscores the fact that Thomas is still seeing natural law as a particular effect of God's universal providence. And second, since "inclination" is thus a more common effect of providence, the move from inclinations to precepts is a move from the general to the particular. This sort of move is extremely typical of Thomas's teaching. I-II, q. 94, a. 2 is itself filled with such moves.

So the perspective is remaining quite "metaphysical." Finnis stresses this.[65] However, is there any reason to think that Thomas is suddenly no longer speaking about the order in which things "fall into the apprehension of all,"[66] or indeed, about the order in which they fall into the *practical* apprehension of all? He referred explicitly to this order in presenting the first precept: the good is what "falls first in the apprehension of practical reason."

If we adopt the assumption that the inclinations to which the other precepts correspond are pre-rational, then indeed we may have grounds for thinking that the order given here is incidental to practical reason's apprehension of the goods. This in fact is Finnis's view.[67] But if we take them to be rational, then surely we must regard the order as the apprehension's own. The *vision* being offered of it is something metaphysical.[68] But it is a metaphysical vision of practical reason itself. It is an overview of the natural principles by which the rational creature "becomes a sharer in providence" (I-II, q. 91, a. 2).

The order goes, once again, from the general to the particular. It begins with the inclination to that good "which is according to the nature that man shares with all substances."[69] After this is the inclination to what is according to the nature he shares with all animals. Last comes the incli-

---

[65] See *Aquinas*, 92-94.

[66] Following the Leonine edition.

[67] He calls it an "irrelevant schematization" (*Natural Law and Natural Rights*, 95) and a "metaphysical stratification" (*Aquinas*, 81).

[68] This is not at all to say that it contributes nothing to practical knowledge of the goods; see Kevin Flannery, *Acts Amid Precepts. The Aristotelian Logical Structure of Thomas Aquinas's Moral Theory* (Washington, D.C.: The Catholic University of America Press, 2001), 48-49.

[69] Even this is to be seen as inclination in the properly human "mode," intellectual. On the intellectual mode of this inclination, see I, q. 75, a. 6. More generally on the community and diversity of "natural inclination" in intellectual and non-intellectual beings, see I, q. 60, aa. 1 & 5; I, q. 62, a. 2, ad 2. There would also be some difference between the angelic and human modes, since the human intellect naturally thinks of itself (and its effects) in terms taken from physical things: I, q. 87, a. 3, ad 1. Pertinent here is II-II, q. 108, a. 2 (cf. I-II, q. 87, a. 1).

nation to the good that is according to the nature of reason, which is proper to man.[70]

Why is this the order? I think the answer is quite simple. Thomas is talking about what "practical reason naturally apprehends to be human goods." The apprehension is of goods *as human*. This means, as pertaining to "what a man is." They are the perfections whose measure, and a principle of whose intelligibility, is the nature of man. At each turn, he speaks of what is according to some dimension of human nature. There is an order in the natural understanding of these dimensions.[71] And Thomas leaves no doubt about its shape. Proceeding from the general to the particular is not just a way that he happens to be fond of. He sees it as the primary way in which *all* human understanding proceeds.[72]

One last question: if the order is that of practical apprehension, does it have any practical bearing? I do not think that by itself, it implies an order among the goods *as goods*, a rank in their *value*.[73] The order is only in reason's acquaintance with them. Yet it does, I believe, have at least two practical implications, one direct and one indirect.[74]

Directly, even if it is not a ranking of the goods in themselves, it does seem to suggest a certain subjective ranking, a gradation in the care that people are naturally apt to give to the goods.[75] Some inclinations are more deeply ingrained than others. We do, I think, find people generally tending, both individually and collectively, to be more concerned about

[70] In the next article Thomas even arrives at an inclination *proper* to man through a reasoning from general to particular.

[71] This of course is not the same as scientific knowledge of man (just as the practical understanding discussed here is not the same as the science of ethics). But all intellectual cognition of things, scientific or not, is some sort of apprehension of their natures.

[72] His fullest presentation of this view is I, q. 85, a. 3.

[73] Even less does it imply that the goods are "commensurable"; see Flannery, *Acts Amid Precepts*, ch. 4, esp. 105-108.

[74] I am not talking here about what the scientific determination of the order contributes to practical knowledge of the goods (see above, n. 66), but about possible upshots of the order itself, as a feature of "natural reason," in human conduct.

[75] Although they do not refer to I-II, q. 94, a. 2, Grisez, Boyle, and Finnis do acknowledge the existence of rankings of this sort; see the section entitled "Natural Priorities among the Basic Goods" in "Practical Principles, Moral Truth, and Ultimate Ends," 137-139. Of course they deny any hierarchy among the goods themselves, as goods; *ibid.*, 139-40.

human survival than about the family, and more about these than about the demands of social life or the knowledge of God.[76] And taking this strictly as a general tendency, is it not, after all, quite rational?

The indirect implication is related to the last article in q. 94, on whether precepts of natural law can be "deleted from the human heart." Thomas says that knowledge of the so-called secondary precepts, which involve some reasoning, can be obliterated altogether. The common, strictly "natural" ones, those "known to all"—the ones surveyed in article 2—cannot be deleted *in universali*, i.e., absolutely or in themselves. But even they can be deleted *in particulari operabili*. Reason can be impeded from using them to guide conduct. This is "on account of concupiscence or some other passion"—some non-rational inclination. What I think is implied by there being an order in which they are known is that reason is less liable to be anesthetized in some areas of natural law than in others.[77] The order of the precepts would be a kind of scale (obviously not the only one) measuring the degree to which people may be living in the grip of passion. This could be useful when looking for the appropriate remedy.

But perhaps more important are the implications of the general thesis that the inclinations that Thomas is talking about are rational. In aligning the true, intelligible human goods with natural inclinations, he is not suggesting that if some *non-rational* inclination is inborn, as e.g. homosexuality is said sometimes to be, its object is therefore a true good of the person in question. The further implication is that its object need not seem a true good even to the person himself. The inclination only makes the object seem *delectabile*, not *honestum*. While it may pervert particular judgments, impeding the application of what is naturally understood, it does not positively alter that understanding. It does not denature the very light of the mind. This I think is an encouraging conclusion.

---

[76] These are the goods cited in I-II, q. 94, a. 2.

[77] Such a difference is suggested in I-II, q. 100, a. 5, ad 1.

ACTION, INTENTION AND SELF-DETERMINATION
E. Christian Brugger

INTRODUCTION TO THE PROBLEM

A scene from the 2004 Sci Fi film, *Alien v. Predator*, illustrates a point that has troubled philosophers of action theory for over sixty years. The dilemma is this. A team of unlucky scientists, exploring an ancient pyramid frozen 2000 feet beneath the icy surface in Antarctica, find themselves in the middle of an epic battle. A dragonesque parasite, called Alien, who turns his victims into living incubation pods before bursting out their chests like a virus has risen from a hundred year slumber to face off against his ancient rival, a steel-clawed, gladiatorial space invader, Predator, who hunts down and mutilates his victims for sport. Exploration team leader Alexa Woods discovers her unfortunate comrade, Sebastian de Rosa, pinned against a wall in the "sacrificial chamber" with an alien parasite growing inside his chest cavity. She pulls her .44 magnum pistol. Sebastian yells, "Kill it before it reaches the surface!" She freezes. In an instant she reasons: "If I shoot, I'll kill the monster; but I'll kill Sebastian too–*for sure*." "If I don't, the monster may escape and the consequences could be disastrous." She aims at his chest, shouts "I'm sorry!," and shoots Sebastian three times at point blank range and kills both.

If a third party happened on the scene an instant before the shooting, that person might be tempted to conclude that Alexa shot Sebastian *to* kill him. It would seem quite clear: the range of the shot, Alexa's proximity and body position vis-à-vis Sebastian, the deadly caliber of the handgun, the undeniably deliberate pulling of the trigger and Sebastian's immediate death. Increasing the apparent clarity would be the spectator's correct conclusion that Sebastian's killing was—how could it be otherwise?—not only foreseen by Alexa, but foreseen with near certitude. If someone asked the spectator, "What did she do?" he would say, "Isn't it obvious? She killed him. Anyone can see that." And in one sense this is quite true. Alexa did shoot Sebastian in the chest; and her shooting did kill him. One can even say that she killed Sebastian purposely, inasmuch as she did so to kill the incubus, which meant killing him as well.

The morally relevant question here is not one of identifying what outcome was produced by outward behavior. The question is what did Alexa *do.* Did she shoot Sebastian *in order to* kill him? Was getting him dead (at least) a proximate end of hers. Even more importantly, did she kill him in order to kill the incubus? She could not kill the incubus without killing him too, so was killing him a means to getting at it? That she intended to shoot him seems undeniable. But in shooting him did she intend his death as either an end or a means? According to the account of intention defended in this essay (which is consistent in most respects with the account proposed by John Finnis, Germain Grisez and Joseph Boyle), the killing of Sebastian need not have been intended either as an end or a means; Alexa need not have been shooting *to* kill him. Though his killing *could* have been intended (Alexa could have taken advantage of the extraordinary circumstances to bump off a rival), it need not have been. Sebastian's killing could have been a tragic and regrettable foreseen *side-effect* of an otherwise legitimately intended act of self defense against a gravely harmful aggressor.

Some theorists think this is implausible. Even if Alexa *wanted* to direct her intention away from the killing of Sebastian, they say, in intending to shoot him, she just *did* intend to kill him. Some effects, in other words, are of such a kind that they cannot be said *not* to be chosen. Most who argue in this way do so from one or more of the following premises (formulated as conditionals): if the harm-causing behavior of the agent is proximate to or close-in to or physically carried out on the person who suffers the harmful effect; if the effect follows immediately from the cause; if given a similar state of affairs the same effect would follow invariably from the same kind of cause; if the effect was clearly foreseen; then the effect is part of what is intended despite what the agent may say about what he intended.[1] One cannot simply perform some inner

[1] Various formulations of these premises include: Warren S. Quinn, "Actions, Intentions, and Consequences," in *The Doctrine of Double Effect: Philosophers Debate a Controversial Moral Principle*, ed. P.A. Woodward (South Bend, Ind.: University of Notre Dame Press, 2001), p. 26; Philippa Foot, "The Problem of Abortion and the Doctrine of the Double Effect," in *The Doctrine of Double Effect: Philosophers Debate a Controversial Moral Principle*, ed. P.A. Woodward (South Bend, Ind.: University of Notre Dame Press, 2001), p. 145; H.L.A. Hart, "Intention and Punishment," in *Punishment and Responsibility: Essays in the Philosophy of Law* (OUP, 1968), p. 120; G.E.M. Anscombe, "Medalist's Address: Action, Intention, and 'Double Effect'," in *The Doctrine of Double Effect: Philosophers Debate a Controversial Moral Principle*, ed. P.A. Woodward (South Bend, Ind.: University of Notre Dame Press, 2001), p. 63; Nicanor Pier Giorgio Austriaco, OP, "On Reshaping Skulls and Unintelligible Intentions," *Nova et Vetera*, vol. 2, no. 2

act of directing one's attention away from one description of an act and toward another and then claim that the resulting description is the morally relevant one.[2] Common sense tells us that some effects are intrinsic to what is chosen. The proximity of cause to effect and the physical circumstances of the act limit what description is and is not valid. Although it might be the case that our wishing can be separable from the limits the world imposes upon us (e.g., I can wish I could fly like Peter Pan), our intendings are, at least to some degree, beholden to that structure; and that is not changed by wishing. When a person stands three feet from another and shoots him in the heart with a .44 magnum, it is nonsense to say she did not shoot *to* kill.

Because it corresponds to a common intuition of many morally conscientious people, this objection needs to be addressed. It raises the question of the nature of intention. In particular, the question of whether intention is an internal act separable from the physical behavior that carries it out or whether or to what degree external behavior is necessarily intended. In Catholic moral tradition since Aquinas intention has been judged to be the central moral determinant of human action.[3] If one's intended end or means is at odds with human good, one's act is wrong. But if one's intention is upright, it can be (though not always is) legitimate to bring about side-effects that would be wrong to intend.

FREE CHOICE MATTERS

The underlying assertion of my entire essay is this: *reasons lead people to choose and those reasons, as principles of choice, become principles of self-determination.* Let's tease this out a bit. As principles of action, the reasons that lead me to choose are, precisely stated, the possi-

---

(2004), p. 89; Kevin Flannery, S.J., "What is Included in a Means to an End?" *Gregorianum* 74 (1993), pp. 511-12.

2 "After all we can *form* intentions; now if intention is an interior movement, it would appear that we can choose to have a certain intention and not another, just by e.g. saying within ourselves: 'What I *mean* to be doing . . . ' The idea that one can determine one's intentions by making such a little speech to oneself is obvious bosh." G.E.M. Anscombe, *Intention* (Oxford: Basil Blackwell, 1957), p. 42.

3 "Now moral acts take their species according to what is intended, and not according to what is beside the intention (*praeter intentionem*)." Aquinas, *Summa Theologiae* (*ST*), II-II, q. 64, a. 7c.

bilities for human fulfillment promised by choosing in a certain way (or which I believe are possible by choosing in a certain way). Before I choose, however, there may be other reasons or sets of reasons that I find attractive, each promising fulfillments (benefits, goods) different enough to establish it as a rival alternative in my mind. If each of a set of alternatives promises goods I am interested in, and if no single alternative promises all the goods I am interested in or all the goods promised by any other alternative or combination of others, then I need to choose among the alternatives. I must make my own one set of reasons with the fulfillment they promise rather than any other set of reasons with their promised fulfillment. And assuming the choosing is free, not constrained by something outside itself, I myself settle which alternative I take. Thus, by free choices I fulfill myself in some goods and set aside others. A graduating college senior, for example, deliberating over whether to go to medical school after graduation with a view to marrying and having a family or whether to enter religious life, must in the end settle on one of the two alternatives, and unless her choice is to set aside both in favor of a third alternative (which might be to put off choosing either for the time being), her choice for medical school or religious life will open up for her real self-determining possibilities, real sorts of human fulfillment, futures with very different kinds of possibilities. It will also *close down* possibilities. Christians who have conscientiously discerned their state-in-life will be familiar with the scenario I describe here, including the conflict experienced as they contemplated not only the real gains promised by choosing one state in life, but the real losses promised by not choosing the other.

Not all choices organize one's life as widely and deeply as choices for one's state in life. Some merely reinforce existing components of one's moral self, like the choice of a scholar to attend an academic conference, or of a music lover to buy season's tickets to the opera and forego the convenience of extra pocket money, or the choice of a young married man to remain on a professional fast track with what it implies—good and bad—for marital and family relationships. Others introduce new dispositions for better or worse into one's persisting character, for example, the choice of spouses to have their first child, or the choice of a woman to nurse her aging mother at home and not commit her to an institution, or the choice of a man to finally yield to the solicitations of a courtesan. The one thing they all have in common is all free choices contribute in different ways and to different degrees to the determining of the kind of people we become. *Choices are principles of the creative self-shaping of moral character.* This is a traditional insight. The great 4th century Eastern Church Father, Gregory of Nyssa, writes:

> All things subject to change and to becoming never remain constant, but continually pass from one state to another, for better or worse. . . Now, human life is always subject to change; it needs to be born ever anew. . . But here birth does not come about by a foreign intervention, as is the case with bodily beings . . .; it is the result of a free choice. Thus we are in a certain way our own parents, creating ourselves as we will, by our decisions.[4]

The insight is not unique to the Christian tradition. Plato in his *Laws* writes:

> He who does not estimate the base and evil, the good and noble . . . and abstain in every possible way from the one and practice the other to the utmost of his power, does not know that in all these respects he is most foully and disgracefully abusing his soul, which is the divinest part of man; for no one, as I may say, ever considers that which is declared to be the greatest penalty of evil-doing—namely, to grow into the likeness of bad men. (*Laws* V, 728b)

The reflexive, self-determining character of human choice, an aspect of the theory of action largely ignored in the philosophical literature, is central to our discussion of the relevance of and relations between intention and side-effects. The link between what I do and what my doing does to me (i.e., who I become), the relationship between self-directed action and human action's (often unrecognised) self-shaping quality, will shed light on why two pieces of human behaviour, identical in appearance from the outside, but differing in intention from the internal perspective of the act-

---

[4] Gregory of Nyssa, *On the Life of Moses*, II, 2-3: *PG* 44, 327-328; quoted in John Paul II, Encyclical Letter *Veritatis Splendor* (1993), no. 71.

ing person, can be very different moral acts[5] (e.g. a genital act between husband and wife can be either an act of selfish self-gratification or self-giving love).

FREE CHOICE AND INTENTION

Free choice is a necessary condition for the moral goodness or bad-ness of human beings.[6] According to Aquinas, human action involves a dynamic interplay between reason and will. Through reason we envisage intelligible possibilities for action; we deliberate over suitable means for realizing those possibilities; and we judge which means we think best here and now: reason apprehends, deliberates over and proposes for choice what is good. But it is through will (*voluntas*) that we move to action. Will is one's responsiveness to reasons put forward by *ratio*.[7] John Finnis helpfully sets forth in tabular form the main elements of Aquinas' account of the relation between *ratio* and *voluntas* in human action in *Aquinas: Moral, Political and Legal Theory* (Oxford: Oxford University Press, 1998), p. 71. Aquinas analyzes several varieties of vol-untariness–several types of actualizations of will. They are: *voluntas simplex*[8]—simple willing (i.e., will's general openness to and interest in human good); *intentio*[9]—intention (interest in, movement towards, a pur-pose envisaged by reason); *consensus*[10]—consent (i.e., will's openness to and interest in certain alternatives as real possibilities of realizing good); *electio*[11]—choice (i.e., the definitive movement of the will toward some

---

[5] I do not mean to imply that doing good in the world through one's moral agency is not important. Consequences are morally relevant, but not decisive in the directing of practical reason. Only a small percentage of the consequences we cause by our behavior can be foreseen.

[6] But not for other aspects of their goodness or badness, e.g., the goodness of being made in God's image and likeness, or the badness of their nearsightedness, or bad back.

[7] "Intention is a movement of the will to something already ordained by the reason." *ST*, I-II, Q. 12, a. 3,

[8] *ST*, I-II, q. 12, a. 1, ad 4, q. 15, a. 3c.

[9] *Ibid.* at q. 12.

[10] *Ibid.* at q. 15.

[11] *Ibid.* at q. 13.

good); *usus*[12]—execution (i.e., will's carrying out of the choice once made); and *fruitio*[13]—enjoyment (will's enjoyment of the "sweetness" of the end attained through choice).[14] The two with which I concern myself here are *intentio* and *electio*.

Aquinas' analysis of voluntariness at times distinguishes between *intentio* and *electio* by distinguishing between the willing (intending) of ends and the willing (choosing) of means: "in so far as the movement of the will is to the means, as ordained to the end, it is called *electio*: but the movement of the will to the end as acquired by the means, is called *intentio*."[15] But he does not mean to say by this that intention and choice are different acts of the will. Aquinas says the will stands in a threefold relation to the good.[16] The first is the will's ordinary openness to and interest in human good (what was called above *voluntas simplex*). Second is the will's resting in the good (i.e., experience of satisfaction in the good once realized, or *fruitio*). The third is the will's movement towards ("stretching towards," Lt. *intendere*) the good which constitutes *intentio*. This third relation, the stretching towards the good, also defines the relationship of the will to the good in choosing (*electio*). Choice, Aquinas says, is "the act whereby the will tends to something proposed to it as being good, through being ordained to the end by the reason."[17] Aquinas' distinction, then, between intending and choosing is a formal distinction of the relatedness of the will to ends and means, not a distinction between different types of acts of the will.

When I will certain means for the sake of a certain end, I will also that end. The intending of the end is part of the same act of the will as the choice of the means.[18] Said in another way, that for the sake of which I choose my means (i.e., the intelligible benefit that I believe is possi-

---

[12] *Ibid.* at q. 16.

[13] *Ibid.* at q. 11.

[14] See Finnis, *op. cit.,* at 69-71; see also his "Object and Intention in Moral Judgments According to Aquinas," *The Thomist,* 55, 1 (1991), pp. 1-27.

[15] *ST*, I-II, q. 12, a. 4, ad 3.

[16] *Ibid.* at q. 12, a. 1, ad 4.

[17] *Ibid.* at q. 13, a. 1c.

[18] *Ibid.* at q. 12, a. 4c & sed contra.

ble–my end) is part of what I will in choosing my means. For example, when I say I wish to give my wife flowers (my means) in order to make her happy (my end) I signify the same movement of the will.[19] My willing to give her flowers includes the will to make her happy.

But Aquinas seems also to say that the willing of the end is called intention only *when means are adopted*, that it is not till one has resolved upon some means for realizing some end that one has formed one's intent to realize that end;[20] before this we might be interested in Y and wish for it, but we *intend* Y only we set about to get it by means of something else: "for when we speak of intending to have health, we mean not only that we will have it [i.e., that we are interested in having it], but that *we will have it by means of something else*."[21] This is not to say the end, as a state of affairs to be realized (Aquinas' "*res*"), is identical with the means that one concludes are adequate for realizing that end; in this regard ends and means are distinct objects of the will. Their union lies rather in the fact that insofar as the end is the reason (that for the sake of which) I will my means, the end and the means are one and the same willed object.[22] So, for example, when I shoot you to incapacitate you to steal your money, stealing your money *and* shooting you to incapacitate you form my object (*"unum et idem obiectum"*).

The willing of ends and means both involve an *intentio* (a "stretching towards") on the part of our wills. That towards which our wills stretch (i.e., what we intend) is some state of affairs *(res)* envisaged as an intelligible possibility desired *for its own sake* or *the sake of something else*.[23] When I drink a cup of coffee in the morning in order to help myself wake

---

[19] *Ibid.*

[20] "*Motus autem voluntatis qui fertur in finem, secundum quod acquiritur per ea quae sunt ad finem, vocatur intention*", *ibid* at a. 4, ad 3.

[21] *Ibid.* at a. 2, ad 4, emphasis added; cf. *De Veritate*, q. 22, a. 13c; Finnis argues convincingly for this interpretation in *Object and Intention*, pp. 7-9, see especially note 18, pp. 8-9 where he addresses the objection that the last statement of q. 12, a. 4, ad 3 ("*intentio finis esse potest, etiam nondum determinatis his quae sunt ad finem, quorum est electio*") contradicts this interpretation.

[22] "*Inquantum est ratio volendi id quod est ad finem, est unum et idem obiectum.*" *Ibid.*, at a. 4, ad 2; cf. Finnis, *op. cit.,* at 9.

[23] Finnis, "Intention and Side-effects," in *Liability and Responsibility: Essays in Law and Morals*, eds. R.G. Frey and Christopher W. Morris (Cambridge: CUP, 1991), pp. 61-62.

up, my will stretches towards both my desired end of waking up and my preferred means of drinking a cup of coffee. Both together–what I am willing here and now and why–define my plan of action. To choose, Finnis writes, is "to adopt a plan or proposal."[24] Whatever is included within that plan of action is chosen. It is correct to say also, in light of what we said above, that whatever is included within that plan is *intended*.[25]

So we intend both our ends and our means. This is intelligible even within an idiom that considers ends alone as intended. Intention regards ends; but means are close-in ends with respect to the means necessary to their realization.[26] If we move from A to C through B, C is an end with respect to A and B, but B is an end with respect to A.[27] "Intention," Aquinas says, "is not only of the last end . . . but also of an intermediary end. A man intends at the same time, both the proximate and the last end."[28] And again, "for things which act for an end, all things intermediate between the first agent and the ultimate end are as ends in regard to things prior, and as active principles (means) with regard to things consequent."[29] Ends and means therefore are linked together in the plan we adopt through choice. That plan is something intelligible we try to bring about (to realize, to make happen) in order to accomplish something.[30]

---

[24] Finnis, "The Act of a Person." *Persona Verità e Morale: Atti del Congresso Internazionale di Teologia Morale (Roma, 7-12 Aprile 1986)*, pp. 159-75, quote on p. 168 (Roma: Città Nuova Editrice).

[25] "What one does is done 'with intent to X' if X is a part of one's plan either as its end (or a part of its end, or one of its ends) or as a means." Finnis, *op. cit.* at 168. Philippa Foot says something similar: a person "intends in the strictest sense both those things that he aims at as ends and those that he aims at as means to his ends." Philippa Foot, *op. cit.,* at 144.

[26] "A terminus (end) is something last, not always in respect of the whole, but sometimes in respect of a part." Aquinas, *ST*, I-II, q. 12, a. 2, ad 2.

[27] *Ibid.* at q. 12, a. 2c.

[28] *Ibid.* at a. 3c.

[29] Aquinas, *Summa Contra Gentiles (SCG)*, bk. 3, ch. 2, no. 5; see also *De Malo*, q. 2, a. 2 ad 8.

[30] "There is a plan or proposal wherever there is *trying*, or doing (or refraining from doing) something *in order to* bring about something or *as a way of* accomplishing something." Finnis, "Intention in Tort Law," in *Philosophical Foundations of Tort Law*, ed. David G. Owen (Oxford: Clarendon Press, 1996), p. 229; see also Joseph M. Boyle, Jr.,

INTENTION AS COMMITMENT TO HUMAN GOOD

This is relevant to our consideration of the relationship between intention and side-effects. If what one chooses one intends; and if (as we said above) *reasons* lead us to choose,[31] and those reasons taken together constitute our plan or proposal for acting; then what we do is defined by those reasons. I said above that choice matters first and foremost because the reasons that lead us to choose act as principles of self-determination shaping the persons we become. As I have shown those reasons, formulated as our plans and purposes, include both ends and means. So it is our intended ends and means that we resolve, try, stretch toward, to bring about. The unintended side-effects we bring about, however, are not the reasons that lead us to choose. Though we bring them about, and if foreseen, we bring them about voluntarily, they are not what we resolve to bring about. They are not part of our proposal adopted by choice. *They do not motivate us to act*; sometimes it is quite the reverse; sometimes they cause us to hesitate, when serious enough, they move us not to choose an envisaged plan of action.[32] In short, they are neither means chosen nor ends intended; they do not pertain to the "object" morally specifying an act.

"Praeter Intentionem In Aquinas," *The Thomist*, 42 (1978), pp. 649-665, esp. p. 664.

[31] The proposition "reasons lead me to choose" is commonly accepted among philosophers; for example, Donald Davidson writes: "The primary reason for an action is its cause"; an "intentional" action is one that is "done for a reason"; Davidson, "Actions, Reasons, and Causes" (1963), in *Essays on Actions and Events* (Oxford: Clarendon Press, 1980), pp. 3-19, quotes on p. 4 and p. 6 respectively. P.M.S. Hacker, commenting on Wittgenstein, writes: "Intentional actions . . . are actions for which *it always makes sense to ask for the agent's reasons*." P.M.S. Hacker, "Wittgenstein: Mind and Will," *An analytical commentary on the Philosophical Investigations*, Volume 4, Part I, (Oxford: Blackwell Publishers, Inc., 2000), p. 240; cf. Anscombe, *op. cit.,* at 9.

[32] Boyle writes: "The foreseen consequences of one's bringing about an intended state of affairs are often considered in deliberating, but not as reasons *for* the action–rather, they are sometimes conditions *in spite of which* one acts. It is not for the sake of such conditions that one selects an option; it is not these effects to which one is committed in acting." Joseph M. Boyle, Jr., "Toward Understanding the Principle of Double Effect," in *The Doctrine of Double Effect: Philosophers Debate a Controversial Moral Principle*, ed. P.A. Woodward (South Bend, Ind.: University of Notre Dame Press, 2001), pp. 7-20, quote on p. 15.

This is important. Such unintended consequences stand outside our reasons for acting, and hence outside of the relationship of means to ends that constitutes our chosen proposal. Such effects are not our goal; they are not what we judge to be choiceworthy; there is no commitment to bringing them about; they are not what an agent "sets his or her heart on."[33] We intend only what we have positive interest in bringing about. By this I do not mean having positive feelings or sentiments. This may or may not be the case. Rather I mean having rational and volitional interest. I am interested in bringing about the states of affairs I intend; in this sense I *want* to bring them about, even if sometimes my feelings register repugnance. A hit man may find the shooting of his victim emotionally repugnant; but if he wants his money, he makes the object of his rational interest the bringing about of his plan; he resolves, tries, sets about to kill his victim. In this sense he *wants* his victim dead.[34] The side effects we bring about are not part of our plan or purpose. In *this* sense we do not want to bring them about. We have no committed interest in their realization. They do arise as a result of intended purposes. But *they* are not what we intend; they do not move us. If we could realize our purpose without bringing them about, we would. They are not our reasons.[35]

Why is this relevant to self-determination? Because when I intend I envisage as ends and means states of affairs in which instances of basic human goods like friendship, human life, knowledge and the appreciation of beauty, marriage and friendship with God, or means that do or appear to promote such conditions, as objects of choice, are engaged by my will. These goods we might say are *committed* to my will, delivered into its charge. Or, if you will, my will is committed towards these goods, positively or negatively. Should I intend to destroy a good, damage it or

---

[33] *Ibid.* at 17.

[34] The term "want" is accurately used if it is taken to mean rationally invested in or committed to bringing something about, but can be misleading if it is taken to mean having positive feelings in relation to one's intended ends and means. Davidson acknowledges the problem of using the term "want" in reference to one's reasons for acting, but argues that nevertheless "in a vast number of typical cases, some pro attitude must be assumed to be present if a statement of an agent's reasons in acting is to be intelligible." Davidson, *op. cit.* at 11.

[35] Boyle, "*Praeter Intentionem* In Aquinas," p. 664.

impede its realization, even for good reasons, I set my will and hence myself at odds with it. "What one thus adopts is, so to speak, synthesized with one's will, i.e., with oneself as an acting subject; one *becomes* what one saw reason to do and chose and set oneself to do."[36] Through the intending of ends and means one forms, reinforces, deepens, hardens, uproots and reforms one's moral disposition in relation to human good. This is the primary element in the formation of character.[37] Though it is not the only element.

INTENTION, FORESEEN SIDE-EFFECTS AND SELF-DETERMINATION

I said above that one's accepting of foreseen side-effects is an expression of voluntariness. It is voluntariness in the sense that in bringing about certain harms that we think we are likely to bring about through our intending, we voluntarily bring about those harms. Anscombe agrees saying such effects are "voluntary though not intentional."[38] Some scholars, wishing to maintain a link between intention and foresight, say such harms are brought about by an "oblique intention" (to be distinguished

---

[35] Boyle, "*Praeter Intentionem* In Aquinas," p. 664.

[36] Finnis, *Intention and Side-effects*, pp. 61-62. This "synthesis," he says elsewhere, "is a real, empirical (though spiritual), and inbuilt effect of one's adopting a proposal. Whatever consequences lie *outside* one's proposal, because neither wanted for their own sake nor needed as a means, are not synthesized into one's will." Finnis, *Intention in Tort Law*, p. 244.

[37] Wittgenstein relates intention and character as follows: "Why do I want to tell him about an intention too, as well as telling him what I did? – Not because the intention was also something which was going on at the time. But because I want to tell him something about *myself*, which goes beyond what happened at that time." Ludwig Wittgenstein, *Philosophical Investigations*, tr. G.E.M. Anscombe, 3rd edition (Oxford: Blackwell, 2001), no. 659, p. 141. Commenting on this, Hacker states that to reveal to another one's intention "may be to reveal something about one's character. It is to lay bare one's objectives at that time . . . In appropriate contexts, it is to disclose something about what considerations moved one to action or tempted one to action." Hacker, *op. cit.,* at 259.

[38] Anscombe, *Intention*, p. 89; see also Stephen Brock, *Action and Conduct: Thomas Aquinas and the Theory of Action* (Edinburgh: T & T Clark, 1998), p. 197.

from "direct intention").[39]   Finnis maintains the link by saying such harms are *not* caused *un*intentionally, since unintentionally implies "accident or mistake or lack of foresight," but thinks the term "oblique intention" is an unfortunate piece of jargon derived from an unsound account of intention.[40]   Whatever voluntariness accurately describes our causality in the bringing about of unintentional harms, our description is always implicitly qualified by some form of the verb "to accept": i.e., "willingly *accepting* harmful side-effects. . .," "voluntarily *accepting* . . .," "intentionally *accepting* . . ." This qualification is telling. It connotes awareness and willingness, so it seems appropriate to say with Finnis that such harms are not entirely unintentional.[41] But it also connotes a lesser degree of active engagement of voluntariness. The two statements: "I accept that my action will bring about harm X," and "I intend harm X," both describe the engagement of the voluntary self, but at different depths. Catholic moral tradition, while always making a distinction between those evils we intend and those we merely bring about, has agreed that we are responsible for both, though not in the same way. One's responsibility for foreseen side-effect lies precisely in the fact that they are foreseen and voluntarily accepted, and hence could have been avoided by not choosing in a certain way.[42] As Grisez writes: "since side effects are freely accepted,

---

[39] H.L.A. Hart, "Intention in Punishment," in *Punishment and Responsibility: Essays in the Philosophy of Law* (Oxford: Clarendon Press, 1968), pp. 120-21; Glanville Williams, *The Mental Element in Crime* (The Hebrew University of Jerusalem, Lionel Cohen lectures) (Jerusalem & Oxford: Magnes Press, 1965), p. 10.

[40] Finnis, *Intention and Side-effects*, pp. 47-48.

[41] One might even say they are done "intentionally" in a loose sense in which whatever one brings about not by accident but voluntarily, fully aware that one's behavior will cause it, is done intentionally. But they are not intended in the stricter sense of being chosen as means or sought as ends.

[42] In Catholic tradition the question of the precise way in which, or degree to which we are responsible for harmful unintended side-effects has been systematized principally through two concepts: *proportionality* and *material cooperation in other's wrongdoing.* For a consideration of the former see Brugger, *Capital Punishment and Roman Catholic Moral Tradition* (Notre Dame: University of Notre Dame Press, 2003), pp. 184-85; for a helpful discussion of the latter see Grisez, *Difficult Moral Questions* (Quincy, Ill.: Franciscan Press, 1997), appendix 2, pp. 871-897.

it makes sense to ask whether one ought to accept them."[43] But because they are not among the reasons moving us to act, not among the states of affairs desired for their own sakes or for the sakes of something else, the voluntariness that brings them about is weaker, less self-engaging and hence less self-determining than the voluntariness of intending. The voluntariness entailed in intending is voluntariness in its fullest sense.[44]

INTENTION AS A SPIRITUAL ACT

At the outset of this essay I raised the question of whether intention is an internal act separable from, though usually accompanied by, the physical behavior that carries it out; or whether or to what extent external physical aspects of our behavior and close-in effects caused by our behavior are necessarily intended. My contention is that it is the former, that intention is a spiritual act, an act of the will,[45] an act of the existential self, initiated and commanded by reason, and, ordinarily, but not necessarily, carried out by bodily behavior. Intention is first and foremost a spiritual act. One might object saying this is too dualistic, that it makes mind and will one thing, and body another, intention all in one, and body just there to do the mind and will's bidding. The objection is important and flags an error in mind-body theory that must be avoided; the error holds that body is instrumental to mind and will, ancillary to the self of consciousness and freedom: my body is not me, though I *use* my body to execute many of my purposes in a material universe.

I think my account avoids this error. It presupposes, with Catholic tradition, that the human person is a unified integrated whole constituted of a material body and an immaterial soul. In man reason and freedom are intrinsically linked with and mediated through man's organic self. Just as intellectual acts are spiritual though dependent on sensations, so volitional acts are spiritual though linked to emotions. Body and soul are inseparably one.[46] I am not saying that intention 'happens in mind' and not 'in

---

[43] Germain Grisez, *Christian Moral Principles* (Chicago: Franciscan Herald Press, 1983), p. 240.

[44] Boyle, *Toward Understanding the Principle of Double Effect*, p. 14; Finnis, *Intention and Side-effects*, p. 62.

[45] Aquinas, *ST*, I-II, q. 12, a. 1c; q. 13, a. 1c.

[46] John Paul II, Encyclical Letter *Veritatis Splendor* (1993), nos. 48-49.

body', since everything that 'happens' in and to a human person happens in and to a conscious free bodily being. I am contending that this spiritual-embodied person has multiple capacities the realization of which may be bodily (e.g., growth), spiritual (e.g., thought) or bodily-spiritual (e.g., biofeedback). Intending is not an actualization of an organic capacity. It is the actualization of the freedom that separates human persons from non-personal creatures. The volitional resolving we call intending is an existential self-determination. As such it is the actualization of a capacity that is not per se outwardly observable. In fact, one can intend to do anything one thinks one can do, and sometimes chooses to do what is impossible. For example, Smith offers Jones ten grand for killing Brown and Jones agrees. But Brown, unbeknownst to both Smith and Jones, is already dead. Moreover, immediately after agreeing, Jones himself may suffer heart arrest, never get beyond saying "it's a deal," yet go straight to hell for murder. Intending therefore is rightly referred to as an internal act separable (though not mutually exclusive) from the external behavior that carries it out. It follows that what I intend and what I accept as side-effects is not settled by looking at outward behavior.

WHAT I INTEND IS NOT SETTLED BY LOOKING AT OUTWARD BEHAVIOR: OBJECTIONS

I said above that the view that holds that some effects (e.g., Sebastian's death), because of their physical circumstances (e.g. proximity to Alexa's shooting), are necessarily intended seems like "common sense." Despite seeming commonsensical, the view proceeds from a conception of intention that fails to characterize intent consistently in terms of the intelligible reasons moving an agent to act but rather in terms of what is outwardly observable.[47] This failure to characterize action from the "inter-

---

[47] Jean Porter's analysis and criticism of the action theory of Finnis/Grisez/Boyle proceeds predominantly from a third party perspective; for example: "As long as the agent acts in pursuit of an aim which is admittedly good . . . it will always remain possible to describe the act in question in terms of the attainment of the good which is sought, omitting any reference to the bad which it brought about. And if this is so, then there is no way to rule out the possibility that the agent's intention is determined by the good which he seeks, and not by the bad effect which he brings about." Porter, *op. cit.,* at 626-627; see Finnis, Grisez and Boyle's reply to her essay: ""Direct" and "Indirect": A Reply to Critics of Our Action Theory," *The Thomist* 65 (2001), pp. 1-44.

nal" perspective of the person acting and *not* from the perspective of an inquisitive honest observer, is common in the philosophical literature on intention.[48] Two common 'hard case' examples in which it plays out are the cases of the fetal craniotomy and the "fat man in the cave." In the first example, the question is posed whether a doctor performing a life-saving emergency procedure on a pregnant woman can extract from her birth canal a pre-born baby whose head is too large to fit through her birth canal by crushing the baby's skull, and do so without intent to kill the baby? A relevant circumstance is that without performing the procedure both the mother and baby will die.[49] Therapeutic recourse to craniotomy was more common before the advent of modern surgical procedures like the cesarean section. But it is still faced today in the developing world where medical resources or knowledge are limited. In the second, the question is whether a group of spelunkers (potholers) can extract a fat man from the lone egress hole in a cave in which he's got himself stuck by dynamiting him out of the way, and do so without intending to kill him? A relevant circumstance is that water is rising in the cave and unless the hole is opened all the potholers will die. The actions carried out in these two cases, as in the Alien v. Predator case, conform to criteria articulated above: the harmful cause is close-in to the harmful effect (i.e., the behavior is carried out on the one harmed); the harmful effect follows immediately from the causal behavior; and the harmful effect is foreseen. So, many suppose that the deaths of Sebastian, the fetus, and the fat man are necessarily intended by those whose voluntary behavior brings those deaths about.

Kevin Flannery, S.J., argues that defenders of the unintended killing thesis in the case of craniotomy resort to euphemism in order to argue for its liceity: "in order to separate off from the compass of the means the

---

[48] Austriaco, for example, proposes a procedure of "questioning" agents about how they understand their own actions to see if their intention seems intelligible to us: "In performing the procedure of extracting the gravid uterus (which leads to the death of a non-viable fetus), the surgeon may either be an abortionist or a healer. It all depends upon what he desires through his actions, and *we would have to ascertain this* by questioning him about his intention until it is intelligible." Austriaco, *op. cit.* at 92, emphasis added.

[49] This example is particularly sensitive to U.S. pro-lifers who have fought valiantly and against serious opposition to ban the gruesome killing procedure known as partial birth abortion, an elective procedure designed specifically for killing late term babies.

killing of the fetus, it is necessary to redescribe the act of craniotomy, calling it a cranium-narrowing operation."[50] But it is not at all clear that any illicit renaming has gone on. The baby's death is *not* what saves the mother, and his or her death is *not* what the doctor aims at.[51] The baby's being removed from her birth canal is what saves the mother; for the baby to be removed, his or her skull needs to be narrowed sufficiently so it can fit through the birth canal; the only way to narrow the baby's skull is to crush it. However, in the case of this example the morally relevant point, *constantly* missed or mischaracterized by critics in the literature, is this: the crushing is not done *to* kill the baby, but *to* narrow its skull; the *what* of the act is "narrowing;" the *why* is "to be able to remove the baby;" the unneeded and unwanted and foreseen tragic side-effect is the child's death.[52] Defining craniotomy as skull reshaping (or narrowing) is *not* a euphemism for killing. It is *what* the doctor does *in order to* save the mother. The baby's death contributes nothing to the mother's healing. The evidence is that, if the baby is already dead and the corpse is removed in exactly the same way as if it were still alive, the benefit to the mother is exactly the same. The thesis does not dodge the violence of the act or its repugnant nature. And it is not euphemistic. It is specifying precisely the intelligible plan the doctor sets himself to realize. The term craniotomy etymologically means incision in the skull. And both Webster's 9th and the New Shorter Oxford dictionaries define it as "opening the skull" with *no* mention that it entails killing. Is defining it as "opening

---

50 Flannery, *op. cit.,* at 511. The same 'redescribing' argument has been made by other scholars; see Austriaco, op. *cit.*, at 83-84; Stephen Brock, *op. cit.,* at 204-205, n. 17; Anscombe, *Medalist's Address: Action, Intention, and 'Double Effect',* 63; Jean Porter, ""Direct" and "Indirect" in Grisez's Moral Theory," *Theological Studies*, vol. 57 (1996), p. 620.

51 Warren Quinn words it this way: "It is not death itself, or even harm itself, that is strictly intended, but rather an immediately physical effect on the fetus that will allow its removal;" Quinn, *op. cit.,* at 25, see also note 6.

52 Leonard Geddes writes, "The surgeon must remove the child from the mother's womb; the dimensions of the child are such that if the surgeon attempts to remove it without changing these dimensions the mother will surely die. He therefore alters these dimensions in certain ways. A necessary but quite unneeded and unwanted consequence of the procedure is that the child dies." Leonard Geddes, "On the Intrinsic Wrongness of Killing Innocent People," *Analysis*, 33.3 (1972), pp. 94-95; quoted in Boyle, "Double Effect and a Certain Type of Embryotomy," *Irish Theological Quarterly*, vol. 44 (1977), p. 308.

the skull," also 'artificially redescribing' the act? No, it is only a more precise description. Flannery's refutation from renaming is therefore unsound.

Flannery makes another argument. He says there is a difference in the logical structure between the classic case of a hysterectomy that brings about the death of a fetus, and a craniotomy that brings about the same thing: a hysterectomy is performed *upon* the woman, and a craniotomy is performed *upon* the fetus; further, a hysterectomy brings about a good for the woman upon whom it is performed, but a craniotomy brings about no good for the fetus upon whom it is performed. (Although he admits in passing that the craniotomy does aim at a good, namely the woman's health.) His conclusion is that given the logical structure of the craniotomy, "the death of the fetus is only artificially separated off from the means," meaning that in *reality* it is part of the chosen means.[53] This argument can be formulated more precisely as follows: if harmful behavior is performed on an individual; and it is performed not for the good of the individual upon whom it is performed, but for some other good (e.g., the good of another person, like the fetus' mother); then the harming is necessarily part of the intended means. Is this argument sound? If it is, then by implication the reasoning of Aquinas specified in his famous discussion of killing in self defense is unsound.[54] Aquinas says that an act of self-defense can have two effects, one good, namely saving one's life, the other bad, namely the killing of the aggressor. If one's intention is to save one's own life, and the measure of force used is no more than necessary to bring this about, then one blamelessly uses such force, even if the force kills the aggressor: "It is not necessary for salvation that a man omit the act of moderate self-defense in order to avoid killing the other man."

Joseph Boyle applies this reasoning to the case of craniotomy:

> The structure of the craniotomy case is precisely similar. There is a piece of behavior—the craniotomy—which has two effects: the killing of the fetus and the saving of the mother's

53 Flannery, *op. cit.,* at 513.

54 Aquinas, *ST,* II-II, q. 64, a. 7c.

life. The latter alone is intended. The lethal effect of the craniotomy follows from the minimum required to save the
woman's life. If the killing of the fetus is a means to saving
the mother's life then so would the killing of the attacker be a
means to saving one's own life. If either were a means then the
death in each case would necessarily be the state of affairs
defining the act. The behaviour in one case is the craniotomy,
in the other—perhaps—shooting a gun. What is intended in
the latter case is one's self-preservation—what one is doing is
defending himself or more immediately, thwarting an attack.
In the other one's intention is saving the mother—what one is
doing is saving her life—or more immediately changing the
dimensions of the skull. I can see no distinction: like the act
of self-defense, the craniotomy is an act with two effects—one
deadly, one lifesaving.[55]

An objection might be made that a fetus cannot be considered an
aggressor, much less an unjust aggressor, since it in no way can be held
morally responsible for the danger that its presence threatens to its mother. But Aquinas does not make his analysis of the lawful use of lethal
force by private persons dependent on the moral responsibility of the
aggressor. He specifies only that the one upon whom the force is used is
an "aggressor" (*invadens*), which implies that such a one may not be
morally responsible for his aggression.[56] Nevertheless, the question of
whether the fetus can be termed an aggressor, or, as in the tradition, mate-
rially unjust, is not relevant to the question of whether his killing is direct
or indirect (although it *is* relevant to the question of whether there is proportionately grave reason to use force against him, and if so, to what
degree). If, for example, we imagined a fetus with adult consciousness
and bad will, who had the extraordinary ability to expand his head to
twice the normal size, who, in an attempt to harm his mother, intention-

[55] Boyle, *op. cit.,* at 311.

[56] This conclusion is explicitly stated in papal teaching. Considering the lawful use of
lethal force against aggressors in self defense *Evangelium vitae* teaches: "the fatal outcome is attributable to the aggressor whose action brought it about, *even though he may
not be morally responsible because of a lack of a use of reason.*" John Paul II, Encyclical
Letter *Evangelium Vitae* (1995), no. 55, emphasis added.

ally expands his head as he is being born *precisely in order to* get stuck in his mother's birth canal so she will die. Knowing that his deliberate act puts both his own and his mother's life at risk, could the choice to narrow his skull to the degree necessary to remove him from his mother's birth canal be done without the intent to kill? Is foreseeability or inevitability of effect the determining factor? Or take for example the case of a deranged (and hence not morally responsible) man in a suit of armor, rushing at me with an ax shouting that he's going to kill me. I have a gun. Because of his armor, there is no place on his body against which a bullet would have any effect, except, because his helmet visor is open, the flesh of his face. The only act of self defense proportioned to the end of stopping his aggression is my shooting him in the face. But I foresee that shooting him there will kill him, for argument's sake, let's say with at least the same certitude with which the craniotomy doctor knows his procedure will kill the baby. Can my shooting him in the face—very clearly an act of self-defense, very clearly proportionate to the end of rendering him incapable of causing harm, and very clearly lethal—be chosen without intending his death? It seems to me that it can. It is not his death that I am after, that I commit myself to bringing about, but his being rendered harmless. And so I intend an act of self defense and I carry out the act upon the person himself and he immediately dies as a result. Inevitability of outcome is not what is central to determining my intention, even though it sometimes can be an indication of intent. What is central is the specific proposal adopted by choice by the acting person in response to deliberation over relevant goods at stake. But since my life is preserved by stopping his attack, and his attack is stopped by behavior that not only incapacitates him but kills him, his death is mistakenly thought to be the chosen means of preserving my life—whereas, should my shot in his face hit the bone of his forehead and glance off but have enough force to knock him out but not enough to kill him, my life would be preserved just as well. The causal sequence alone therefore is not determining. The plan of action I set before myself is. It is not my purpose to kill him, not the proposal I put before myself, not what I am trying to bring about. Although I intended man-killing behavior, I did not intend it under the morally relevant specification of killing. I intended it as an act of proportionate self-defense. The same can be said of the acts in the three examples stated above.

Flannery's confusion seems to stem from wider confusions about act analysis in general.[57] His criteria for determining whether something is intended or *praeter intentionem* are difficult to determine from his somewhat elliptical account. If I am correct, he argues that in the mind of an agent certain harmful effects caused by that agent's behavior cannot be logically (conceptually?) "separated off" from what he intends: "If in the craniotomy case, the killing of the fetus cannot be separated off from the crushing of its skull, then it must be included in the agent's intention." In just three pages of text, Flannery uses in this way the term *separate* (and its derivatives *separable, separated, separability*) ten times; a few examples include: "[Boyle's premise] presupposes that it is always possible to separate out in a way that has bearing on the moral situation two aspects of the sort of act in question, calling one aspect 'the means' and the other 'the indirect effect'"; "Boyle has left unexamined the presupposition that it is always possible to separate out two aspects of the act in question, identifying one as the means the other as the side-effect"; "the soundness of this argument depends on whether one can separate in a morally significant way the "killing" from the alteration of the dimensions of the child's skull."[58] He even implies that defenders of the thesis (whom he refers to by the pronoun "we") separate the two *while really knowing* that the killing is part of their intended means: "if we want to make it clear that we do not wish to include it [i.e., the killing] within the means, we must artificially separate off an aspect of the operation which we regard as truly (and solely) within the compass of the means."[59] Finally, he

[57] For example, he makes the error of saying that if a hysterectomy is performed on a pregnant woman's cancerous uterus, but the cancer is not immediately life threatening, "the hysterectomy becomes not just performing an hysterectomy but also a direct killing." But the killing need be no more direct than it would be if the cancer were immediately life threatening; what's different about the two scenarios is that in the first there is what the tradition has called "proportionately grave reason" for tolerating the harm to the fetus, in the second there is not grave reason, which means it would be immoral to proceed with the operation knowing the harms it will cause; see Kevin Flannery, S.J., "Natural Law *Mens Rea* Versus the Benthamite Tradition," *The American Journal of Jurisprudence*, 40 (1995), pp. 377-400, quote on pp. 394-95.

[58] Flannery, *What is Included in a Means to an End?,* pp. 504-506.

[59] *Ibid.,* at 511-12.

argues that defenders of the unintended killing thesis "fail ever to argue for the notion that one can separate off from the compass of the means the death of the fetus in the craniotomy case."[60]

If my thesis is correct that intending is an internal act, an actualization of human freedom not outwardly observable, then *conclusive* evidence can never be evinced by me or any agent that one *really* has not intended to kill when carrying out behavior that looks like one has.[61] This does not mean that when one intends something one's intention is not related to some objective state of affairs, that intention is just a matter of focusing one's mind on something or describing to oneself what one wants one's intention to be. Someone wills the end (something in itself desirable) and that part of reality which one thinks one needs to bring about in order to bring about the end. So, our willing of the end causes us to will the means. Does this mean one can intend something that is impossible? In one sense, yes. Because intention is an intelligible plan to bring about some state of affairs, one can intend only what one thinks is possible to bring about. It might in fact not be possible. But to the extent that one sees some state of affairs as desirable to bring about; and to the extent that one believes one can realize that state of affairs through acting; to that extent can one intend to bring about that state of affairs. It might be the case that there is an objective impossibility standing between me and the realization of my intention. It seems to me this does not mean we cannot intend it. Settling oneself to bring about the impossible might of course mean one is not in one's right mind. But it might merely mean that one has made a mistake in judgment.

What convinces Flannery that a person *cannot* form a plan of action that excludes elements one foresees one will bring about? He provides no analytic argument. His contention ultimately rests on an unstated erroneous proposition: that intention is reducible to a combination of

---

[60] He suggests we can "go further than this and say that there is positive reason *not* to separate off the death in this fashion"; *ibid.*, at 510.

[61] This is *inter alia* because in telling others one's intention one can always deceive them.

inevitable foreseeability and proximity of acting agent to caused effect.[62] But as I have said, what is intended and unintended is determined by an agent's settling himself on an intelligible plan of action judged choiceworthy for itself or for what it promises by way of bringing about some more remote end. And though in a fallen world dissimulating is unfortunately often intertwined in peoples' self-justification of their behavior, it is not to their self-justifications that we turn in identifying intention, but rather to the reasons they themselves have for doing what they do. One who intends X knows he intends X; he may not want anyone else to know; but he knows, not because he has privileged access to his mental files; not because he peers into his mind and observes his intention there as he might if he were trying to imagine what something looks like, or remember a face when he hears a name; not by observation of his outward behavior; he knows he intends X because his intention consists in his adopting of his own reasons for acting; and he knows his own reasons because he formulated them himself. *He* formed his intention; the plans and projects he pursues are the plans and projects *he* came up with.[63] If a doctor performing a hysterectomy or craniotomy or cesarean section intends to kill the baby during the procedure, that is his working plan of action. He has identified *the death* (among perhaps other things) as choiceworthy, and aims at it; and knows he does. If the baby does not die, his plan to that extent fails.

A similar but inverse question might be asked: will a doctor performing a craniotomy, specified precisely as cranium narrowing for the sake of the baby's removal for the sake of saving the mother, *know* with the

---

62 For example, Flannery asserts: "If and when that happens [i.e., when medical science advances sufficiently], the logical structure of the act [of craniotomy] will have changed in conjunction with the state of medical technology." *Ibid.*; in other words, when the possibility becomes a real living alternative, the foreseeability of the baby's death will not be certain; one *then* will be able to conceptually "separate out" the effect from the "compass of the means"; foreseeability is the determinative factor.

63 Wittgenstein holds that we do not come to know our intention based upon observation or evidence: one does not assert 'I intend to X' on the basis of evidence, or have a hunch one is intending then examine one's mind to see if there is any evidence. Hacker, *op. cit.*, at 258.

same clarity that he is *not* aiming at the baby's death when he performs the act? I grant that the psychology of the act is likely to be different from the previous example. The 'closer in' the harm causing behavior to the harmful effect, and the more foreseeable the harm, likely the more intense will be the felt experience that one is causing the harm. And indeed one is. To someone ordinarily disposed to reverence, protect and promote human life, especially vulnerable human life like that of the unborn, the feeling is likely to be vexing. The person will *know*, however, that the baby's death was not what he was aiming at; death offered him no gain, only loss; when he extracts the baby, we can imagine him looking down anxiously to see if, by some grace, *the baby is still alive*, though he knows this almost certainly will not be the case. But if by a miracle the baby was alive, the intention would still have been *entirely fulfilled because the baby's death was not part of it.*

The doctor who aims at death might also feel reluctant; grasping the baby's head, he might hold his breath, crinkle his brow, close his eyes before he squeezes as tightly as he can; he then withdraws the baby, and, perhaps with an overwhelming feeling of repugnance, looks down *to make sure it's dead!* If it is still alive, his plan to that extent *fails*. It is clear that this doctor is justly characterized–morally speaking–as being *a killer*. I do not think it is fair to say the same of the first doctor.

Certain opponents of this view hold that both doctors intend death;[64] it follows that if they do so for the same end (i.e., for the sake of the life of the mother), then ceteris paribus they *do* the same act. This erroneous simplification of moral analysis collapses intention into a combination of foreseeability and physical causal consequences. Nicanor Austriaco, for example, articulates the erroneous principle as follows: "No reasonable agent can posit as an indirect object an end that results from his action if that end is linked to his action by an immediate causal chain of events. All such ends can only be, properly and reasonably, direct objects of

[64] See Nancy Davis, "The Doctrine of Double Effect: Problems of Interpretation," in *The Doctrine of Double Effect: Philosophers Debate a Controversial Moral Principle*, ed. P.A. Woodward (South Bend, Ind.: University of Notre Dame Press, 2001), p. 122; Nicanor Austriaco, *op. cit.,* at 98.

human acts. Again, to claim otherwise would be unintelligible."[65] If immediate physical causality is the necessary determinant of intention then the soldier in a foxhole who willingly throws himself on a live grenade to save the life of his comrade in the hole with him intends to kill himself; and the woman who shoots her armored aggressor in the face to save herself from rape intends her aggressor's death; and the F-16 fighter pilot who shoots down a passenger airplane that terrorists are about to crash into a crowded skyscraper intends to kill everyone on board; and the bomber who in wartime drops a bomb on an enemy's dangerous weapons depot knowing civilians are inside intends to kill those civilians; and the woman who throws herself out a 10th story window to escape engulfing flames intends to kill herself; and the sailor who closes and locks his submarine's flood doors before his vessel swamps locking out fellow sailors unable to reach the door in time intends to kill his fellow sailors; and when I say "no" to my four year old daughter knowing my words will be linked immediately to her becoming sad, I intend my daughter's unhappiness; and of course Alexa intended to kill Sebastian?[66] A superficial consideration of the so called "action narrative"[67] of each of these events, links the killing or harming in an immediate causal series with someone's choice to do something in order to bring about some good. But it is

---

[65] Austriaco, *On Reshaping Skulls and Unintelligible Intentions,* 89. The question might be asked whether one can intend something that is impossible. Because intention is an intelligible plan to bring about some state of affairs, one can intend only what one thinks is possible to bring about. It might in fact not be possible; but to the extent that one sees some state of affairs as desirable to bring about; and to the extent that one believes one can realize that state of affairs through action; it seems right to say to that extent can one intend. It might be the case that there is an objective impossibility standing between me and the realization of my intention. It seems to me this doesn't mean we cannot intend it. For example, if the half-giant Hagrid believes he can squeeze the grumbles out of his good friend Harry Potter who is in a beastly mood, and, settling on this plan, proceeds to squeeze Harry to death, is there any doubt that Hagrid intended to squeeze the grumbles out of Harry? Settling oneself to bring about the impossible might of course mean one is not in one's right mind. But it might merely mean that one has made a mistake in judgment.

[66] Austriaco's essay is marked from beginning to end with the erroneous methodological approach to the determining of intent that adverts to the perspective of what a reasonable third party observing the event would be warranted in concluding is being intended.

[67] Austriaco, *op. cit.,* at 90.

unreasonable to say that in each case the harmful effect was intended. Intention is not assessed by looking at "action narratives" or "immediate causal chains of events" or anything else except the intelligible proposal that one's reason sets before one's will in order to attain some intelligible benefit. This and this alone determines intent and this should be what we consider when analyzing what a person does.

SEBASTIAN'S DEATH WAS *PRAETER INTENTIONEM*

Two points by way of conclusion. First, the morally significant difference between the responsibility one has for the harms one intends and the harms one brings about as unintended side effects is not grounded in a difference between the extent of the harms that result in the two cases. The extent of the harms could be exactly the same, as they are when a physician prescribes narcotics to end the life of a burn victim whom he considers better off dead, while the nurse, while foreseeing the drug's lethal effect, administers them solely to deaden the patient's pain. The two agents' responsibility differs because their wills with respect to the effects differ. In the first, the effect's intelligibility precisely *as harmful* is willed, is volitionally (even if not always emotionally) embraced; ipso facto the orientation of that will towards the harmed human good is determined. A disposition against the good is incorporated into the agent's will. In the second, the intelligibility of the effect's harm is foreseen and tolerated but never embraced; the harm is never made the operative aim of the will's actualization. Warren Quinn answers the question with a Kantian reply, different from but consistent with what I have proposed: the former treats those harmed as *for the sake of* the agent's purposes, while the latter does not.[68]

Second, to say that some harms are not intended is *not to say* the acts that bring them about are thereby morally legitimate. Opponents of the view I'm defending often protest saying that if this account of intention is correct, then all one needs to do to justify acts like therapeutic abortion is 'not intend' to kill.[69] This is a caricature. Actions not bad by virtue of their intended objects can be bad in other ways. They might, for exam-

---

[68] Warren Quinn, *Actions, op. cit.,* at 35.

[69] "But this has the counter-intuitive result that nearly any evil result of an action could be a side-effect." Flannery, *op. cit.,* at 507.

ple, violate the Golden Rule by being selfishly partial in the goods they prefer and the harms they tolerate. I might, for example, restrain my own children from playing in the back yard that I have freshly dusted with rat poison, but allow my neighbor's children to play there, wrongly tolerating the harms that might come to them, without ever intending their harm. Consistent with Catholic moral tradition, my account assesses the morality of causing harm not only in the light of the agent's intention but also in terms of whether causing harm under the circumstances is reasonable to permit, *even if not intended.* The condition for reasonableness has sometimes been called the principle of proportionality (or proportionate reason).[70] Aquinas formulates it in relation to the question of lawful killing in self-defense as follows: "Though proceeding from a good intention, an act may be rendered unlawful, if it is out of proportion to the end. Wherefore if a man, in self-defense, uses more than necessary violence, it will be unlawful: whereas if he repel force with moderation his defense will be lawful."[71] In the case of Alexa this would mean using no more

---

[70] This is not to be equated with "proportionate reason" as used among proportionalist ethicists, the most influential of whom in the past 50 years was Richard McCormick, S.J.; he uses the term proportionate reason to mean a state of affairs–"morally relevant circumstances"–that justifies one in intending means (objects) traditionally termed intrinsically evil:

> Common to all so called proportionalists . . . is the insistence that causing certain disvalues [i.e., intending an evil object in the traditional sense]. . . in our conduct does not by that very fact make the action morally wrong . . . . These evils or disvalues are said to be premoral when considered abstractly, that is, in isolation from their morally relevant circumstances. But they are evils. . . The action in which they occur becomes morally wrong when, all things considered, there is not a *proportionate reason* in the act justifying the disvalue.

Richard A. McCormick, "Killing the Patient," *Considering Veritatis splendor*, ed. John Wilkins, (Cleveland, Ohio:The Pilgrim Press, 1994), p. 17, emphasis added.

[71] Aquinas, *ST*, II-II, q. 64, a. 7c. The *Catechism of the Catholic Church* (1997) teaches: "One is not exonerated from grave offense if, without proportionate reason, he has acted in a way that brings about someone's death, even without the intention to do so." (No. 2269)

force and causing no more harm than is necessary for bringing about her good end (i.e., of protecting the world from the alien); under the circumstances she judges she needs to kill the alien; since it is growing rapidly inside Sebastian's chest, and since she has good reason to fear that if it bursts out she will be unable to stop it before it overtakes her, she judges that she needs to shoot it while it is still in Sebastian; she accepts the harm to Sebastian. If there was a reasonable alternative, that included preserving Sebastian's life and killing the alien, and had Alexa apprehended that alternative, she would have been morally obliged to choose it; in other words, Alexa would not have been justified in shooting the alien while still inside Sebastian, *not* because she would have thereby intended Sebastian's death, but because unintentionally, but with foreknowledge, she would have caused more harm than was necessary to bring about her good end. This would be a grave injustice against Sebastian and hence a grave moral wrong.

The assertion, therefore, that the baby's death in the case of the craniotomy can be unintended, does not imply that it would always—or ever—be morally legitimate to accept.

DOUBLE EFFECT REASONING AND CARE AT THE END OF LIFE: SOME CLARIFICATION AND DISTINCTIONS
Daniel P. Sulmasy, OFM

The Church has no philosophy of her own nor does she canonize one particular philosophy in preference to others.
Fides et Ratio, n. 49.

From different quarters, then, modes of philosophical speculation have continued to emerge and have sought to keep alive the great tradition of Christian thought which unites faith and reason.
Fides et Ratio, n. 59.

No less important is philosophy's contribution to a more coherent understanding of Church Tradition, the pronouncements of the Magisterium and the teaching of the great masters of theology, who often adopt concepts and thought-forms drawn from a particular philosophical tradition. Fides et Ratio, n. 65.

INTRODUCTION

The distinction between ordinary and extraordinary means of care (O/E) is often considered an application of the rule of double effect (RDE). This has become a common contemporary belief, shared by parties on both sides of some recent debates within the Church about care at the end of life.

Frs. Benedict Ashley and Kevin O'Rourke, for instance, write that, "… 'letting die' when therapy will not benefit the patient (indirect killing in accord with the principle of double effect) is ethically justifiable."[1]

They make a similar claim that forgoing extraordinary means of care can be distinguished from suicide by the invocation of the rule of double effect.

> Therefore, by the principle of double effect, the choice of another good may justify the *indirect* surrender of human life either for oneself or for another. In these circumstances, one

---

[1]Benedict Ashley, O.P. and Kevin O'Rourke, O.P., *Health Care Ethics: A Theological Analysis*, 4th ed. (Washington, DC: Georgetown University Press, 1997), p. 421.

does not choose death. Rather, one chooses another good, foreseeing that death will result as an unwanted and indirect result of that choice.[2]

The same conflation of O/E and RDE appears in the so-called New Natural Law theory, although less explicitly stated. These authors sometimes treat the O/E distinction with grave suspicion because of the potential they see for its abuse.[3] But their treatment of the O/E distinction is distinctive in other ways. They tend to treat it ahistorically. They cite no sources prior to Pius XII in their discussions of this topic, and frequently cite late 20th century U.S. legal opinions that *do* distort the meaning of the O/E distinction, lending credibility to their suspicions about its potential for abuse. At the very least, they caution that we should be very clear about what the O/E distinction means.

When the New Natural Law theorists do discuss the O/E distinction, however, they tend to translate it into their "basic reasons for acting" theory, in which the rule of double effect plays a critically important role. To notice this, one must be a very careful reader. Perhaps more importantly, one should pay attention to what is lost in this translation. As an example of how subtly this happens, consider the following passage from Grisez. In discussing the case of a man's duties to his wife who suffers from a condition of post-coma unresponsiveness, he writes:

> Since life is inherently good, there is still a reason to sustain and care for the gravely debilitated person in every appropriate way; but this reason cannot be considered decisive in determining moral responsibility. Otherwise, everyone would always be obligated to use every available means to sustain every person's life. But sound principles of morality do not entail such an exceptionless obligation, in practice nobody acts on it, and the Church implies that it does not exist because some means can be considered extraordinary and nonobligatory. Therefore, when resources that could be used to sustain someone's life are needed to meet some other serious responsibility, one may use them for that other purpose, provided

[2] *Ibid.* at 425.

[3] Germain Grisez and Joseph Boyle, *Life and Death With Liberty and Justice* (South Bend, Indiana: University of Notre Dame Press, 1979), pp. 105-7; 257; 418.

there is not some reason in addition to human life's inherent
goodness for using them to sustain life.[4]

The move between the last two sentences is interesting. Grisez interprets the O/E distinction in terms of a conflict between competing moral
obligations to promote the basic human goods. His move is understand-
able since this view is fundamental to the New Natural Law theory.[5]
However, there is a suppressed premise. Framing the case as a conflict
between a positive duty to promote one basic human good and a negative
duty not to violate another basic human good involves one immediately
in the double effect reasoning that is fundamental to the New Natural Law
theory. Double effect has a special preeminence in this theory because
New Natural Law theorists posit that one may never act except to instantiate one of the basic goods (life, knowledge, play, aesthetic experience,
friendship, practical reasonableness, religion, and marriage), and one cannot act against one of these goods except as an indirect consequence of
acting to promote another. All the principles of Catholic medical morals
appear to become applications of the RDE in this theory.[6] Thus, the
moment one casts the O/E distinction in terms of the New Natural Law
theory, one has cast that distinction in terms of double effect reasoning.

Here is another treatment of the topic by another member of this
school, John Finnis. In describing the difference between refusing "ordinary" care and "abstaining from excessive measures," he writes:

> ...it is not suicide to choose to refuse treatment precisely
> because it—having the treatment and undergoing its afteref-
> fects—is burdensome, and one chooses to reject the burden.
> One's death is not chosen, for it is neither one's end, nor a

---

[4] Germain Grisez, *Difficult Moral Questions*, vol. 3. (Quincy, Illinois: Franciscan Press, 1997), p. 222.

[5] See, for instance, John Finnis, *Natural Law and Natural Rights* (Oxford: The Clarendon Press of Oxford University Press, 1980), pp. 118-125; Joseph Boyle, "Medical Ethics and Double Effect: The Case of Terminal Sedation," *Theoretical Medicine and Bioethics* 25 (2004): 51-60.

[6] Even the amputation of a gangrenous limb to save a life is construed, on this account, to be an unintended side-effect at a 3rd order level of moral abstraction. Thus, the Principle of Totality becomes explicitly re-interpreted as an application of the RDE (see John Finnis, *Aquinas: Moral, Political, and Legal Theory* (New York: Oxford University Press, 1998), pp. 279-80.)

means to one's end, but a side-effect, foreseen and accepted
(but not intended, not chosen), of one's choice to reject the burden. Such choices may in certain cases, perhaps many cases,
be unjustified (cowardly, selfish), but need not be suicidal
(homicidal).[7]

Again, while not explicit, Finnis' language implies that what he is
offering the reader is an interpretation of what has come to be known as
the distinction between ordinary and extraordinary means. The language
he uses to interpret that distinction, with its talk of "means" and "side-
effect," however, is the language of double-effect. While he may want to
distance himself from the label 'double effect',[8] it seems fairly certain
that he is interpreting the O/E distinction using double effect reasoning.

So, despite their differences, Ashley and O'Rourke and Grisez and
Finnis appear to have at least this much in common. They appear to consider the withholding and withdrawing of extraordinary means of care an
application of the rule of double effect.

I want to argue that it is mistaken, however, historically and logically,
to consider the forgoing of extraordinary means of care to be an application of the RDE. The RDE and the O/E distinction are distinct, have different historical origins, and the latter is not reducible to the former. Not
all moral reasoning that involves a condition of proportionality and a
division between intention and foresight is an application of the Rule of
Double Effect. As Anscombe once observed, the denial of the RDE "has
been the corruption of non-Catholic thought, and its abuse the corruption
of Catholic thought."[9]   The idea that the O/E distinction is an application
of the RDE may be an instance of that corruption.

THE HISTORICAL ARGUMENT

In his definitive history of the O/E distinction, Cronin catalogues possible principles and circumstances that might excuse an individual from

---

[7] John Finnis, "The 'Value of Human Life' and 'The Right to Death': Some Reflections
on Cruzan and Ronald Dworkin," *Southern Illinois University Law Journal* 17 (Winter,
1993): 559-571, at 565.

[8] Finnis, Natural Law and Natural Rights, op. cit., at 123-4.

[9] G. E. M. Anscombe, "War and Murder," in *War and Morality*, ed. Richard A.
Wasserstrom (Belmont, CA: Wadsworth Publishing, 1970), pp. 42-53.

the precepts of natural law regarding self-conservation.[10]   This list includes non-culpable ignorance,[11] physical impossibility,[12] and the rule of double effect.[13]   But he dismisses each of these as the source of the O/E distinction. His historical analysis suggests that it is derived from the last category on his list, "moral impossibility."[14]   He writes:

> It is a rational presumption then that since man is not always and everywhere, under every circumstance, bound to do something positively good, he would not be always and everywhere bound to fulfill an affirmative precept. Hence, moral impossibility, while not freeing an individual from the basic obligation of the natural law, excuses him from the present observance of an affirmative precept of that law.[15]

Cronin states that what constitutes a moral impossibility is that circumstances have made the obligation one "not commonly experienced by men in general,"[16] fraught with fear, repugnance, difficulty, danger, or inconvenience. Hence,

> The law that demands the conservation of one's own life also commands that he employ the means necessary to conserve life. Since, however, this law is an affirmative law and a licit application of the doctrine on moral impossibility may be made, theologians commonly divide the means of conserving life into two categories. The first includes those which are obligatory for everyone. The second is comprised of those whose use would constitute a moral impossibility either for human beings in general or for one particular individual. The former they term *ordinary means*; the latter, *extraordinary means*.[17]

[10] Daniel A. Cronin, "Conserving Human Life," in *Conserving Human Life*, ed. Russell E. Smith (Braintree, Massachusetts: The Pope John Center, 1989), pp. 1-145, at 23-31.

[11] *Ibid.*, pp. 23-25.

[12] *Ibid.*, p. 30.

[13] *Ibid.*, pp. 26-29.

[14] *Ibid.*, pp. 29-31.

[15] *Ibid.*, p. 30.

[16] *Ibid.*, p. 31.

[17] *Ibid.*, p. 31.

Thus, Cronin suggests the derivation of the O/E tradition is from a principle that he distinguishes from double effect—namely—the tradition of moral impossibility as an exculpatory factor in the fulfillment of a positive precept of natural or human positive law.

ST. THOMAS AND THE SCHOLASTICS

In considering whether the Catholic moral tradition of ordinary and extraordinary means has been an application of the RDE, it is also important to remember that the RDE arose in a historical line of scholastic and casuistic commentary completely distinct from the O/E distinction. Aquinas is silent on the topic of extraordinary means of care. However, both the O/E distinction and the RDE arose from commentary on his work. Nonetheless, the histories of these discussions are distinct. The RDE arose in discussions regarding Thomas' treatment of the morality of killing in self-defense.[18] As Magnan has pointed out in his classical work on the RDE, it was not until the first edition of Gury in the 19th century that there was such a well-formed principle.[19] The RDE was not applied to medical care in Catholic discussions until the 20th century—in discussions of the use of morphine at the end of life and discussions of surgery for ectopic pregnancy.

By contrast, the O/E distinction arose from commentary on Thomas' treatment of suicide,[20] and mutilation.[21] It is also invoked in discussions of the virtue of temperance and about the limits of fasting.[22]   Neither

[18] St. Thomas Aquinas, *Summa Theologiae*, II-II q. 64, a. 7.

[19] Joseph T. Mangan, S.J., "An Historical Analysis of the Principle of Double Effect," *Theological Studies* 10 (1949): 41-61.

[20] St. Thomas Aquinas, *Summa Theologiae*, II-II q. 64, a. 5.

[21] St. Thomas Aquinas, *Summa Theologiae*, II-II, q. 65, a.1. It seems plainly obvious that Finnis interprets this passage though the heuristic of the New Natural Law theory by claiming that this is an application of the RDE (Finnis, *Aquinas*, pp. 279-280). Just two articles before this in the *Summa*, in discussing self-defense, Aquinas uses the phrases *duo effectus, duplex effectus, bona intentione, praeter intentionem*, and *proportionatus fini*. This is the language of double effect. It seems quite a stretch to claim that this was the reasoning Aquinas was employing in his defense of amputation of a gangrenous limb when none of these phases or anything remotely resembling them is used in his argument.

[22] See Cronin, *op. cit.* at 38; 45-46; also Francisco de Vitoria, O.P., *Reflection on Homicide and Commentary on Summa Theologiae IIᵃ-IIᵃᵉ Q. 64*, John P. Doyle (Milwaukee, Wisconsin: Marquette University Press, 1997), pp. 172-3.

Thomas' discussion of killing in self defense nor the RDE are ever mentioned in these discussions. The O/E distinction became an explicit moral principle beginning in the 16th century, 300 years before the RDE became an explicit principle.

CRONIN'S HISTORY OF THE SCHOLASTIC DISCUSSION
In Cronin's study of the history of the O/E distinction, not a single author cites the RDE or uses the phrase 'double effect.' Not one of them casts this as a conflict of obligations between the duty to conserve one's life and some other obligation. One's duty to conserve one's life is limited by various aspects of one's finitude as a creature.

For more than five centuries, the question has always been, as Kelly would later put it, "How much does God demand that I do in order to preserve this life which belongs to God and of which I am a steward?"[23] The answer has been, as Cronin amply documents through several centuries, "No more than is reasonable." And "reasonable" has never been defined as "until you reach the point of a conflict with other duties," but in terms of a frank recognition of the limits of human physical, mental, emotional, and spiritual resources. That is to say, the duty holds to the point of "moral impossibility," which has been defined as "a proportionately grave inconvenience which excuses from the present observance of the law."[24] Although Cronin suggests that this line of reasoning is at the root of every discussion of the O/E distinction, he attributes the explicit use of the language of moral impossibility to Vitoria, Sayrus, Mazzotta, Tournley, Marc-Gestermann, Aertnys-Damen, Lehmkuhl, Kelly, and Paquin.[25]

What counted as proportionately grave inconveniences during this history? According to Cronin, Catholic casuists suggested that treatments could be considered to have associated with them disproportionately grave inconveniences (i.e., to be "extraordinary") under the following conditions: (1) when there is a lack of hope of benefit or (2) the treatments are associated with too much difficulty, (3) lack simplicity, (4) are

[23] Gerald Kelly, SJ, *Medico-Moral Problems*, St. Louis, MO: The Catholic Hospital Association of the U.S. and Canada, 1958, p. 132.

[24] Cronin, *op. cit.* at 100.

[25] *Ibid.* at 100-101.

not commonly used, (5) are out of proportion to one's physical, psychological, financial, or social condition; (6) when there is intense pain associated with the treatment or its aftermath, or (6) excessive hardship in attaining or undergoing the treatment; (7) when one has great fear of the treatment or the condition in which one would be left by it, or (8) repugnance at the treatment or the condition in which one would be left by it; and (9) when the treatment requires great effort or (10) is very costly.[26]

These do not seem to constitute some set of inchoate, enthymatic double-effect arguments. These are a set of justified limits to a duty. They are invoked without reference to double effect reasoning. The mere fact that there is a condition of proportionality in the O/E distinction does not imply that it is an instance of double effect reasoning. As I shall discuss in greater detail below, the proportionality considered in the tradition regarding ordinary and extraordinary means of care is between the burdens and the benefits associated with undergoing the treatment, relative to reason, given one's condition, granting that the treatment might conserve one's life. It is most certainly not a proportion between the good effect of the treatment (conserving one's life) and the associated burdens of the treatment. Nor was it ever historically construed as a proportion between the expected good effects of discontinuing a treatment (i.e., relieving one of the burdens caused by the treatment) and the bad effect of causing one's earlier death.

This difference is subtle but crucial to understanding the tradition. The tradition has appropriately applied double effect in addressing various *other* questions in the ethics of care at the end of life. The case of morphine is one appropriate application of the RDE. So is the case of so-called "terminal sedation," at least when it is done appropriately and licitly.[27] But the questions raised in these cases are distinct from the question of when it is appropriate to forgo a life-sustaining intervention.

[26] *Ibid.* at 84-112.

[27] See Daniel P. Sulmasy, OFM and Edmund D. Pellegrino, "The Rule of Double Effect: Clearing Up the Double Talk," *Archives of Internal Medicine* 159 (1999): 545-50; also Lynn A. Jansen and Daniel P. Sulmasy, "Sedation, Hydration, Alimentation, and Equivocation: Careful Conversation About Care at the End of Life," *Annals of Internal Medicine* 136 (2002): 845-849.

GURY AND THE MANUALIST TRADITION

Over centuries of reflection and refinement, Catholic natural law casuistry has carefully distilled a panoply of important moral principles and distinctions. They are actually quite numerous and various. Within that tradition, the RDE and the category of moral impossibility were never treated as the same thing, nor was it ever suggested that one could be reduced to the other. In the 1946 edition of Gury's *Theologia Moralis*, the RDE is treated as a general principle of morality for managing conflicting moral obligations.[28]   Among the cases referenced are ectopic pregnancy and the unintentional killing of non-combatants in war. There is no mention of end-of-life care. Many pages later, in the exposition of general ethical principles catalogued in Volume I of the *Theologia Moralis*, the conditions that excuse one from carrying out one's duties under human positive law and natural law are laid out for the reader. These include external causes, invincible ignorance, physical impossibility, and moral impossibility.[29]   It is clearly specified that the condition of moral impossibility applies only to affirmative precepts, not to negative precepts. The examples that follow are about the conditions under which one could be exempted from the Lenten fast, and when a religious could be exempted from reciting the breviary.

In Vol. II of Gury's *Theologia Moralis*, in discussing suicide, there is a brief discussion of extraordinary means of care,[30] suggesting that one may forgo these interventions licitly "by reason of the fact that one is required to serve life only by ordinary means." The text then lists some possible reasons a treatment may be considered extraordinary, such as cost, pain, etc. The classic case of forgoing an amputation is given as an example of an extraordinary means of care. There is also a discussion of

27 See Daniel P. Sulmasy, OFM and Edmund D. Pellegrino, "The Rule of Double Effect: Clearing Up the Double Talk," *Archives of Internal Medicine* 159 (1999): 545-50; also Lynn A. Jansen and Daniel P. Sulmasy, "Sedation, Hydration, Alimentation, and Equivocation: Careful Conversation About Care at the End of Life," *Annals of Internal Medicine* 136 (2002): 845-849.

28 Thomas A. Iorio, SJ, *Theologia Moralis*, 3rd ed., vol. I, § 23 (Napoli, Italy: M. D'Auria, Holy See Apostolic Publishers, 1946), pp. 104-105.

29 *Ibid.* at § 122, pp. 94-96.

30 Thomas A. Iorio, SJ, *Theologia Moralis*, 3rd ed., vol. II, §165, no. 3 (Napoli, Italy: M. D'Auria, Holy See Apostolic Publishers , 1946), p. 104.

how it is licit for a consecrated virgin to refuse medical examinations or treatments involving her genitalia by virtue of her repugnance at the idea that a man might touch her there. The text of this section on extraordinary means does not mention the RDE. Ten sections later, the RDE is referenced with respect to the use of morphine under a discussion of one's duty not to kill the innocent.[31]

GERALD KELLY: 20TH CENTURY CATHOLIC CASUISTRY

In the middle of the 20th century, Gerald Kelly's *Medico-Moral Problems* affirms this historical distinction of the O/E from the RDE, and their distinct justifications. In the first chapter of this book, he sets forth "Basic Notions and Principles," including fundamental principles such as "Totality," and "Bodily Integrity." In this chapter, he addresses as his second separate principle the distinction between "doing good" (*affirmative* precepts) and "avoiding evil" (*negative* precepts), and notes that while negative precepts always bind, "there is a limit to the duty of doing good." He explicitly states that "there is a reasonable limit to a man's duty to care for his health," and promises that "practical applications of these limits to the duty of doing good will be found particularly in the [chapter] concerning means of preserving health and life."[32] One must bear in mind that this book was intended for medical professionals and not professional theologians. It may be for this reason that he does not use the explicit phrase "moral impossibility" here. But his meaning is clear enough.

Later in this chapter, he treats the RDE as his fourth distinct principle, and gives examples such as operations for ectopic pregnancy. He does not mention the O/E distinction in the context of discussing the RDE.[33] Obversely, his chapter on ordinary and extraordinary means makes no mention of the RDE, but justifies it by stating "there are reasonable and proportionate limits to one's duty of doing good."[34] In his chapter on euthanasia he refers to the RDE obliquely in his defense of the distinction

---

[31] *Ibid.* at § 176, p. 122.

[32] Kelly, *Medico-Moral Problems, op. cit.*, at 4.

[33] *Ibid.* at 12-16.

[34] *Ibid.* at 131.

between using sedatives to "kill pain" and euthanasia to "kill the patient."[35]

Kelly explicitly invokes the phrase "moral impossibility" in his famous scholarly article on this topic in *Theological Studies*, stating simply, "an extraordinary means is one which prudent men would consider at least morally impossible with reference to the duty of preserving one's life."[36]

CONTEMPORARY CHURCH DOCUMENTS

Contemporary Church documents discuss both the RDE and the O/E distinction, but none of these treat the O/E distinction as an application of the RDE. The *Catechism*, for instance, cites the RDE in its discussion of self-defense,[37] but make no mention of it in its discussion of ordinary and extraordinary means of care.[38] *Evangelium vitae* (no. 65) states that extraordinary means may be foresworn if they "are disproportionate to any expected result or impose an excessive burden on the patient and his family."[39] There is no mention of competing moral obligations or the RDE. The reason given to explain why forgoing extraordinary care is not the equivalent of suicide or euthanasia is, in accord with the discussion above, the acceptance of human finitude—an "acceptance of human finitude in the face of death." The *Declaration on Euthanasia* (§ 4) states that one must use "due proportion in the use of remedies." In accord with centuries of tradition, the justification for distinguishing the abatement of extraordinary means of treatment from euthanasia or suicide is neither that one has a conflicting obligation, nor because one can appropriately apply the RDE to such cases. The Declaration grounds the non-suicidal nature of the abatement of extraordinary means of treatment in the recognition of human finitude and in the virtue of charity, stating, it represents either the "acceptance of the human condition, or a desire to avoid the

---

35 *Ibid.* at 115.

36 Gerald Kelly, S.J., "The Duty of Using Artificial Means of Preserving Life," *Theological Studies* 11 (1950): 203-220.

37 *Catechism of the Catholic Church*, § 2263 (Cittá del Vaticano: Libreria Editrice Vaticana, 1994), p. 545.

38 *Ibid.*, § 2278, p. 549.

39 Pope John Paul II, *Evangelium vitae*, March 25, 1995, no. 65. http://www.vatican.va/edocs/ENG0141/_INDEX.HTM

application of a medical procedure disproportionate to the results that can be expected, or a desire not to impose excessive costs on the family of the community."[40]   These reasons are clearly consistent with casting the O/E distinction squarely within the tradition—as an application of "moral impossibility," not the RDE.

The only official Church document I could find that invokes the RDE with respect to the O/E distinction is in the Allocution of Pius XII to anesthesiologists in 1957 in which he states (in an infrequently quoted passage),

> ...even when it causes the arrest of circulation, the interruption of attempts at resuscitation is never more than an indirect cause of the cessation of life, and one must apply in this case the principle of double effect and of *voluntarium in causa*.[41]

Yet he did not invoke the RDE in the first and more detailed explanation of the O/E distinction within the same allocution, in which he famously stated,

> But normally one is held to use only ordinary means—according to circumstances of persons, places, times, and culture— that is to say, means that do not involve any grave burden for oneself or another. A more strict obligation would be too burdensome for most men and would render the attainment of the higher, more important good too difficult. Life, health, all temporal activities are in fact subordinated to spiritual ends.[42]

In addition, it must be noted that this was neither an encyclical nor a serious work of theological scholarship, and so the utmost care might not have been devoted to every word. For example, most scholars distinguish sharply between double effect and *voluntarium in causa*. It is uncertain why these phrases are in this document. One might speculate that since

---

[40] Congregation for the Doctrine of the Faith, *Declaration on Euthanasia*, May 5, 1980, §4.
http://www.vatican.va/roman_curia/congregations/cfaith/documents/rc_con_cfaith_doc_19800505_euthanasia_en.html

[41] Pope Pius XII, "The Prolongation of Life: An Address of Pope Pius XII to an International Congress of Anesthesiologists," *The Pope Speaks* 4 (1958): 393-398, at 397.

[42] *Ibid.* at 395-6.

the pope had invoked the RDE in his discussion of morphine in February, 1957,[43] it was still on his mind when he discussed forgoing ventilator support in November, 1957. This reference to double effect may represent an early instance of the conflation of the RDE and the O/E distinction that has, as I have suggested, deviated from the Tradition, apparently unwittingly. All told, I am not inclined to think that this isolated, almost offhand reference, was a serious and well-thought out attempt to alter the theological grounding for the O/E distinction as I have outlined it.

HISTORICAL CONCLUSIONS

These considerations suggest that the O/E distinction has been cast as a natural limit to one's duty to carry out an affirmative precept of the natural law, not as an application of the RDE in a situation in which one's duty to carry out an affirmative precept clashes with one's duty never to violate a negative precept. The casting of the question is crucial. The tradition treats these as distinct modes of moral reasoning, and does not consider one reducible to the other. Moral impossibility is a limiting principle based upon an acceptance of natural limits and a recognition of the finite physical, intellectual, emotional, and spiritual resources of human beings. It does not require a conflict with another duty to establish this limit. In other words, it is sufficient to decide that a treatment is extraordinary by judging that one has met the limits of reasonability in doing what is necessary to fulfill one's duty to preserve life. In other words, "Enough is enough," is a good enough answer. The duty to preserve life has never been construed in Catholic thought as requiring that one meet the much higher standard of judging a proposed life-preserving intervention to be extraordinary (morally optional) only when it conflicts with some other, competing basic reason for acting. The historical basis of the O/E distinction in the Catholic tradition is moral impossibility (i.e., grave inconvenience), not the RDE.

A misinterpretation of the Catholic tradition can cause one's evaluation of cases to go awry, and might either make one's evaluation of what

---

43 Pope Pius XII, "Allocution to Doctors on the Moral Problems of Analgesia," Feb. 24, 1957. http://www.acim-asia.com/Allocution_To_Doctors.htm

Catholics are bound to do under penalty of mortal sin too lax or too harsh. Revisionism is dangerous whether it is liberal or conservative. Tradition serves to keep us in check. There are times when it is necessary to adjust the tradition to new circumstances, but we must be careful not to do so without extremely good reasons and the utmost of care.

DIFFERENCES BETWEEN THE RDE AND TRADITIONAL O/E REASONING

I will next argue that, historical considerations aside, from a purely structural point of view, when one applies the RDE correctly and consistently to cases involving end of life care, cases are classified differently than they would be under a traditional understanding of the O/E distinction. Among the reasons for this are that O/E reasoning and double effect reasoning differ in the content of their respective proportionality conditions, in how intention and foresight are distinguished, and in the focus of moral agency when considering surrogate decision making.

A CASE

To see why classical O/E reasoning and double effect reasoning differ, consider the following hypothetical case. A wealthy man develops a rare neurological condition that does four things: (1) It produces a complete expressive aphasia in which he is awake and alert but is totally unable to express himself in any communicative form—spoken, written, hand signals, etc. (2) Although it is hard to tell because of his aphasia, he appears to have problems with information processing and decision making. He is simply docile. The MRI shows some frontal lobe abnormalities of uncertain significance. (3) The condition is also associated with a severe, lancinating, neuropathic facial pain syndrome similar to that of *tic douloureaux*, completely unresponsive to all forms of medical therapy. This is often described as the most severe, agonizing pain syndrome to affect the human species. Thirty-minute episodes of this pain occur at random, multiple times each day. (4) The condition also attacks the medullary respiratory centers and renders him unable to breathe on his own. The condition came on suddenly, but is now stable and has not progressed over the last year. He has undergone a tracheostomy and is cared for at home on a portable ventilator. After the initial expenditure, this is very inexpensive to maintain. He has a home oxygen concentrator, so that he need not purchase oxygen, and really only uses this at night. During the day the ventilator just pumps air. He is not paralyzed, so he can accomplish most of his own care without burdening others. He left no advance directive and we have no direct evidence about what his beliefs would have been about continuing this treatment, and no way of finding out now due to his aphasia and organic brain syndrome. Is it morally permissible to discontinue his ventilator?

The patient must, sadly, be declared lacking in decision making capacity since he cannot communicate any decisions, even if it seems that he has at least a rudimentary understanding of what is going on. Accordingly, the decision whether to forgo ventilator support must be made by surrogates. Suppose the surrogate, his wife, is instructed to look to the RDE for guidance about how to proceed. According to the classical formulation of the RDE, one may undertake an action that has two effects, one good and one bad, only if:

1. the act is not intrinsically evil;
2. one sincerely intends only the good, foreseeing but not intending the bad;
3. the bad effect one claims not to intend is not the cause of the good one claims to intend;
4. the good effects are disproportionately greater than the bad effects.

How would our case be analyzed under the RDE if it were asked whether his wife could authorize the physicians to discontinue the ventilator? The first condition of the RDE is easily satisfied—discontinuing the ventilator is not intrinsically evil. Second, let us suppose that his wife really does not want him to die,[44] but merely foresees his death. Third, relieving his pain would seem to be a good reason for acting, so she might seem on her way to stopping the ventilator. However, straightaway there is a problem. How could she stop his pain except by making him dead? The ventilator is not causing the pain, so no pain relief follows as a direct consequence of stopping the ventilator. She could only be construed as intending to relieve his pain by making him dead, and thereby disvaluing

---

[44] Desire and intention are not the same, but let us grant this conflation for present purposes.

the quality of his life as not worth living. And this would be homicide, pure and simple. Under the RDE, she could not authorize discontinuing the ventilator.

Could this be construed otherwise under RDE reasoning? Let us suppose that she does not intend to relieve the neuropathic pain by discontinuing the ventilator, but intends to relieve the burdens of the ventilator itself, foreseeing his death as a side-effect. However, what sort of suffering does the ventilator itself cause in this case, and how does it compare in proportion to the value of keeping the patient alive? Positive pressure breathing is a bit of an unusual feeling at first, but people get used to it. In fact, hundreds of thousands of persons now manage to sleep through the night using continuous positive airway pressure (CPAP) as treatment for obstructive sleep apnea. The tracheostomy is not uncomfortable, and plenty of people live with one for many years after major head and neck operations. Maintaining it requires little effort once it is in place. How does the wife's duty to relieve her husband of these very minor discomforts compare in proportion to the wife's duty to preserve his life? The discomforts of the ventilator itself pale in comparison. In fact, by discontinuing the ventilator, she would actually increase his discomfort since he would then experience shortness of breath, so it is implausible, under the RDE, to suggest that she would have a proportionate reason for discontinuing the ventilator if her intention were to relieve him of the discomfort caused by the ventilator.

What about burden to others? Suppose she were to argue that care for her husband was conflicting with her duties to others? Well, the care her husband requires is actually minimal. He is mostly a "self-care" patient and can even feed himself, although he is not able to cook for himself. She and her children have no need for any specialized nursing assistance to help them in caring for him. The expenses are minimal, and he is rich anyway. So the burdens of caring for him seem small compared with the value of his life, and not a proportionately grave reason for discontinuing the ventilator.

But she is deeply troubled. She wishes something could be done to stop her husband's pain. She becomes distraught watching as the episodes of neuropathic pain bring him to tears multiple times each day. His pain has not responded to opioids, non-steroidal anti-inflammatory drugs, antidepressants, anti-epileptics, or even the surgical severing of his facial nerve root. She considered sedating him permanently, again invoking the RDE, but realizes that this would deprive him of all consciousness indefinitely. Because he is on a ventilator, she realizes the RDE would not even apply to a possible plan to sedate him since sedation would not stop him from breathing and could not thereby hasten his death. It would only make him persistently unconscious and alive on a ventilator, and she is not certain that would really be better. Nor would such a move relieve her of her duty to continue the ventilator support because it would not change the conditions for the correct application of the RDE to the decision about discontinuing the ventilator. And so, she feels that she has misunderstood Catholic moral tradition, which she previously took to have permitted patients to forgo extraordinary means of care. As it has now been explained to her using the RDE, the continued use of the ventilator is ordinary care and must be continued.

A TRADITIONAL READING OF THIS CASE AS EXTRAORDINARY CARE

A traditional reading of the case would invoke the O/E distinction, however, and not the RDE. The moral and spiritual advisor would ask the wife to consider how much she thought her husband could reasonably be asked to bear in order to satisfy his obligation to conserve his life. Would he have wanted to be kept alive in this condition? How much pain would he need to bear? Having tried everything to stop the pain, having given ample time to see if the condition would reverse itself, realizing that the ventilator did nothing to reverse the underlying condition but only supported one of several neurologically damaged functions, would he be prepared to say, with St. Paul, "I have fought the good fight, I have finished the race, I have kept the faith" (2Tim 4:7)? Does she think he would consider all of the burdens and benefits associated with the condition and its treatment proportionate to the reasonable fulfillment of his duty to preserve his life? The ventilator supports his breathing and that keeps him alive. But it does not reverse the aphasia, the dementia, or the pain. There are no prospects for its success in doing anything more. Her intention would never be to make him dead, but simply to discontinue a treatment that only partially treats an underlying lethal pathophysiologic condition. She values him, loves him, cherishes him, prays for him, and despite his dementia tries to get him to pray with her. She would rather that he be cured. But she can't bear to see what this disease has done to him—for his sake. She realizes it would be selfish of her to make him persist under such heroic conditions merely because she does not want to lose him. She authorizes the discontinuation of the ventilator as an extraordinary, disproportionate means of care.

This analysis seems a correct one, consistent with the tradition. The RDE analysis of the case, by contrast, seems incorrect. Perhaps there are those who believe the traditional analysis is incorrect, and would put more faith in the RDE than in the Tradition. But I think this would only demonstrate a revisionist tendency to interpret the entire Catholic moral tradition through the RDE, even if it demands more of the faithful than the Tradition would demand. It therefore pays to look more closely at precisely how the RDE analysis and the Tradition differ in their application to cases.

DIFFERING VIEWS OF PROPORTIONALITY

Not every moral principle that contains a condition of proportionality is an application of the rule of double-effect. For example, in the *jus ad bellum* aspect of just war theory, a nation is required to meet a condition of proportionality before undertaking armed conflict. Traditionally, this means that not only must the cause be just and the prospects of success reasonable, but the anticipated results must be worth the anticipated bloodshed. Such an invocation of proportionality is obviously not reducible to an application of the RDE. Clearly, in war, the good effect can only be achieved by means of the bad effect. Factories are destroyed. Ships are sunk. Soldiers are killed. Ultimately, one hopes, the war will thus be won and the injustice righted. But if this is how proportionality works in the theory of *jus ad bellum*, it cannot be the case that it is an application of the RDE. Standard discussions of *jus ad bellum* do not invoke the RDE.[45]

One should not be confused by the use of the RDE in other aspects of just war theory, however. Once a nation has undertaken armed conflict in a morally justified war, discussions of *jus in bello* appropriately invoke double-effect reasoning to discuss whether one may endanger non-com-

---

[45] Robert L. Holmes, "Just War Theory," *Cambridge Dictionary of Philosophy*, ed. Robert Audi (Cambridge, UK: Cambridge University Press, 1995, p. 397.

batants in carrying out attacks on combatants.[46]   Since there is an agreed upon negative precept that one cannot directly attack innocent civilians, but the attacking of armed combatants and/or the destruction of the means of making war are justified in a just war, double-effect reasoning can be invoked in evaluating how one conducts a just war. The upshot is that one may not make the death of civilians one's direct intention, nor can one accept their being killed as the means by which one will wear down the will of the people and thus end the war.

This invocation of the RDE is but one aspect of *jus in bello* theorizing. My main point is that in just war theory, the proportionality condition invoked in discussions of *jus ad bellum*, as described above, is not an application of the RDE. And one exception is sufficient to prove that not every invocation of proportionality implies the RDE.

Therefore, one of the first differences to note is that the concrete content of the proportionality conditions of the traditional O/E distinction and the RDE differ. Under RDE, one may only consider the effects that flow directly from one's action. In the classical morphine example, these effects are analgesia and respiratory depression. In applying the RDE to the withdrawal of extraordinary means of life-sustaining care, one can only consider the direct effects of this action. The good effect that results directly from the discontinuation of the treatment is the cessation of pain or other discomfort caused by the treatment itself. The bad effect is death. This sets an extremely high standard for determining that the discontinuation of life-sustaining treatment is morally licit. It would seem that one could only consider a treatment "extraordinary" if the treatment itself caused suffering proportionately graver than the evil of shortening life.

Alternatively, one could construe the discontinuation of life-sustaining treatment as a double-effect dilemma for an agent with some responsibility for distributing scarce resources. One could say (after the insurance had run out, but not before), "I only have so much money. I can either feed my children or care for my loved one. All human lives are equally valuable, but I have three young children and therefore it seems that I

---

[46] See Iorio's discussion in Gury's *Theologia Moralis*, vol. I, *op. cit.*, § 23, pp. 104-105 and John C. Ford, S.J., "The Morality of Obliteration Bombing," *Theological Studies* 5 (September 1944): 261-309.

have a proportionately grave reason for stopping the life-sustaining treatment. By choosing to feed my children, I forsee but do not intend the death of my loved one." Of course, this also sets an enormously high standard—the treatment must be so expensive that it consumes enough resources to threaten the lives of others from whom those resources are being siphoned. By such standards, almost every Western person who has ever authorized the discontinuation of life-sustaining treatments for a comatose loved one since the 1970s has committed a grave moral error.

By contrast, the genuine Roman Catholic tradition regarding ordinary and extraordinary means is much more organic and natural in its considerations of what constitutes a proportionately grave inconvenience—moral impossibility. The burdens and the benefits are not considered as competing direct effects of the act of discontinuation balanced against each other, but are considered together with the condition of the patient, in proportion to practical reason.

> Since the dictate of the natural law which commands a man to conserve his life is obviously a reasonable law, the means to fulfill it need only be within reason. Hence, any inconvenience or difficulty that is unreasonable is not obligatory.[47]

So, the proportionality of the O/E distinction is not between the benefits caused by the treatment (preserving life) and the burdens caused by the treatment (pain, cost, etc.), but the proportion of the burdens and the benefits associated with the treatment considered together in proportion to practical reasonability, given the fact that one accepts that there is a natural duty to preserve one's life.

What constitutes this standard of practical reasonability beyond which an intervention becomes extraordinary? It will obviously not be possible to give a precise definition, and it will vary according to the physical, intellectual, emotional, spiritual, social, and economic resources of the individual. Those considerations Cronin cites include "a difficulty...not commonly experienced by men in general,"[48] or what "exceeds the nor-

[47] Cronin, *op. cit.*, at 102-103.
[48] *Ibid.*, at 31.

mal strength of men in general,"[49] or "the common estimate of men"[50] or
what is deemed not to be a "reasonable and moderate means."[51] Kelly
calls this standard "a prudent communis aestimatio."[52] To the conster-
nation of those who demand more precision than this, one can only cite
Aristotle's famous observation in the Nichomachean Ethics that one can
only demand from a science the precision that its subject will allow.[53]

Traditional writers never imagined the possibility of contemporary
life-sustaining treatments. They discussed treatments that were generally performed only once, such as an amputation. They concentrated on the
expenses and pains caused by the treatments themselves, with the general presumption of cure or death. They did not say much about treatments
that would not cure the disease but would be continuously or recurrently
needed to sustain life in a condition of great suffering. For the most part,
this simply did not happen before the great medical developments of the
latter half of the 20th century.

However, the scholastics and later casuists were not completely silent
about whether the state of the patient, independent of the treatment, could
be included in their calculus of the benefits and burdens of treatment with
respect to reason. Bañez, for instance, writes simply that one need not
preserve one's life in the face of "certain and horrible pain," without necessary reference to the fact that the treatment itself would cause the
pain.[54] According to Cronin, these classical casuists also took into
account "the quality and duration" of the state one would be in after treatment.[55] One's condition after the treatment could render the treatment
extraordinary—for example, a "troublesome convalescence."[56]
Repugnance at the state one would be in after treatment, such as of living

[49] *Ibid.*, at 73.

[50] *Ibid.*, at 73.

[51] *Ibid.*, at 99.

[52] Kelly, "The Duty of Using Artificial Means of Preserving Life," *op. cit.*, n. 35.

[53] Aristotle, *Nichomachean Ethics* 1098a.26;1137b.29, Terence Irwin, trans.
(Indianapolis, Indiana: Hackett, 1985), pp.18; 145.

[54] quoted in Cronin, *op. cit.* at 42.

[55] Cronin, *op. cit.* at 88.

[56] *Ibid.*, at 75.

without a limb, could also render a treatment extraordinary.[57]   Finally, discussions of "reasonable hope of benefit" contained some consideration of the difference between sustaining life with a disease and curing the disease, however speculative that discussion might have been given the science of the day.

The most definite classical consideration of the idea that the suffering associated with the condition itself, independent of the treatment, is part of the burden to be considered in judging whether a life-sustaining treatment is ordinary or extraordinary is found in the writings of the 17th century Cardinal DeLugo.[58]   He draws an elaborate analogy based upon a man trapped in a fire. The man in the fire is said to have easy access to water, certainly something common, inexpensive, and natural. He is certain that he can calm the flames, extend his life, and even give himself some temporary relief by dousing himself with water. But he is certain that he cannot extinguish the fire and cannot ultimately escape. Must he use the water? DeLugo's answer is a resounding, "No." If he could extinguish the flames and effect a "cure" it would be obligatory, but if it only prolonged the suffering, it would be an "extraordinary means." It is critical to note that the suffering in this example is caused not by the treatment, but by the condition in which he finds himself. The "therapy" that is declined in this case does not cause suffering, and, in fact, will temporarily relieve it. In this sense, the proportionality condition of the O/E distinction differs dramatically from the proportionality condition of the RDE. O/E proportionality permits consideration of the suffering associated with the patient's condition, not merely the suffering caused by the treatment itself.

Thus, in the 20th century, Sullivan concluded that the tradition would permit the discontinuation of intravenous feeding as "extraordinary" if it merely prolonged the pain of a man dying of cancer.[59]   Likewise, Kelly could judge, "There are degrees of 'success.' It is one thing to use oxy-

[57] *Ibid.*, at 73-74.

[58] *Ibid.*, at 49-55.

[59] Joseph Sullivan, *Catholic Teaching on the Morality of Euthanasia* (Washington, DC: Catholic University of America Press, 1949), p. 72.

gen to bring a person through a crisis; it is another merely to prolong life when hope of recovery is practically negligible."[60]

The observations of Sullivan and Kelly, who wrote 50 years ago, are only more correct today. And DeLugo's 17th century analogy aptly describes much of what medicine faces today—many treatments that sustain life do not cause suffering in themselves, but neither do they cure the disease. Rather, they prolong a state in which at least some of the suffering caused by the disease persists. In some cases, such as the use of insulin by an 18 year old newly diagnosed Type I diabetic, the burdens and benefits of treatment seem clearly proportionate to a prudent *communis aestimatio*, and anyone who said otherwise would be beyond the bounds of reason unless other circumstances or moral considerations came to bear upon this 18 year old's duty to preserve his life. But the situation facing the man in our case of aphasia, dementia, neuralgia, and ventilator care would seem to be well beyond the limits of what most prudent people would judge a reasonable expectation of what a good man must do in fulfilling his duty to preserve his life. His wife would be justified in using this standard to stop the ventilator. She does so by relying upon a traditional Catholic O/E analysis, not the very narrowly constrained proportionality condition of the RDE.

DIFFERING VIEWS OF THE INTENTION/FORESIGHT DISTINCTION

The distinction between the foreseen and the intended is critical to good moral thinking. Intention is, as Aquinas taught, the "form" of the moral act. Acting with the intention of making someone dead (prescinding from discussions about war and capital punishment, and from debates about self-defense and rescue) is morally wrong. To create a new lethal pathophysiological condition in a patient with the specific intention-in-acting of making a patient dead is euthanasia. However, to forgo an intervention that interferes with a pre-existing lethal pathophysiological condition in a patient could also be morally wrong, precisely if one does so with the specific intention in acting of making the patient dead. Nonetheless, the O/E tradition holds that such forgoings of treatment are

[60] Kelly, "The Duty of Using Artificial Means of Preserving Life," *op. cit.*, n. 35.

not morally wrong (provided certain other conditions are met) if one's intention in acting is not to end the patient but to end the treatment. One foresees death, but one's intention is that there should be no such treatment, not that there should be no such patient. This is the traditional way of understanding the intention/foresight distinction in the O/E tradition.

The RDE formulates the distinction differently. I cannot overestimate the importance of seeing this subtle but crucial distinction. According to the RDE, two effects must follow directly from one's action. One must intend the good effect, but not the bad, which is merely foreseen. In the case of using morphine for dying patients, this fits perfectly. Morphine has at least two effects—easing pain and slowing respiratory drive. One can act intending to ease pain, foreseeing the possibility of slowing respiratory drive as an unintended side-effect, provided the pain is great enough, the life expectancy short enough, etc.[61]

Nonetheless, it is inappropriate to apply the RDE to the withdrawal of life-sustaining treatments, for the reasons I have already given in detail. But one further consequence of conceiving of the withdrawal of extraordinary means of treatment as an application of the RDE is that the way its framing of the intention/foresight division under the RDE differs from that in the traditional O/E distinction. The RDE demands that one see one's action as a causal fork, leading to two outcomes, one intended and the other unintended. One asks the physician or surrogate, "What are you doing?" and demands that the answer be framed as, "I am intending to p, foreseeing that doing p will have two effects, q and r. I intend r, foreseeing but not intending q," where:

p = withholding or withdrawing of the life-sustaining treatment
q = the death of the patient
r = the good one is aiming to accomplish, e.g., relief of suffering, redistribution of these resources to help others, etc.

☐ = the event is intended by the agent

61 I should in no way be construed as arguing against the importance of the RDE in medicine and elsewhere. I am arguing only that its use be limited to cases in which it is appropriate and necessary. The RDE is indispensable to morally sound medical practice.

This is depicted in Figure I, below:

I Causal Fork of the RDE

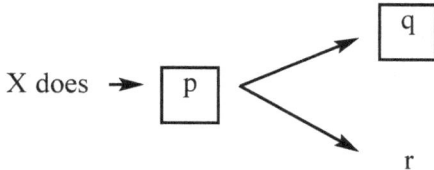

When this construal of causation, intention, and foresight is applied to the ventilator case described above, and the conditions are such (as they often are) that the treatment is not causing much suffering in itself, is not very expensive relative to one's resources, and one's motive is to relieve the suffering of the patient or to cause the resources to be used elsewhere, then one is led to the conclusion that the conditions for the RDE's division of intention and foresight cannot be met. The RDE requires a causal fork, and there is none in this case. One could only bring about the intended good by means of the death of the patient, violating the 3rd condition of the classical RDE. The agent could only claim the intentional stand depicted in Figure II, below:

II Causal Chain Precluded by the RDE as Irrational

In other words, the agent would need to say, "In stopping the ventilator, I intend to relieve the patient's suffering, but don't intend the patient's death." However, the RDE would hold that this construal of causation, one's intentions, and one's foresight is simply irrational. One cannot reasonably claim to intend to do p, knowing that it brings about q as the means by which r comes about, intending r but not intending q. In other words, if someone claims II, he or she is either self-deceived or disingenuous. One cannot say I intend to relieve the patient's suffering by way of the patient's death without also intending the patient's death as one's chosen means. One must interpret anyone who claims II to really be claiming III.

III Rational Casual Chain Precluded by the RDE as Immoral

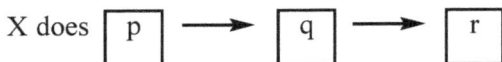

X does [p] ⟶ [q] ⟶ [r]

One is intending the bad event (the death of the patient) as the very means by which one achieves the good effect (relief of suffering, re-distribution of resources, etc). The powerful argument that one can never claim to foresee but not intend an admittedly bad means by which one brings about a desired end is at the heart of the RDE. It seems indisputable. But if it is applied to the ventilator case, then one must conclude that one cannot claim to be relieving the patient of his or her suffering except by causing his death. And this is precluded by the RDE. Thus, in the hypothetical case I have described, one could not stop the ventilator.

However, the intention/foresight division of the O/E distinction does not require any double effect, and never has historically, as I have explained above. One's intention, simply stated, is to stop the treatment, not in order to do anything else, but because one has reached a limit; because one has done enough to fulfill one's duty to preserve one's life. In other words, one intends p, foreseeing but not intending q. This intentional stand is depicted in IV:

IV Rational Causal Chain Invoked in the O/E Distinction

X does [p] ⟶ q

This is a causal chain, not a causal fork. One intends to remove the ventilator (p), because continuing it is more than what one reasonably believes the patient would need to do to fulfill his duty. This is the object of the act. The outcome (q, death) is foreseen and unintended. Yet it is not properly described as a side-effect since there is no causal fork. This is how all the classical authors described the difference between forgoing extraordinary means and suicide. Vitoria says, "it is one thing not to protect life, and it is another thing to destroy it."[62]   Suarez says, "The reason is that although a man may never kill himself, he is not bound, however, to conserve his life always and by every means..."[63] De Lugo says,

> ...the "bonum" of his life is not of such great moment, however, that its conservation must be effected with extraordinary diligence: it is one thing not to neglect and throw it away, to which a man is bound: it is another, however, to seek after it and retain it by exquisite means as it is escaping away from him, to which he is not held; neither is he on that account considered morally to will or seek his death.[64]

One can rationally intend one event along a causal chain while foreseeing but not intending events that follow it. If the unintended event that one foresees were not to come about, one would not say, "I have failed, let me try another way." Karen Ann Quinlan's parents expected her to die if her ventilator were discontinued. But their aim (their intention) was to eliminate the ventilator, not to eliminate their daughter. They had no other aim. The resources were not an issue. They merely thought that her dying was being averted by a means that went beyond what a reasonable person could be expected to do to sustain her life. When she started breathing after the ventilator was turned off they were surprised; perhaps even disappointed. But they did not fail in fulfilling their intention.

This sort of moral psychology is ancient. Aquinas for instance, writes,

> As stated above, intention regards the end as a terminus of the movement of the will. Now a terminus of movement may be taken in two ways. First, the very last terminus, when the movement comes to a stop; this is the terminus of the whole movement. Secondly, some point midway, which is the beginning of one part of the movement, and the end or terminus of the other. Thus in the movement from A to C through B, C is

---

[62] Cronin, *op. cit.* at 36.

[63] *Ibid.*, at 44.

[64] *Ibid.*, at 53.

the last terminus, while B is a terminus, but not the last. And intention can be of either. Consequently though intention is always of an end, it need not be always of the last end.[65]

It is common for human beings to adopt this sort of intentional stance. One recognizes a limit and ceases effort, foreseeing but not intending some further consequence along a chain of consequences. One need not have another intention, something else that one intends to accomplish by way of having ceased the effort (i.e., a double effect), but merely an acknowledgment that one has done enough. For instance, suppose I am taking a math test. I come to the last problem that I just can't figure out. I'm pretty certain that I didn't answer everything else on the test perfectly, and I know that this problem counts for 25% of the grade on the test, while the passing grade is 75%. Thus, I foresee that if I don't answer it I will almost certainly fail. Suppose it is the final exam and I have been given 8 hours to take the test. I answered everything else in an hour. After two hours puzzling over this last question I am the only person left in the room. I reason that perhaps with more time I could figure it out, but after 3 ½ hours I just give up. I need give no other reason than that I think it is too hard. I do not need to invoke a double effect. I do not need to say that I can better use my time studying for another course or helping little old ladies to cross the street. I can simply decide, "I give up." And in doing so, did I thereby intend to fail the test? I think the answer is no. I *did* intend not to answer this question, foreseeing the likelihood that I will fail as a consequence, but I did not intend to fail the test. If, by some miracle, I were to pass, I would be delighted. Perhaps by some miracle the teacher will be merciful and throw out that question or assign a few extra points for any scribble in attempting to answer that question that I committed to paper, so that I will pass. But I know such miracles are unlikely, and I foresee that I will fail.

This is all the intention/foresight division that is necessary for invoking moral impossibility. This is all the intention/foresight division that is needed for the O/E distinction. It is a mistake to force the forgoing of life-sustaining treatments into the intentional constraints of the RDE.

---

[65] St. Thomas Aquinas, *Summa Theologiae* I-II, q. 12, a. 2.c.

THE LOCUS OF AGENCY IN SURROGATE DECISION MAKING

The classical casuists never considered making decisions about discontinuing life-sustaining treatments for persons lacking decision making capacity. Before the mid-20th century, coma was simply fatal. People who could not breathe or swallow due to neurological impairment simply died. The questions that concern us now are iatrogenic—they concern not just powerful but far from perfect treatments, but also medical conditions caused by medical treatment. Many contemporary treatments are powerful in sustaining particular impaired natural functions, but not powerful enough to cure. In other cases, the condition rendering the person incapable of making decisions has come about as a side effect of medical treatment. Our contemporary epidemic of Alzheimer's disease, for example, has come about because more people are living long enough to develop this disease, at least in part because they are not dying earlier of other diseases such as myocardial infarction or cancer. Anoxic post-coma unresponsiveness is most commonly the result of heroic efforts undertaken to resuscitate someone who had already met the cardiopulmonary definition of death. No one receives the diagnosis of anoxic post-coma unresponsiveness without huge sums of money first having been spent on cardiopulmonary resuscitation, ventilator support, and intensive care necessary to bring the person (who could have been declared dead at the start and subsequently could have had extraordinary means of treatment stopped at innumerable junctures along the way) to the point of being alive in a state of post-coma unresponsiveness.

Because they never imagined such conditions or treatments, the classical casuists only considered the point of view of the patient. There was almost no medical surrogate decision making in their societies. So, they asked whether *the patient* had the obligation to undergo the treatment, given his physical, intellectual, emotional, social, economic, and spiritual resources? They put the question to the patient. In considering whether the religious superior could direct a monk or nun to undergo extraordinary treatments, the classical casuists answered no. The question was not framed in terms of the superior's duty to preserve the life of the religious, but from the perspective of the monk or nun.

In the 20th century, millions of persons now face the burden of deciding for others. And what moral perspective should they assume in discerning whether a treatment is ordinary or extraordinary? Long before lawyers developed the legal doctrine of substituted judgment, the Catholic medico-moral tradition taught that third parties should assume the perspective of the patient. They were advised to ask questions of the following form: Would the patient deem this burden extraordinary? Is this proposed treatment, as best you know the patient, more than he or she could reasonably be expected to bear? Cronin summarized this nicely in the mid-20th century,

> Since the doctor is unable to ascertain the patient's own wishes in the matter, he should make a reasonable effort to determine what the patient's wish would be if the patient personally could respond. In the event that relatives are present, they should try to make the decision in the name of the patient, and the doctor is obliged to follow their wishes. If there are present no relatives nor persons entrusted with the care of the patient's welfare, then it is up to the doctor to make the decision. His obligation in justice to the patient binds him to take reasonable care of the patient. He must consider the spiritual, physical, financial and social condition of the patient. Perhaps, the doctor will require the aid of others in making this consideration, but in the last analysis, it is the doctor's duty to do what he thinks will bring about the greater good of the patient.[66]

However, some recent writings have drifted from traditional analysis to concentrate not on the physical, intellectual, emotional, social, economic, and spiritual resources of the patient but on those of the caregivers. Perhaps in part this is due to unvoiced suspicions about the moral legitimacy of substituted judgments, or due to a deontological focus on the duties of the decision-maker. This is not clear. But for these commentators, when patients are unable to participate in decision making and have left no directives about their wishes regarding life-sustaining treatments, the question changes from, "Is it reasonable to judge that the patient has reached the limits of his obligation to preserve his life?" to "Have I reached the limit of my obligations to keep the patient alive?" If I have not reached these limits, then I must continue to do so unless doing so conflicts with other obligations. Then, using RDE analysis, one simply calculates the benefits and the burdens that flow directly from the provision of the treatment by the third party. As Grisez puts it, if one is not

[66] Cronin, *op. cit.* at 130.

certain of the patient's wishes, the question becomes simply whether pro- viding a treatment for incompetent patients "significantly benefits them and others concerned without still more significantly burdening either [them] or others concerned," without any reference to the patient's point of view.67   Finnis argues that in the absence of clearly expressed patient wishes to forgo a treatment, one should presume an intention on the part of third parties to "terminate" the patient unless proven otherwise.68

Once again, this drift in perspective is subtle but critical. People who are healthy always have more resources than the sick. This change in per- spective makes the standard for declaring a treatment extraordinary high- er than the standard proposed by the Tradition.

Proponents of the New Natural Law worry about allowing third par- ties to construe altruism on the part of patients who lack capacity. Their concerns are well-placed. It does seem to invite abuse to allow people to say, "Aunt Tilly wouldn't have wanted us to have spent her whole inher- itance on her health care, right?"   However, it does *not* seem disingenu- ous to say, "Aunt Tilly never said what she would have wanted, but we just don't think she would ever have wanted to have been kept alive indefinitely in this state, cut off from all the rest of us, unable to speak to us or understand us. She has suffered enough. She has lived a good life. She has done more than enough to try to care for the gift of her life. We'd love to keep her with us, but it is time for us to let go. *Nolo tangere.* Let God take her." This reasoning, however, is not permitted by some current analyses.

Further, an additional peculiarity is added when one turns to the per- spective of the caregivers. Some writers emphasize the witness value of the care provided by family members as a reason for continuing care.69 This seems to me to be at least as worrisome as attributing altruism to incompetent patients as a reason to discontinue their life support. On this analysis, Aunt Tilly becomes instrumentalized. She becomes a pretext for others to use their care for her in order to witness to the world regarding their commitment to Christian reverence for life. If the focus is on the

67 Germain Grisez, "Should Nutrition and Hydration be Provided to Permanently Comatose and Other Mentally Disabled Persons?" *Linacre Quarterly* 57(May, 1990): 30- 43.

68 John Finnis, "Bland: Crossing the Rubicon?" *Law Quarterly Review* 109 (1993): 329-337.

caregivers, this might seem reasonable. But if the focus is on the patient, one would hesitate to say, "Aunt Tilly would have wanted us to keep her alive in this state so that we could show the world how much we care about the vulnerable." I think one must be extremely cautious about invoking this rationale for continuing care.

The locus of analysis in the O/E tradition has always been on the moral obligation of the patient to continue treatment. This was extended in the 20th century, in considering patients unable to speak for themselves, to judgments made by the family about the reasonable limits to that obligation as the patient would judge them. Shifting the moral analysis to the RDE moves the focus to the moral obligations of the third parties authorizing or performing the act of forgoing treatment. This has affected the analysis of what constitutes an extraordinary means of care in ways that have not been fully appreciated.

SOME POTENTIAL COUNTER-ARGUMENTS

Let me consider several potential counterarguments. One such counterargument would be that while it can be granted as historically true that O/E distinction preceded the formalization of RDE, the idea of the RDE, *ex hypothesi*, has been central to Catholic thinking about forgoing care at the end of life since at least the time of Basil the Great. One could argue that it was there all along, standing as the silent but central tenet from which other principles were derived, but was simply never codified or made explicit. Therefore it is wrong to argue that the RDE is not the basis for the O/E distinction.

This hypothesis is certainly possible. Yet no one has presented the case for this. The New Natural Law theory *does* present itself as an authentic interpretation of St. Thomas' moral teaching,[70] although not without substantial controversy.[71] And Ashley and O'Rourke have claimed the Thomistic tradition as well. But Thomas never discussed the O/E dis-

---

[69] Grisez, "Should Nutrition and Hydration be Provided?" *op. cit.*

[70] John Finnis, *Aquinas, op. cit.*, n. 6.

[71] See, for example, Russel Hittinger, *A Critique of the New Natural Law* (Notre Dame, IN: University of Notre Dame Press, 1987); Ralph M. McInerny, *Aquinas on Human Action: A Theory of Practice* (Washington, D.C.: Catholic University of America, 1992); Anthony J. Lisska, *Aquinas' Theory of Natural Law: An Analytic Reconstruction* (New York: Oxford University Press, 1996). McInerny once wrote: "Whatever fallacy there

tinction. And many debate whether his discussion of self-defense is the actual origin of the rule of double effect. So, it is hard to claim St. Thomas as the basis for deciding that the O/E distinction is an application of the RDE. And none of these authors (nor any others of whom I am aware) have attempted to establish by any sort of logical or historical argument that the O/E distinction sprang from the inchoate idea of the RDE. Rather, I think these authors have simply assumed what I take to be a conflation. In the absence of evidence to the contrary, the mere possibility that it might be mistaken provides no sound reason to doubt the historical analysis I have provided.

Further, the prospects for an historical analysis that would refute mine seem slim. If the differences in moral justification, logical structure, treatment of proportionality, manner of distinguishing between intention and foresight, and focus of moral agency differ between the Tradition's understanding of the forgoing of extraordinary means and the application of the RDE, then it would not seem possible to make such a claim on any grounds. On the basis of these structural arguments, any historical claim that the O/E distinction was derived from the RDE would only seem to indicate that history had been mistaken.

A variation on this argument might be that the RDE is a necessary doctrinal development that finally allows one to make sense of what "moral impossibility" means. How does one know when one has done "enough" in fulfilling a moral duty to conserve one's life? According to this analysis, one knows one has reached one's limits when doing one's duty interferes with one's other duties so that, on proportionate balance, more harm is done. But as I have pointed out, such clarity comes at too high a price. Its abstract, deontological emphasis obscures the human reality of finitude. Given the intrinsic value of life and the anti-dualistic, hylomorphic conjunction of person and body, respect for the value of human life would entail an almost absurd priority for the use of life-sustaining treatment. On the one hand, it seems to signify an undignified reluctance to accept one's creaturehood and attendant finitude. On the other hand, it demands

---

may be in passing from Is to Ought—and no one seems able to say what precisely the fallacy is—Grisez's insistence on it threatens to undercut his own procedure as well as St. Thomas's." (*Ethica Thomistica: The Moral Philosophy of Thomas Aquinas* (Washington, D.C.: Catholic University of America, 1982), p. 56).

too much—more than the faithful can reasonably be expected to bear. What a person can reasonably be expected to do is not merely determined by duties external to the person. It is determined by the individual's makeup as a human person integrally considered, including the individual's physical, moral, intellectual, emotional as well as social and economic resources. And those sorts of limits are not the stuff of competing, abstract, deontological duties, but the stuff of moral impossibility, which depends on a robust philosophical anthropology.

A second potential counter-argument would be that the case example I gave is fictional, and that the claims I have made have nothing to do with the real world. One might argue that this was simply a philosopher's "burning lorry" case, one that, if not completely fictional, is of so rare a type as to be not worth considering. However, this charge can be readily dismissed. The case was designed to keep certain other controversies fixed in order to concentrate on the issue at hand. Questions such as whether comatose persons can suffer, or how the foregoing analysis is applied to feeding tubes are important. But if these were made features of the case, discussion would likely become bogged down in addressing these controversies rather than the narrower question of whether the withdrawal of extraordinary care is an application of the RDE. Further, all of the individual features of the case are genuine. Patients, sadly, often are rendered awake and aphasic by neurological diseases. There are such things as untreatable neuropathic pain syndromes. Home ventilators and oxygen concentrators are already in widespread use, and they are inexpensive to operate once purchased.

But most importantly, the argument works in much simpler cases. If a patient is comatose and on a home ventilator, and has left no advance directives, then the ventilator in itself causes no suffering. If it is cheap and the family has the means, then the only way to discontinue the treatment under double effect analysis would be by way of deciding that the state of being in coma was in itself a source of suffering, and that the only way to relieve a patient of that suffering would be by means of the patient's death. This intentional stance would be homicidal and wrong, and not permitted by the RDE. And this seems a very different analysis than one would arrive at by way of the O/E analysis.

Third, the authors I have cited might claim that I have misunderstood their positions. Ashley and O'Rourke are explicit in explaining the withholding and withdrawing of extraordinary means of treatment as an application of the RDE, so it would be hard to be accused of misinterpreting them. I think they would be better off admitting that I am correct and that their references to the RDE as the basis of forgoing extraordinary means were too hastily considered. They are generally quite traditional in their analyses and would be better off, in my judgment, emphasizing the tradition of moral impossibility as their justification for forgoing extraordinary care. Importantly, this would allow them to escape criticisms that in certain of their analyses they are disvaluing human life or instrumentalizing human life—criticisms leveled at them when they say that treatments for certain classes of patients are of no benefit or futile. They would not need to make this claim. They would only need to say that it is reasonable to construe that at least some patients lacking capacity would consider the state they are in to be a state of suffering, and that if they were able to speak for themselves would consider continued treatment in this condition more than they could be expected to do in order to fulfill their duties to conserve their lives.

The situation of the New Natural Law perspective is a bit more complicated. These authors are not so explicit about linking the RDE to the forgoing of extraordinary means. If they were to say that I have misconstrued them as holding that the forgoing of extraordinary means is an application of the RDE, I would be delighted. I would encourage them to commit to that position in writing because I think I have at least made the case that their writings on the topic to date certainly suggest the conflation of the RDE and the O/E distinction.

Yet I fear they would resist this, because I do not think they are prepared to say that the intention/foresight distinction applies to causal chains as well as to causal forks. I also suspect they would resist the idea that the scope of the proportionality condition invoked when forgoing extraordinary treatments includes the suffering associated with the patient's medical condition in addition to the suffering caused by the treatment itself.

But if that is the case, and if they do wish to argue that the forgoing of extraordinary means of care is an application of the RDE, then I think their judgments about the moral permissibility of forgoing treatments such as ventilator care may have been based upon overestimates regarding the costs and the amount of suffering caused directly by many life-sustaining treatments in themselves.   If patients have permanently implanted intravenous catheters for parenteral medication or alimentation, or are treated with home ventilators, the principles put forth by the New Natural Law theorists should lead them to insist that these relatively cheap and non-burdensome treatments must almost always be considered ordinary and morally obligatory in cognitively impaired patients who have left no advance directives. Many, many more treatments that are currently considered extraordinary will become ordinary according to their analyses. And medical progress and increasing wealth will only lengthen the list of "ordinary" care. To the extent that this widens the gulf between their philosophy and traditional Catholic thinking, they would need to consider whether they might wish to adjust their philosophy to align more with traditional Catholic thought regarding these matters.

Presuming they would wish to do this, at least two courses would be open to them. One would be to reject the naturalistic fallacy, accept a full-bodied, ontologized natural law theory, and with it a wider number of rules and principles upon which to draw, including a recognition of something like a principle of moral impossibility that could be applied even to persons who cannot speak for themselves because one would be able to appeal to an ethical standard based on a robust philosophical anthropology—a conception of the kind of thing these patients are—finite human beings.

However, this would be a marked revision of their philosophical system and would be an unattractive option for proponents of the New Natural Law. The only other option would be to tweak their system of basic human goods to reflect more fully an appreciation of human finitude. One way to accomplish this might be to expand the list of basic human goods to include the recognition of one's physical, intellectual, emotional, social, economic, and spiritual finitude as a basic human good. Then one could construe the decision to withdraw life-sustaining treatment from the severely cognitively impaired not as intending the patient's death in order to achieve relief from suffering, but as a double effect—promoting the good of recognizing human finitude, foreseeing but not intending the patient's death. But it seems a stretch to call the recognition of human finitude a basic human good, and this solution seems very ad hoc.

Perhaps a principle akin to the traditional category of moral impossibility could be teased out of one of their already existing basic goods—e.g.—the basic human good of practical reasonability. One could surmise that practical reasonability encompassed a recognition not just of financial resources, but of inner human resources as well. Towards this, proponents of the New Natural Law theory do seem to recognize the category of "repugnance" as a reason to call a treatment extraordinary, and repugnance has long been one of the criteria for moral impossibility according to the classical O/E tradition. These authors allow a conscious patient's expression of repugnance at the thought of being fed by a feeding tube to serve as a sufficient reason to forgo that treatment.[72] But they seem to limit this to repugnance at the idea of the treatment in itself, and seem strongly to resist the thought that one could be repugnant about the state in which the treatment left one as a patient. But it seems plain that what horrifies most people about the prospect of an amputation is not so much the operation (for which they can now be anesthetized) as the thought of being left limbless. Should it be possible for a patient to express such *vehemens horror*, should it not also be possible to make a substituted judgment that an incapacitated spouse or child would harbor such repugnance? The O/E tradition has long permitted this view, without worry that this necessitated the belief that one's life was not worth living, or that limbless or otherwise damaged human beings were thereby devalued as human beings, or that they would therefore no longer be counted as persons. If that view has seemed practically reasonable and faithfully Catholic for 500 years, shouldn't our 21st century philosophies be able to embrace a similar view? At the very least, accusing those who hold this traditional view of a heretical disvaluation of human beings and demanding that all Catholics adopt the views of a philosophical system that departs from that tradition seems to privilege one philosophical view over the tradition. And that does not seem very Catholic.

POTENTIALLY WORRISOME QUESTIONS

At least two potentially worrisome issues need yet be addressed. The first concerns the slippery slope considerations invoked by many who favor taking a very hard line about abating treatment as a way of protecting vulnerable individuals from being euthanized. Certainly, it is possi-

---

[72] Grisez, "Should Nutrition and Hydration be Provided?" *op. cit.*

ble to euthanize a patient either by performing a motor action or by omission. One might refrain from performing the motor action of starting a life-sustaining treatment with the specific intention-in-acting of making the patient dead, or one might perform the motor action of withdrawing a life-sustaining treatment with the specific intention-in-acting of making the patient dead. Both would be intentional human acts, for which their agents would be morally responsible. These acts of allowing to die would be every bit as morally wrong as active euthanasia, in which one created a new, lethal pathophysiological state with the specific intention-in-acting of making the patient dead.[73]   Since the morality of these acts depends heavily (but not exclusively) upon the intention of the agent, the problem in acts of withholding and withdrawing becomes one of judging intentions. For active euthanasia, judging intentions is easy. The burden of proof is overwhelmingly upon the agent to say that his intentions were anything other than making the patient dead if he injects 100 mEq of KCl into the right ventricle of a patient. In allowing to die, it is much harder to discern intentions from the outside. One can withhold or withdraw an intervention intending only the cessation of a treatment that is appropriately judged extraordinary, or one can withhold or withdraw the same intervention in a similar case intending the death of the patient, perhaps even with a nefarious motive. But from the position of the outside observer, both look the same. Thus, it is reasonable for society to show its respect for the dignity of all human beings by an absolute ban on active euthanasia. This is an enforceable moral absolute—a negative precept. However, with respect to passive euthanasia, one is dealing with a question of the limits of a positive precept. How far one must go in conserving one's life? A just society must rest content to educate people about the importance of intentions in their own moral lives, of understanding the seriousness of the duty to preserve life, but leaving a wide berth for individual discretion, and reserving the right to prosecute in egregious cases of abuse of the withholding and withdrawing of medical treatment. The policy of prohibiting active euthanasia while generally refraining from judging the intentions of those who withhold or withdraw care has proven enforceable, long-standing, and sustainable without leading to

---

[73] See my "Killing and Allowing to Die: Another Look," *Journal of Law, Medicine, and Ethics* 26 (1998): 55-64.

active euthanasia. I think we can continue to hold the line there, and fear that attempts to ban certain kinds of treatment abatement may, ironically, lead to more support for active euthanasia.

The second potentially worrisome question concerns knowing when to apply which moral principles. It is admittedly much tidier to have just a handful of basic reasons for acting and a single master-principle such as double effect to adjudicate potential conflicts. But the real moral life is considerably more complex. It is not chaotic or unprincipled, but it is not algorithmic. Natural law has moral absolutes, but is also responsive to the finitude of human beings and their complexity. Genuine natural law, like the natural creatures who ought to be guided by it, is an organic theory (at least that form which has been embraced by the Roman Catholic Church for centuries). The question of when to apply which principles is a problem for practical reasoning in general that I cannot discuss in detail in an already lengthy article. Suffice it to say that similar problems in practical reasoning arise not only in ethics, but in jurisprudence and in medicine. When does a judge apply the principle of *stare decisis*? When ought the principle of *nulla poena sine lege* be invoked? When does a physician justly apply Occam's razor? When invoke the principle of *primum non nocere*? When invoke the diagnostic aphorism, "If you hear hoofbeats, don't think of zebras"? There is deep rationality and wisdom in these rules and principles, but a discussion of when which ones apply is extraordinarily complex and beyond the scope of this essay.[74]

CONCLUSION

The forgoing of extraordinary means of treatment is not an application of the RDE. The O/E distinction has a different history, justification, view of proportionality, way of framing the intention/foresight division, and moral focus in making decisions for incapacitated patients. Hence, cases are classified differently by the two approaches. This analysis might help to clarify some points of agreement and disagreement in discussing cases that have proven controversial for Catholic moral thinking.

---

[74] I have proposed a set of conditions for the correct application of the rule of double effect in "'Re-inventing' the Rule of Double Effect," In: *Oxford Handbook of Bioethics*, Bonnie Steinbock, ed. (Oxford: Oxford University Press, forthcoming, 2006).

ETHICAL FORCE IN ARISTOTLE
Kevin L. Flannery, S.J.

Some of John Finnis's finest pages come in his Michael J. McGivney Lectures, where he discusses Aristotle and moral absolutes, arguing compellingly against all comers that the Stagirite holds that certain actions are always wrong.[1] Beginning as early as the second century after Christ, there have been commentators inclined to argue that, when Aristotle says in *Nicomachean ethics* ii,6 that actions of certain types are always immoral, the types themselves are already delimited by a negative moral connotation, so that he would be saying, for instance, not that all lying is immoral but that all immoral lying is immoral. Finnis demonstrates that the types of actions actually mentioned by Aristotle—adultery, theft, and murder—do not admit of such an analysis. As Aristotle himself says, "goodness or badness with regard to such things [does not] depend on committing adultery with the right woman, at the right time, and in the right way, but simply to do any of them is to go wrong."[2]

In the course of his discussion, Finnis mentions, but does not elaborate upon, the Aristotelian concept of force (βία), citing passages in both the *Nicomachean ethics* (*EN*) and the *Eudemian ethics* (*EE*).[3] This concept is essential, however, for a full understanding of moral absolutes since force has a bearing upon what can be attributed to a person's will and therefore upon determining when or to what extent a person has violated a moral absolute. It may be true that strictly speaking one cannot be forced to commit adultery and so adultery never fails in some sense to be

[1] John Finnis, *Moral Absolutes: Tradition, Revision and Truth* (Washington, D.C.: Catholic University of America Press, 1991) 31–37.

[2] 1107a15-17. Often in this essay (as here) I make use of the Revised Oxford Translation of Aristotle [Jonathan Barnes, ed., *The Complete Works of Aristotle: The Revised Oxford Translation* (Princeton: Princeton UP, 1984)], occasionally making adjustments.

[3] Finnis, 33 n.6. To be precise, Finnis mention both βία (force) and ἀνάγκη (compulsion), saying that Aristotle speaks of them "as if they were synonymous" (p.33). For the most part this is true, although there is a place, *EE* ii,8,1225a17, which we shall examine below, where he distinguishes the two. One finds a distinction between βία and ἀνάγκη also in *Magna moralia (MM)* i,15. The abbreviations of classical works used in this essay are to be found in the front material of any edition of Liddel and Scott's *Greek-English Lexicon*.

immoral, but force does have a bearing upon one's level of culpability and upon whether one can be forgiven (say, by one's husband or wife). And in the killing of humans, the presence of force does allow us to characterize an action as not a murder but rather as a mere killing, consequent upon a person's activity but in no way attributable to his will. Consider, for instance, the man who, in self-defense, stabs another who is coming at him with a knife. Even if it is true that murder is identifiable as a type of act independently of its specification as immoral—that is, even if the precept 'Do not murder' does not mean 'Do not murder unjustly'—still, whether or not we apply the word 'murder' depends to some extent on the presence of force in the relevant sense.

So, in this essay I would like to consider ethical force from a specifically Aristotelian perspective. My approach will be very textual, looking closely at a limited number of passages from *EN* and *EE*. Much of what I say will not be immediately related to moral absolutes, although I shall come back to this issue towards the end.

I BRUTE FORCE

Aristotle's understanding of force seems at first glance quite straightforward: it seems, that is, to be equivalent to what we would call 'brute force.' He says in *EN* iii,1, that "that is forced of which the moving principle is outside, being a principle in which nothing is contributed by the person who acts or is acted upon, e.g. if he were to be carried somewhere by a wind, or by men who had him in their power" [1110a1-4]. And in *EE* ii,8, he uses the example of someone who, "taking the hand of someone whose will and appetite both resist, strikes someone [else]."[4] (The person whose hand is taken up is not responsible for the striking since the action has been forced.) So exonerating force seems to be force in which the person involved is wholly passive, all the causality of the action itself being attributed to another agent or some other natural factor.

We find an interpretation along these general lines in Alexander of Aphrodisias—although even here we begin to see that something more than brute force could be involved.[5] In the twelfth of his "Ethical problems," which is a commentary upon *EN* iii,1,1110b15-17 ("The forced

---

4 ὥσπερ εἴ τις λαβὼν τὴν χεῖρα τύπτοι τινὰ ἀντιτείνοντος καὶ τῷ βούλεσθαι καὶ τῷ ἐπιθυμεῖν [1224b13-14].

then, seems to be that whose moving principle is outside, the person forced contributing nothing"), he contrasts actions that are forced and therefore involuntary with what Aristotle calls "mixed acts," such as jettisoning precious goods during a storm or performing a heinous act in order to save the life of a relative. "Generally considered" [ἁπλῶ'ς], says Aristotle, these latter acts are involuntary, although in these particular instances they are voluntary [*EN* iii,1,1110a4-19]. Since forced acts sometimes also appear to be voluntary in their particular instances, Alexander needs to explain what it is that makes them different from mixed acts. He writes:

> Someone who is forced by someone to move one of his bodily parts in a movement which contributes towards what happens by force, will not just for *that* reason contribute through himself to what happens by force. For it is not the case that, if someone who had been pushed by someone fell on someone or knocked something down, moving his legs [κινήσας τὰ σκέλη: 133.8], he would just for that reason be said to contribute to what happened. Rather, if he did this in accordance with his own impulse and purpose, he would contribute; but if he is moved according to some customary and natural locomotion of the legs, no.[6]

At first, Alexander seems to have in mind the involvement of a human

---

[5] I refer to Alexander of Aphrodisias, who flourished at the turn of the third century after Christ, although the work I discuss below might have been written not by him but by a member of his school. See Robert W. Sharples, "Alexander of Aphrodisias: Scholasticism and Innovation," *Aufstieg und Niedergang der Römischen Welt* II.36.2 (1987): 1189–91; also Robert W. Sharples, "The School of Alexander?" *Aristotle Transformed: The Ancient Commentators and Their Influence*, Ed. Richard Sorabji (London: Duckworth, 1990) 85–86; also Arthur Madigan, "Alexander of Aphrodisias: the book of *Ethical problems*," *Aufstieg und Niedergang der römischen Welt* II.36.2 (1987): 1260–79.

[6] Alexander of Aphrodisias, "Ηθικων προβλημάτων βιβλίον α̅ [One book of ethical problems]," *Scripta minora: Quaestiones, De fato, De mixtione*, Ed. Ivo Bruns (Berlin: Reimer, 1892), vol. 2.2 <supplement> of *Commentaria in Aristotelem Graeca* 133.5–12. I make use here of Alexander of Aphrodisias, *Ethical Problems*, trans. R. W. Sharples, *The Ancient Commentators on Aristotle* (London: Duckworth, 1990) 42. The last bit [133.9-11] reads in Greek, ἀλλ' εἰ μὲν κατὰ τὴν οἰκείαν ὁρμὴν καὶ πρόθεσιν ποιήσαι τοῦτο, εἴη ἂν συντελῶν· εἰ δὲ κατὰ συνήθη τινὰ καὶ φυσικὴν μεταφορὰν των σκελων κινηθείη, οὐκέτι... .

body considered as a mere physical object, like a rock which falls on another person. But then one notices that the person's legs might have independent—even intentional—movement and that the person who is said not to contribute to the action might nonetheless be moved in the direction of the person or object knocked down according to some *customary* movement [κατὰ συνήθη τινὰ...μεταφορὰν] of the legs.

Aristotle discusses these matters in the *Eudemian ethics* (*EE*), the less well known of his two ethical works, in a passage that is not without its problems. This is typical of *EE*, which survives in far fewer manuscripts than *EN* and is therefore chockfull of textual difficulties. Moreover, Aristotle (or, perhaps, his redactors) appears to have consigned to *EE* his more subtle reflections on topics treated more synthetically in parallel passages in the *EN*. In any case, the passage, in the Revised Oxford Translation, runs as follows:

> Generally, we speak of enforced action and necessity [τὸ βίαιον καὶ τὴν ἀνάγκην] even in the case of inanimate things; for we say that a stone moves upwards and fire downwards on compulsion and by force; but when they move according to their natural internal tendency, we do not call the act one due to force; nor do we call it voluntary either; there is no name for this antithesis; but when they move contrary to this tendency, then we say they move by force. So, too, among things living and among animals we often see things suffering and acting from force, when something[7] from without moves them contrary to their own internal tendency. Now in the inanimate the moving principle is simple, but in the animated there is more than one principle;[8] for desire and reason do not always agree. And so with the other animals the action on compulsion [τὸ βίαιον] is simple (just as in the inanimate), for they have not desire and reason opposing one another, but live by desire; but man has both, that is at a certain age, to which we

---

[7] The word 'something' translates τι, found in just one rather late (15th century) manuscript. The two oldest manuscripts (P and C) have τις ('someone'), which word moves one's understanding away from brute force and towards other types of force such as could be felt by rational creatures.

[8] ἐν μὲν τοῖς ἀψύχοις ἁπλῆ| ἡ ἀρχή, ἐν δὲ τοῖς ἐμψύχοις πλεονάζει [*EE* ii,8,1224a23-24].

> attribute also the power of action; for we do not use this
> term of the child, nor of the brute, but only of the man
> who has come to act from reason [*EE* ii,8,1224a15-30].

There is some confusion here in the transition from mere animals to humans—due perhaps to Aristotle, perhaps not.[9] One thing is clear, however: force, when it makes its appearance among rational creatures, even when it is described as coming "from without [ἔξωθεν—1224a23]," is tied up with will and intellect, which are, by most accounts, internal. Aristotelian force, therefore, is not necessarily brute force. This is reflected also in Aristotle's reference to things "suffering and acting [καὶ πάσχοντα καὶ ποιοῦντα—1224a22] from force." (We have already seen the same thing in the *EN* iii,1 definition of force: "...in which nothing is contributed by the person who acts or is acted upon..." [*EN* iii,1,1110a2-3].) There are things that we *do* on account of force. So, the force with which Aristotle is concerned in his ethical works is force that concerns in some way the will and the intellect of the person who performs some action or another.

II COUNTERVAILING CURRENTS

The idea, however, that, when he speaks of force, Aristotle does not mean brute force seems to go against a number of things he says in *EN* iii,1, where he sets out the factors—force, but also certain types of ignorance—that cause involuntariness. First of all, there is what he says about mixed acts: these involve factors beyond the control of the agent who throws his goods overboard or commits a heinous act in order to save a family member—and yet he describes them as, in the end, voluntary [1110a18]. If even these acts are voluntary, the involuntary (which is not the result of ignorance) would seem to involve something truly overpowering—such as brute force. Secondly, there are Aristotle's remarks about internal force, which would seem to be the only alternative to brute force. He apparently denies that internal factors—for example, one's attraction toward "pleasant and noble objects" [*EN* iii,1,1110b9]—could count as

9 Perhaps the problem is in the manuscript tradition and we can fix things by emending τοὺς in 1224a24 to τισι, giving ἐν μὲν τοὺς ἀψύχοις ἁπλῆ ἡ ἀρχή, ἐν δὲ τισι ἐμψύχοις πλεονάζει. The idea would then be that in inanimate things the moving principle is simple, but in *some* animated things (i.e., man) it is complex.

the type of force that causes the involuntary. Those who are forced, he says, experience pain; those moved by pleasantness and nobility experience pleasure. Pleasantness and nobility, therefore, do not qualify as "external circumstances" [τὰ ἐκτός—1110b13]. Thirdly, and perhaps most conspicuously, there is Aristotle's definition of force, which we have already seen: "That is forced of which the moving principle is outside, being a principle in which nothing is contributed by the person who acts or is acted upon, e.g. if he were to be carried somewhere by a wind, or by men who had him in their power" [1110a1-4].[10]

This last point is easily dealt with. It could very well be that when referring to men who have another in their power, Aristotle has in mind brute force; but it is now fairly widely acknowledged that "to be carried somewhere by the wind" refers to something that happens at sea (as does, of course, the jettisoning of goods). According to Alexander of Aphrodisias, Aristotle himself elucidates his definition of force by saying that "this happens in the case of voyagers when they are driven off course by some wind."[11] Gauthier points to a passage at *Metaph.* v,30,1025a25-27, which gives the general idea: "Going to Aegina was an accident, if the man went not in order to get there, but because he was carried out of his way by a storm or captured by pirates."[12] This changes our understanding of ethical force: we are to think not so much of a situation the whole of which consists in being picked up physically and dropped somewhere else but rather of a situation in which one might still be active, perhaps as a pilot, trying to deal with a situation brought on by a factor over which one has no control. It could be that a pilot very deliberately maneuvers his ship into the harbor at Aegina; even still, it can be said that he was forced to go there.

[10] See also *EN* iii,1,1110b15-17: "The forced, then, seems to be that whose moving principle is outside, the person compelled contributing nothing."

[11] ὡς ἔδειξεν γινόμενον ἐπὶ τῶν πλεόντων, ὅταν ὑπὸ πνεύματός τινος ἐξωσθῶσιν [Alexander of Aphrodisias, "Ηθικῶν προβλημάτων βιβλίον α [One book of ethical problems]," 133.2–3]. One notes the verbal resemblance between ἐξωσθῶσιν and ἔξωθεν in Aristotle's definition at *EN* iii,1,1110a1.

[12] R.-A. Gauthier and J.Y. Jolif, *L'Éthique a Nicomaque: Introduction, traduction et commentaire* (Louvain: Publications Universitaires de Louvain; Paris: Éditions Béatrice-Nauwelaerts, 1958–59) II,1 172. Gauthier is also good here on the misunderstandings of the wind example in medieval times (in particular by Robert Grosseteste and Albert the Great).

With respect to Aristotle's remarks about "pleasant and noble objects"—his saying, that is, that the desires they provoke do not constitute the force associated with the involuntary—one needs to juxtapose them with other passages which are somewhat more positive toward the idea that some emotions might constitute a type of force. Beginning at *EN* iii,1,1111a24, for instance, he takes up again the issue of whether things done due to passions might be called involuntary. "Perhaps [ἴσως—1111a24]," he says, "it is not well said that acts done by reason of anger or appetite are involuntary"—and he goes on to argue against those who would claim forced involuntariness only for their bad acts. A few lines later he remarks, "but perhaps [ἴσως—1111a29] it is strange to describe as involuntary the things one ought to desire." Why this hesitation? Aristotle appears to be taking seriously the idea that emotions constitute exonerating force. But who could take such an idea seriously?

Well, in a sense, the emotions *do* come from without—i.e., in the sense that we do not create them but we find them "already installed" in our nature. It is not our doing, for example, that humans get angry when struck or insulted: such movements of the soul happen quite naturally and are (in that sense) beyond our control, like the winds that blow a ship off course.[13] Plato speaks of a father's quite properly growing angry when he thinks that his son has done him harm and says that the son must bear with this patiently.[14] And Aristotle, in *EN* v,8, which is also about the involuntary and force, says that "acts proceeding from anger are rightly judged not to be done of malice aforethought; for it is not the man who acts in anger but he who enraged him that starts the mischief" [1135b25-27]. Aristotle apparently has in mind a pair of litigants who have come to blows over an injustice. Who is in the right—or, at least, less guilty—depends on the naturalness of the emotions provoked. Aristotle recognizes just two sources of involuntariness: ignorance (of the relevant type) and force. If a level of involuntariness is to be assigned, it cannot be for

---

[13] Gauthier notes that in *EN* iii,1,1111a24-25 ("it is not well said that acts done by reason of anger or appetite are involuntary") Aristotle is arguing against Euripides [Gauthier and Jolif, II,1 177]; he cites a number of works by Euripides and also fragment 840 (Nauck), γνώμην δ' ἔχοντά μ' ἡ φύσις βιάζεται, offering his own paraphrase: "These passions are inscribed in nature and nature does violence to reason."

[14] *Lg.* iv,717D5-6; see also *Lg.* ix,866D5-867C2 and 878E5-879A2.

want of knowledge of who was being struck or of the other relevant facts of the case, for the wronged man is presumably aware of a real injustice, he knows who committed it, and so on; any involuntariness must therefore be due to the natural force of the emotions provoked. Recalling Alexander's remarks about the man being pushed and falling onto someone else, we might say that, if a litigant did what he did in accordance with his own impulse and purpose, he would be the guilty party; "but if he is moved according to some customary and natural locomotion" of the soul, no.[15]

This helps us to understand a difficult remark at the end of this same chapter (*EN* v,8) where Aristotle, according to the Revised Oxford Translation, says the following:

> Of involuntary acts some are forgivable, others not. For the mistakes which men make not only in ignorance but also from ignorance are forgivable, while those which men do not from ignorance but (though they do them in ignorance) owing to a passion which is neither natural nor such as man is liable to, are not forgivable [*EN* v,8,1136a5-9].

Aristotle is apparently summing up the chapter, over the course of which he talks about acts that are involuntary because performed "in ignorance" (i.e., the persons who act are ἀγνοοῦντες) and acts that are voluntary because performed "from ignorance" (δι' ἄγνοιαν) —a distinction he makes also in *EN* iii,1. A drunk who punches someone acts "in ignorance"; Oedipus killed his father "from ignorance," not knowing who he was. The problem, though, lies in the reference to "a passion which is neither natural nor such as man is liable to." Burnet says that Aristotle is speaking about the condition of people who have become quite inhuman: "a state in which moral insensibility and temporary mental obscuration have been caused by an access of brutality."[16] But Aristotle has

---

[15] Cp. Thomas Aquinas on *EN* v,8,1136a5-9: "Sed illa non sunt digna venia quae aliqui non peccant propter ignorantiam causantem, sed peccant ignorantes propter passionem, quae non est naturalis neque humana, id est ratione regulata; in talibus enim passio causat et ignorantium et peccatum" [*in EN* lb.5 lect.13 ll.233-38 (§1049)].

[16] John Burnet, *The Ethics of Aristotle, illustrated with essays and notes* (London: Longmans, Green, and Co., 1895) II 132.

discussed no such extreme states in *EN* v,8; and, as Aristotle says at *EN* iii,1,1110a24-26, "when one does what he ought not under pressure which overstrains human nature and which no one could withstand," forgiveness is due. It would seem rather that Aristotle's emphasis is not so much on the state of mind of the offender as on the possibility that one can do injury to another owing to passion which *is* natural and human. The second part of the above remark should then be translated with a slightly different emphasis, along these lines: "...those [acts] which men do not from ignorance but in ignorance owing to a passion (one, however, which is neither natural nor such as man is liable to), are not forgivable."17 Both the person who picks the fight and the person who reacts are influenced by passions; but the first is moved by hatred or envy (or whatever), the second by the natural human passions that arise when one is dealt with unjustly. The act of the first is not forgivable, that of the second is.

There is a passage in *EE* ii,8 which makes a similar point. At 1225a14-17, Aristotle says, "For, if in order not to be seized someone groping about were to slay another, it would be ridiculous if he were to say that he acted under force, i.e., that he was compelled; but there must always be some greater and more painful evil which will befall the one not acting."18 The word translated here "groping about" (i.e., ψηλαφῶν· 1125a14) comes out in the Revised Oxford Translation as "[playing] blind man's bluff."19 This is a bit misleading since it suggests that what is ridiculous is applying the word 'force' to what occurs in a mere game.

17 ...ὅσα δὲ μὴ δι' ἄγνοιαν, ἀλλ' ἀγνοοῦντες μὲν διὰ πάθος δὲ μήτε φυσικὸν μήτ' ἀνθρώπινον, οὐ συγγνωμονικά [*EN* v,8,1136a7-9]. It seems to me that the proposed translation better corresponds to the flow of the Greek.

18 εἰ γὰρ ἵνα μὴ λάβῃ ψηλαφῶν ἀπο κτείνοι, γελοῖος ἂν εἴη, εἰ λέγοι ὅτι βίᾳ καὶ ἀναγκαζόμενος, ἀλλὰ δεῖ μεῖζον κακὸν καὶ λυπηρότερον εἶναι, ὃ πείσεται μὴ ποιήσας [*EE* ii,8,1225a14-17]. The word γελοῖος [1225a15] could perhaps be translates as 'funny,' in the sense of strange.

19 See also Michael Woods, *Aristotle: 'Eudemian Ethics,' books I, II and VIII*, 2nd ed. (Oxford: Clarendon, 1992) 134: "The reference seems to be to a game like blind man's bluff." Dirlmeier agrees, citing Rackham and Jackson [Franz Dirlmeier, *Aristoteles: 'Eudemische Ethik'* (Berlin: Akademie, 1962) 284]. A game something like blind man's bluff called χαλκῆ μυῖα ("bronze fly") is described at August Friedrich Pauly, Georg Wissowa, and others, eds., *Paulys Real-Encyclopädie der classischen Altertumswissenschaft: Neue Bearbeitung* (Stuttgart: Metzler, 1893) III 2068.

What Aristotle has in mind is a situation like that of the two litigants example in *EN* v,8, where one of two can legitimately claim to have been seized by a natural passion. Similarly, if a person groping about in the dark is seized by another, he quite naturally lashes out. The ridiculousness has nothing to do with the game but with the linguistic usage: saying that instinctive lashing out involves force or compulsion.

But why would Aristotle say that it is ridiculous to speak of force, given that in *EN* v,8 he seems to accept such an approach? Important here are the words, "if he were to say that he acted under force, i.e., that he was compelled." Other translations join the ideas (1) that the man is forced and (2) that he was compelled, by means of the conjunction 'and'; the Revised Oxford Translation, for example, has, "if he were to say that he acted by force, and on compulsion." But it is perfectly legitimate to translate the word kai; not as 'and' but epexegetically, as we have done. The idea is that it would be ridiculous if the man were to say that he acted under force *in the sense that* he was compelled.[20] So, we could indeed say that the man who lashes out was forced to do what he did; but it would be ridiculous to say he was compelled to do so, which would require the presence of "some greater and more painful evil which will befall the one not acting."

---

[20] As mentioned above, something like this sense of τὸ ἀναγκαῖον (the compelled), as distinct from τὸ βίαιον (the forced) is found also in *MM* i,15: "Let this, then, be our definition of what is due to force [Τοῦ οὖν βιαίου οὗτος ἡμῖν ἔστω ὁ ὁρισμός—1188b12]—those things of which the cause by which men are forced to do them is external (but where the cause is internal and in themselves there is no force). But now we must speak about compulsion and the compelled [ὑπὲρ ἀνάγκης καὶ τοῦ ἀναγκαίου—1188b14-15]. The term 'compulsion' must not be used in all circumstances nor in every case—for instance, of what we do for the sake of pleasure. For if one were to say 'I was compelled by pleasure to debauch my friend's wife,' he would be a strange person. For 'compulsion' does not apply to everything, but only to externals; for instance, whenever a man receives some damage by way of alternative to some other greater, when compelled by circumstances. For instance, 'I found it necessary to hurry my steps to the country; otherwise I should have found my stock destroyed.' Such, then, are the cases in which we have the compelled."

This helps us to understand the immediately subsequent remark, which has also caused difficulties for commentators and editors. It reads: "For thus he [i.e., the person who does not simply lash out in the dark] is compelled and he acts not under force, or at least not by nature, when he does something evil for the sake of good, or for the sake of release from some greater evil... ."[21] Although the manuscripts all include it, a number of modern scholars have eliminated the word 'not' from the phrase, "thus he is compelled and he acts not under force..."; i.e., they have eliminated the second mh; in line 1225a17, arguing that it violates the sense of the remark. But it seems to me that they have not understood the previous remark in which Aristotle associates 'force' with natural reactions such as those which occur when someone is frightened in the dark (or insulted). If one means 'force' in this sense, the compelled person is not forced; the person given a fright is, however, forced, which is to say that at least some aspect of his action is not his responsibility because it is natural.[22]

None of this is to say that natural passions necessarily constitute exonerating force, for obviously a person following natural passions can perform voluntary acts of injustice. The reason for bringing in Aristotle's analysis of naturally arising passions is simply to counteract the notion, suggested by his saying that desires and attractions do not count as force, that force is wholly external in the way that brute force is. In other words, Aristotle's understanding of force ought not to prevent us from moving our analysis of force (including truly exonerating force) into the non-physical realm, i.e., into the realm of things that could have a bearing only upon rational creatures. As Aristotle suggests in the passage from *EE* we examined earlier (i.e., ii,8,1224a15-30), dogs and children are capable of voluntary acts but are subject only to brute force; humans who have attained the age and the use of reason can be truly forced in more complicated and subtle ways.

III MIXED ACTS AND FORCE

But we have not yet discussed the first issue listed above, i.e., the fact that Aristotle says that actions performed under pressure (mixed acts) are

---

[21] οὕτω γὰρ ἀναγκαζόμενος καὶ μὴ βίᾳ πράξει, ἢ οὐ φύσει, ὅταν κακὸν ἀγαθου᾽ ἕνεκα ἢ μείζονος κακου᾽ ἀπο λύσεως πράττῃ... [1225a17-19].

[22] There is a similar issue at *EN* v,8,1135a31-34.

in the end to be considered voluntary. One of the examples he gives is formulated in the following way: "...if a tyrant were to order one to do something base, having one's parents and children in his power, and if one did the action they were to be saved, but otherwise would be put to death..." [*EN* iii,1,1110a5-7]. So, we are talking about situations that involve a great deal of force—and yet the acts performed are considered voluntary. Does this not entail that acts that are involuntary because of force cannot contain any element of the agent's will? If we are not to draw this conclusion, there must be some way of distinguishing the force that—without being mere brute force—implies involuntariness, from the type involved in mixed acts.

A help in this direction is found in what Aristotle says in *EN* iii,1 about why mixed acts are, in the final analysis, voluntary:

> Such actions, then, are mixed, but are more like voluntary actions; for they are worthy of choice when they are done, and the end of the action bears upon the moment. So, the terms 'voluntary' and 'involuntary' are to be applied at the time when a man acts. But he acts voluntarily, for the origin of the moving of the instrumental parts [of the body] in such actions is in him, and the things of which the origin is in a man himself are in his power to do or not to do.23

The phrase "the end of the action bears upon the moment" is obviously crucial. It is best understood as further specifying that which immediately precedes it: "for [mixed acts] are worthy of choice when they are done." The idea then would be that the end enters into the act that is immediately chosen, making *it* attractive—i.e., an object of choice. But

---

23 μικταὶ μὲν οὖν εἰσιν αἱ τοιαῦται πράξεις, ἐοίκασι δὲ μᾶλλον ἑκουσίοις· αἱρεταὶ γάρ εἰσι τότε ὅτε πράττονται, τὸ δὲ τέλος τῆς πράξεως κατὰ τὸν καιρόν ἐστιν. καὶ τὸ ἑκούσιον δὴ καὶ τὸ ἀκούσιον, ὅτε πράττει, λεκτέον. πράττει δὲ ἑκών· καὶ γὰρ ἡ ἀρχὴ τοῦ κινεῖν τὰ ὀργανικὰ μέρη ἐν ταῖς τοιαύταις πράξεσιν ἐν αὐτῷ ἐστίν· ὧν δ' ἐν αὐτῷ ἡ ἀρχή, ἐπ' αὐτῷ καὶ τὸ πράττειν καὶ μή [*EN* iii,1,1110a11-18].

this does not mean that every aspect of such a voluntary act is voluntary.[24]

Note too that Aristotle says that not only the term 'voluntary' [τὸ ἑκούσιον] but also the term 'involuntary'[τὸ ἀκούσιον] are to be applied when a man acts [1110a14]. It might be argued that he is speaking in that sentence of various acts, some of which might be voluntary, others involuntary, depending upon the man's state of mind "at the time" when he acts. But this does not square with what he says immediately afterwards, i.e., "But he acts voluntarily... ." The idea is that the terms 'voluntary' and 'involuntary' are both to be applied when the man acts, but in the end we have to say that he *acts* voluntarily. Aristotle is not talking about acts in general (either voluntary or involuntary) in the first sentence and about the man's particular act in the second; the subject of the subordinate clause in the first—the understood 'a man' in "when a man acts"—is the subject also of the second sentence: "But he acts voluntarily...." Indeed, not only are the subjects the same but so are the verbs: "when a man acts" [ὅτε πράττει] "he acts voluntarily" [πράττει δὲ ἑκών]. So the mixed act *is* in a sense involuntary: the pilot does not want to go to Aegina, although he *acts* voluntarily, for what he does he does of his own free will. As to the reason for the involuntary aspect, it is just barely conceivable that Aristotle has in mind the involuntary that is due to ignorance of particular circumstances (that the cup contained poison, etc.) and yet involve a voluntary act (giving the cup), but he has not yet introduced such factors, which come only in *EN* iii,1,1111a3-21—and, in any case, they do not suit well the jettisoning example. It is more natural to assume that he means any aspects of basically voluntary acts which do not fall under the end—and, in particular, aspects which are not attributable to the agent's will because they are in some sense forced upon him.

To use the example of the tyrant who holds a person's parents and children, let us presume that the end here is 'saving lives' and that the act

---

[24] See Thomas Aquinas's *Summa contra Gentiles* iii,6 (Marietti edition §1907): "...licet malum praeter intentionem sit, est tamen voluntarium..., licet non per se, sed per accidens. Intentio enim est ultimi finis, quem quis propter se vult: voluntas autem est eius etiam quod quis vult propter aliud, etiam si simpliciter non vellet; sicut qui proiicit merces in mari causa salutis, non intendit proiectionem mercium, sed salutem, proiectionem autem vult non simpliciter, sed causa salutis." For a good explanation of how this passage fits into Thomas's action theory, see Stephen L. Brock, *Action and Conduct: Thomas Aquinas and the Theory of Action* (Edinburgh: T & T Clark, 1998) 207–08; see also p.234, where Brock discusses Aristole's jettisoning example.

immediately to be performed by the agent is providing names of his comrades who oppose the tyrant. If we needed to pick out what the agent is doing at the time in question, i.e., at the moment of the betrayal, we need only look to see what falls under the end 'saving lives.' What does he do in order to save lives? He betrays his colleagues. We know that he does that voluntarily since it falls under the end and he chooses to do what he does for that end. There is no denying that the act is voluntary, although other aspects of the act are not: disgracing himself, for example, or "undermining the cause." Not every mixed act involves, however, a base object in this way. Take the example of jettisoning cargo. There again the end might be 'saving lives' (not excluding the agent's own life), and the act immediately performed is throwing goods overboard. He throws the goods overboard because this may save lives, so the act is voluntary; but it is not a heinous act. Indeed, it is quite properly described as a reasonable and praiseworthy act, failure to do which would have been unreasonable and disgraceful, indicative of inordinate attachment to material goods.

What all this suggests is that, when Aristotle speaks of the involuntary by force in *EN* iii,1, he is not simply putting whole acts into different categories. Sometimes force introduces involuntariness only to an aspect of an action. Even if it is true that in the end jettisoning goods is voluntary, there is an aspect that is involuntary—and, in particular, involuntary due to force as defined at *EN* iii,1,1110a1-4 (and 1110b15-17): that whose moving principle is "outside," the agent contributing nothing. The thing is beyond his control.

IV IMPLICATIONS

Why is force in this sense so important for Aristotle? Because it contributes to determining what the agent is doing and whether it is to be characterized as praiseworthy or not. In the jettisoning case, for example, the action is reasonable and praiseworthy only in so far as it is forced, i.e., the result of factors beyond the control of the agent. Were the storm not especially violent, posing no real threat to the ship or to lives, and were the agent in question to throw the goods overboard, we would begin to ask questions about what he is doing: what he is up to. Let us say that he has an insurance policy that pays him richly if certain goods are thrown overboard during a storm at sea. The first squall that occurs, he runs to throw his goods overboard and then to the pilot to get his signature on a form saying, "goods thrown overboard during storm." In this case, the term 'involuntary' is in no way to be applied to the act [cp. *EN* iii,1,1110a14-15]. Moreover, the act of jettisoning no longer falls under the end 'saving lives' but rather under the end 'personal gain': that is why he has thrown the goods overboard. The man can claim to have performed a praiseworthy deed (in the present sense) only if he has been truly forced to do what he did.

The hostage case can be tweaked in a similar manner. Let us say that the man whose parents and children are held would *like* to betray his comrades but is happy also to do so in such a way that they think he is still on their side. The tyrant, who knows nothing of the man's allegiance to some third party, takes the family members; the man betrays his comrades, recovering his family, without jeopardizing his cover. He has not really been forced to betray his comrades since he would have done it anyway. We cannot say, therefore, that his action falls just under the end, 'saving lives.' That would require the presence of force: not brute force but the force that comes with factors wholly outside one's own wishes but such as characterize one's action.

Both these cases, however, i.e., both the jettisoning and the betrayal case, involve mixed acts; and, indeed, most of what Aristotle says about force is connected with such acts. But force is also involved in actions in which the evil or the disvalue brought about is in no way attributable to the will of the agent. Examples featuring such actions become, many centuries after Aristotle, staple fare in discussions of the principle of double effect; they are important, therefore, for determining when a moral absolute is violated since the principle of double effect is invoked when, despite immediate appearances, an evil effect is not to be attributed to the will of an agent. Take, for example, the case of a pregnant woman upon whose uterus there is found a cancerous growth. Defenders of the principle of double effect often say quite flatly that removal of the cancerous uterus is permissible, even though it is certain that the fetus will die, since the doctor would have removed the uterus anyway in order to arrest the cancer. In fact, however, the principle is only applicable in cases where sufficient force is present. Imagine that a doctor in a Catholic hospital discovers such a cancerous growth two or three months before the anticipated delivery date and knows too that the cancer is very unlikely to be a real threat for a year or so: he could easily wait until after the delivery to remove the uterus. For the doctor to perform the abortion, arguing that he is doing nothing immoral but precisely that which is permissible according to the principle of double effect would be like the man in the squall's filling out a form documenting the occurrence of a storm in order to justify his throwing precious goods overboard. The doctor would have violated the relevant moral absolute—"Do not murder"—since without the presence of sufficient force, the killing of the fetus is attributable to his will.

V CONCLUSION

Certainly, there is more work to be done in order to establish with greater certainty and precision how Aristotle understands the role of force in the analysis of human actions. And no doubt too many issues will have to be left undecided, given the state of the pertinent Aristotelian writings that survive (I am thinking especially of the *Eudemian ethics*). But the work is well worth doing since even the lines of thought we can discern are very suggestive of approaches one might take in tackling some of the most difficult problems in the theory of human action. It is typical of his penetrating understanding of ethical theory that John Finnis points us toward the concept of force at precisely the point where it is most important: the consideration of moral absolutes.

MARRIAGE AND ACTS REPRODUCTIVE IN KIND
Patrick Lee

In various venues, including philosophical journals, law reviews, and courts, John Finnis has defended, with clarity and precision, the traditional position that deliberate sexual acts can be morally right only within marriage. According to Finnis, influenced on this point of course by Germain Grisez, the key to understanding the ethics of sex is, first, to understand what marriage is, and, second, to understand how marital sexual acts contribute to marriage. From there, the increasingly controversial propositions of traditional sexual ethics follow. In this paper I will review the case Finnis makes for this position, and defend it against some recent objections.[1]

I MARRIAGE
Every society has some way or regulations for determining the ways and the contexts in which children come to be and are raised. This is a necessity. For, it is both desirable and inevitable that children will come to be. The question for society, and for people who engage in acts (sexual acts) by which children might come to be is the following. What should society and those who engage in such acts do to provide a suitable environment in which children might come? That is, what must society and those in society who engage in sexual acts do in order to be fair to the children who will come to be through sexual acts?

The answer is that those couples who perform sexual acts should first form a community that will be dedicated to the raising and educating of children who might come to be. State-run organizations, business enterprises, even communes (groups composed of sexual partners) are not the groups most suitable for the raising and educating of children.[2] In virtually every society it is generally recognized that the best arrangement for bearing and raising children is to ensure that the parents themselves in some way form a society oriented to bearing and raising children (this is

---

[1] Parts of this essay have appeared in an article I co-authored with Robert P. George, "What Sex Can Be: Self-Alienation, Illusion, or One-Flesh Union," *American Journal of Jurisprudence* 42 (1997), 135-157.

[2] Of course, in some cases, as with the death of one or more of the biological parents, such arrangements are the best that can be had, but they are not optimal.

true of polygamous societies as well, though polygamous marriages violate the equality of man and woman in marriage and are not, in the end, most suitable for raising children).   Thus, marriage is the community formed by a man and a woman who publicly consent to share their lives, in a type of relationship oriented toward begetting, nurturing, and educating of children together.   Even though this or that particular marriage may not result in children, marriage is the *sort* of relationship *that would be fulfilled by* bearing and raising children together.   This openness to procreation, as the community's natural fulfillment, distinguishes this community from other types of community.

Moreover, sexual acts have a tendency, in most people at least, to create a strong feeling of bonding and an expectation of a deeper, non-instrumental relationship.   And the desire to have children is often, and naturally, an outgrowth of a romantic love between and a man and a woman. When they love each other they naturally tend to desire to form a life together, and (often) to have children together.[3]   Thus, marriage is the society whose distinctive purpose is the provision of a stable and protective environment not only for bearing and raising children but also for romantic love, a love that is itself intrinsically linked to bearing and raising children.   Rightly understood, marriage has a two-fold end—one end with two aspects, marital communion and procreation.

Two truths about these two aspects of marriage are fundamental.   First, the relation of marriage to the goal of bearing and raising children cannot (or should not) be one of simple means to end.   Marriage is not a mere contractual union like that of a roof-repair company, or even a tutoring group, where the activity of the group is simply instrumental to an extrinsic end or goal, with the result, also, that once the end is achieved the reason for the unity of the group has also ended.   To view the marriage as merely instrumental would be to denigrate the union of the man and the woman; it would reduce their union to that of a mere means.   So, marriage should be oriented to the union of the man and the woman *for its own sake*, not merely as a means to an end—out of regard for both goods of marriage, namely, the bearing and raising of children, and the communion of the spouses.

[3] Germain Grisez, *The Way of the Lord Jesus: Volume 2, Living a Christian Life* (Quincy, IL: Franciscan Press, 1993), 574-576.

Secondly, marriage is essentially oriented to bearing and raising children, though in a somewhat indirect way. Marriage, the community of the man and the woman, is intrinsically good, but it is the *type* of community that is naturally *fulfilled* by bearing and raising children. Since children are distinct persons, the production of children is not directly the aim of marriage. Rather, the aim of marriage is to form a community that is suitable for bearing and raising children, and to be a community in which children are welcomed as gifts, prolonging the marital community into family—so that children are viewed neither as products nor as mere burdens.[4] Because of its orientation to procreation and the personal communion of the spouses the good of marriage requires a sharing of whole lives (or: an open-ended, all-inclusive unity), permanence, and exclusivity.[5]

II MARITAL INTERCOURSE

Given these points about the nature of marriage, sexual intercourse has a role to play in marriage quite different from how it is often conceived even by some proponents of traditional sexual morality. In marriage, sexual intercourse is neither merely an extrinsic symbol nor a mere pursuit of pleasure. Rather, sexual intercourse is a real, biological unity, and this unity actualizes or renews the multi-leveled (physical, emotional, spiritual, etc) union of the spouses. In sexual intercourse between a man and a woman (whether married or not), a *real* organic union is established. This is a literal, biological point. Human beings are organisms, albeit of a particular type. For most actions, such as sensation, digestion, walking, and so on, individual male or female organisms are complete units. The male or female animal organism uses various materials as energy or instruments to perform its actions, but there is no internal orientation of its bodily parts to any larger whole of which it is a part, with respect to those actions. However, with respect to one function the male and the female

[4] Thus, if a married couple do not have children for some reason, their marriage is fully a marriage and remains good in itself (denied by a view of marriage which reduces it to a mere instrument for procreation) but also lacks its natural fulfillment (denied by the view of marriage, popular today, that views children as a mere appendage to marriage and sometimes even as only a means to the fulfillment of the couple).

[5] Grisez ibid., 555-584.

are *not* complete, and that function is reproduction. In reproductive activity the bodily parts of the male and the bodily parts of the female participate in a single action, coitus, which is oriented to reproduction (though not every act of coitus results in reproduction), so that the subject of the action is the male and the female as a unit.[6] Coitus is a unitary action in which the male and the female become organically one.[7] In marital intercourse, this bodily unity is an aspect, and a physical making-present, of the couple's more comprehensive, marital communion.

When a couple chooses to form the kind of community distinguished by its openness and orientation to procreation, then the organic unity effected in sexual intercourse has a continuity with their community. In sexual intercourse they unite (become one) precisely in that respect in which their community is distinct and naturally fulfilled. So, this bodily unity is not extrinsic to their emotional and spiritual unity. The bodily, emotional, and spiritual are the different levels of a unitary, multi-leveled personal communion. Therefore, in such a community sexual intercourse actualizes the multi-leveled personal communion. The sexual intercourse of spouses is not an extrinsic symbol of their love, or a mere means in relation to procreation. Rather, their sexual intercourse embodies, or actualizes, their marital communion. In that way the chaste sexual intercourse of husband and wife instantiates a basic human good: the good of marital union.

---

[6] It is important to note that the teleology of sexual acts belongs to them as groups primarily. That is, one cannot say that each and every spermatozoon is designed to join with an oocyte, so that if this particular one does not it has failed. If so, it would be hard to explain teleologically why there are millions of spermatozoa ejaculated in intercourse. Rather, the design of the bodies is that *some sperm or other at some time or other* join with an oocyte. The same is true with individual instances of sexual intercourse. That is, the functional orientation belongs to acts of sexual intercourse as a group, primarily, and only indirectly to the individual acts. That is, the individual act of intercourse is not *directly* oriented to reproduction; one could say that it is indirectly oriented to reproduction, as a member of a set, some of which will reproduce.

[7] The reproductive bodily parts are internally oriented toward actuation together with the bodily parts of the opposite sex. So, the same feature which shows that the various bodily parts of a single horse or human constitute a single organism, is found in the bodily parts of the male and the female engaging in a reproductive-type act. So they are truly organically one. Note too that, strictly speaking, men and woman engaging in sexual acts do not choose to reproduce, though they can choose to perform reproductive-type acts, with reproduction as their goal.

It is certainly true that there *are* sexual unions different from genuine marriage. Some men and women, particularly frequently in Muslim countries, form essentially contractual unions that are instrumental to other goods, such as economic flourishing and raising children. In some societies (including, for example, ancient Greece) many men have viewed their wives only as mothers of their children, and have sought romantic relationships elsewhere. Also, many couples today regularly perform sexual acts together, but view their relationships as having nothing in them inherently connected to procreation (and thus view their unity as romantic in essence but not essentially procreative). Both of these types of relationships have at times been called "marriage." But these societies or arrangements are specifically and fundamentally distinct from the intrinsic good of marriage. Moreover, sexual acts performed within these types of communities or arrangements, are *extrinsic* to the personal communion of the couple.[8] Only in *marriage*, that is, only in the one-flesh union of spouses, is the sexual intercourse part of, or constitutive of, the personal bodily communion itself.

III THE IMMORALITY OF EXTRA-MARITAL SEXUAL ACTS

On this position it follows that deliberate extramarital sexual acts of whatever kind are objectively immoral. In particular, sodomitical acts are non-marital and therefore objectively immoral. By "sodomy" here is meant (1) anal or oral intercourse between persons of the same sex, or (2) anal or oral intercourse between persons of opposite sexes (even if married), if it is intended to bring about complete sexual satisfaction apart from vaginal intercourse. If a couple use their sexual organs for the sake of experiencing pleasure or even for the sake of an experience of unity, but do not become organically one, then their act does not actually effect unity. If Susan, for example, masturbates John to orgasm or applies oral stimulation to him to bring him to orgasm, no real unity has been effected. That is, although bodily parts are conjoined, and so there is juxtaposition and contact, the participants do not unite biologically; they do not become the subject of a single act, and so do not literally become "one flesh." They may be doing this in order simply to obtain or share plea-

---

8 Or more, if more than two are engaging in the sexual act.

sure. In that case the act is really an instance of mutual masturbation, and is as self-alienating as any other instance of masturbation.[9] However, they might intend their act as in some way an expression of their love for each other. They might argue that this act is no different from the vaginal intercourse they performed two nights before, except that this one involves a merely technical or physical variation—a rearrangement of "plumbing."

However, in sodomitical acts, whether between persons of the same sex or opposite sexes, between unmarried or married persons, the participants do not unite biologically.[10] Moreover, an experience of pleasure, just as such, is not shared. Although each person may experience pleasure, they experience pleasure each as an individual not as a unit. For a truly common good, there must be more than experience; the experiences must be subordinated to a truly common act that is genuinely fulfilling (and as such provides a more than merely instrumental reason for action). If, on the contrary, the activities are subordinated to the pleasurable experiences, if the physical stimulation administered to one another is merely a means to attain what are (and can only be) individual, private experiences, then a real, biological unity is not achieved.

How *is* unity achieved? What feature must a sexual act have so that one is not merely using another's body (and one's own)? The answer is that it must be an act in which a real good is realized or participated. If this is so, then it is an act in which the two share and therefore become one in jointly performing this act. In that case, their pleasurable experiences will be aspects of a real good, rather than their acts being subordinated to the pleasurable experiences. In the case of chaste marital intercourse, spouses participate in the real good of marital bodily union. In marital intercourse the man and the woman become organically one in an act of copulation, and this physical union initiates or renews their total marital communion: that is, distinct from the pleasurable *experiences*, there is an identifiable, real act and basic good in which they share, name-

---

[9] On the immorality of masturbation, see Grisez, op. cit., 646-651; Patrick Lee and Robert P. George, "What Sex Can Be: Self-Alienation, Illusion, or One-Flesh Union," loc. cit., 137-142.

[10] John Finnis, "The Good of Marriage and the Morality of Sexual Relations: Some Philosophical and Historical Observations," *American Journal of Jurisprudence* 42 (1997), 118-134.

ly, the act of initiating or renewing their marital union in their becoming organically one.

IV OBJECTIONS

Objection 1

The principal objection to this argument, of course, has been that it would entail that the sexual acts of sterile married couples are also immoral, and everyone recognizes that is not the case. It has been claimed that the sexual act of an infertile married couple lacks any intrinsic relation to procreation, but that it is clearly morally permissible. On the same grounds (it is argued) one should concede that sexual acts between partners of the same sex, though also lacking in procreative potential, can be morally justified.[11]

However, there *is* a clear difference between *what* homosexual couples do and what infertile married couples do. No one could have children by performing sodomitical acts. Yet, this is not true of the *type of act* performed by infertile married couples when they engage in vaginal intercourse. People who are not temporarily or permanently infertile *could* procreate by performing *exactly* the act which the infertile married couple perform and by which they consummate or actualize their marital communion. The difference between sterile and fertile married couples is not a difference in *what they do*. Rather, it is a difference in a distinct condition which affects what may *result* from what they do. However, the difference between any heterosexual couple engaging in vaginal intercourse and a homosexual couple is much more than that. The lack of complementarity in homosexual couples is a condition which renders it impossible for them to perform *the kind of act* which makes them organically one. As Finnis expresses it:

> The marriage of a sterile couple is true marriage, because they can intend and do together *all* that any married couple *need* intend and do to undertake, consummate, and live out a valid marriage.[12]

11 For example, Stephen Macedo, "Homosexuality and the Conservative Mind," *Georgetown Law Journal* 84 (1995), 261-300, at 278.

12 John Finnis, "The Good of Marriage and the Morality of Sexual Relations: Some Philosophical and Historical Observations," *American Journal of Jurisprudence* 42 (1997), 127.

If a married couple becomes infertile, it is obvious that this does not change what they have been doing in bed: they still perform the same kind of act they have been doing perhaps for years. Similarly, a fertile married couple may have sexual intercourse several times during a week. If conception results, they may not know which act of sexual intercourse caused it. Still, all of their acts are *the kind of acts* which could result in procreation. Their sexual acts later in life, for example, after the female spouse has become infertile, are still the kind of acts which could result in procreation—the difference is not a difference in *what they do*—the kind of act—but in a condition extrinsic to what they do.

Thus, the infertile heterosexual couple performs the kind of act that, given other conditions, reproduces; a homosexual couple (or indeed a heterosexual couple engaging in sodomy) performs acts on each other (for they do not engage in a unified act) which of themselves are not apt, in any conditions, to reproduce. This difference is indeed morally significant. The heterosexual couple who engage in a reproductive-type act truly become biologically one, one body. If they have given marital consent, then this act initiates or renews their marital communion. Their intercourse will be an aspect of this multi-leveled union and so will embody or renew that union. By contrast, the homosexual couple lacks not just a condition enabling their act to be reproductive, but, first, a prerequisite for the formation by them of the kind of personal union which is initiated or renewed by sexual acts, and, second, the biological complementarity enabling them to become biologically one. Of course, men have friendships with other men, and women have friendships with other women; but sexual acts performed on each other do not biologically unite them and so do not actualize or embody such friendships.

Still, one might object to this, as Andrew Koppelman has, that the sexual acts of a sterile or elderly couple *cannot* be described as reproductive in kind, since *these* acts do not have the power to procreate. Koppelman objects that our definition of *marriage* (that is, the definition proposed by traditional morality) is not adequately warranted, that it is in fact arbitrary: "Finally, there is not adequate warrant for accepting the NNL [new natural lawyers'] definition of marriage."[13] But to support that claim he

---

[13] Andrew Koppelman, *The Gay Rights Question in Contemporary American Law,* 86

argues that our classification of marital *acts*, as essentially distinct from homosexual acts, is unwarranted and arbitrary:

> What sense does it make to postulate one type of sexual activity as normative in this way [our definition of marital acts], so that heterosexual intercourse is held to be an act of a reproductive *kind* even if reproduction is not intended and is known to be impossible? Why is it not equally plausible to say that all acts of seminal ejaculation are reproductive in kind, or to say that no acts of seminal ejaculation are reproductive in kind, and that reproduction is only an accidental consequence that may ensue under certain conditions? There is nothing in nature that dictates that the lines have to be drawn in any of these ways.[14]

The class of sexual acts we have described as reproductive in type, or "as such suitable for procreation," Koppelman later says might be just "an ex post mental construct."[15] After quoting John Finnis, who said that a marital act, even of a sterile or elderly couple, is of reproductive type because it is "behavior which, as behavior, is suitable for generation,"[16] Koppelman replies that such an act cannot be suitable for generation if the organs are not suitable for generation, or do not have the power to procreate. He then adds:

> A sterile person's genitals are no more suitable for generation than an unloaded gun is suitable for shooting. . . . Dependencies of deception and fright aside, all objects that are not *loaded* guns are morally equivalent in this context . . . . But the only aspect of reproductiveness that is relevant to the natural lawyers' argument, namely the reproductive *power* of the organ, does not inhere in *this* organ.[17]

So, Koppelman's claim is that one should not hold that marriage as we have defined it is normative, and that it is arbitrary for us to single out heterosexual vaginal intercourse, which includes that of sterile and elderly

14 Ibid., 86-87.
15 Ibid., 87.
16 John Finnis,
17 Koppelman, op. cit., 88.

couples, as morally significantly different from other types of sexual activity, such as homosexual sex acts.

Koppelman's argument has two parts, one about marriage and the other about sexual acts. First, let me reply to the part about marriage. Contrary to Koppelman's claim, marriage is not simply an historical accident which can now be modified as our culture—or a small fraction of our culture—might choose. As explained above, the complexity of marriage stems from the fact that one of its distinctive purposes—bearing and raising children—requires a stable and loving environment formed by the children's parents. In order to form a stable and loving environment this union cannot be a mere contractual and instrumental agreement entered solely for the sake of children—this would depersonalize both the children and the parental union. Hence the parents—and any couple who might become parents—should form a stable union of love *for each other*, an interpersonal union that is in itself good but that would be naturally fulfilled by bearing and raising children. But since this type of interpersonal union of man and woman is in itself good even if this natural fulfillment is not reached, it follows that sterile couples must be included within the extension of this kind of community—otherwise, marriage will be reduced to a mere means in relation to an extrinsic end and would cease once that end was completed or if it was found to be impossible of realizing.

Moreover, man and woman are complementary physically, but also emotionally, psychologically, and spiritually. So the union of a man and a woman, a union of complements, and in such a way as to provide a suitable environment for whatever children might come to be—such a community is scarcely an arbitrarily drawn class. Rather, the basic welfare of children, and the romantic inclinations toward fulfillment in love in men and women, are the bases in the natures of man, woman, and children, for delineating those committed man-woman couples and families as belonging to one class.

The *normativity* of this class stems from its being a basic and irreducible good perfective of human persons. Marriage, so defined, that is, defined as it has been for centuries in our civilization, is a basic good, and therefore is worthy of pursuit, promotion, protection, and respect.

The second part of Koppelman's argument centers on reproductive-type acts. Here he claims that the classification of all heterosexual vaginal sexual acts as reproductive in kind is arbitrary. In turn, in the course of defending this argument, he makes two claims: (a) that marital acts performed by sterile or elderly couples are *not* reproductive in kind, but also (b) if they *are* considered reproductive in kind, then *any* seminal ejaculation could be classified as reproductive in kind. As to claim (a), the key assumption in Koppelman's argument here is the following:

> No act which cannot succeed (in a suitable environment under certain circumstances) in producing X can be of the kind that is oriented toward X.

Or, put more specifically:

> No act in which the agents (or parts of the agents) lack the full internal resources (in a suitable environment, under certain circumstances) to produce X can be internally oriented toward X.

Because the sterile man does not have all of the internal resources to procreate (together with a woman), then, says Koppelman, his sexual acts cannot be oriented toward procreation. In fact, says Koppelman, his sexual organs in that case are not genuinely reproductive organs at all—they are reproductive, he says, only in some "taxonomic" sense,[18] which seems to mean they merely can be classified that way, but without any present basis for that classification.

But these claims cannot be true. A composite entity may have several constituents internally arranged so as to cooperate to produce X. But this composite may have, or have acquired, a defect that prevents it from producing X. For example, a hand is oriented toward grasping objects, and remains oriented toward that, even though a defect—a broken bone, for example—prevents it from actually doing so. So a reproductive organ remains a reproductive organ in fact and not just in name (merely "taxonomically"), even if some defect in the agent makes actual reproduction impossible.

A similar point applies to a reproductive-type *act*. In the generative act the male and the female perform an act (intercourse) in which the sperm is deposited in the vaginal tract of the female. This act, performed

[18] Ibid.

by the male and the female together, is the first part of the process of reproduction. In performing this first part of the reproductive process together, the male and the female act as a single unit, even if the second part of the process cannot, for any of a variety of causes, be completed. Of course, if the process continues, they continue to act as a unit (though at a distance, by means of their gametes). A condition, or even a defect, which prevents the second part of the process cannot change the fact that the male and the female did become organically one by completing the first part of that process.

Moreover, just as marriage is more complex than most other communities, so genuine sexual intercourse is more complex than other acts. The orientation of the first part of the process (sexual intercourse) is not related to the rest of the process in the same way that a simple means is related to a single end. Rather, the orientation of the sexual acts toward procreation belongs to the set of sexual acts, not directly to each act. And the only behavior which the couple have direct control over is the sexual intercourse itself in such a way that the male sperm is deposited in female vaginal tract—this is the only act, the only behavior, which they directly perform which disposes them to procreation. So, in doing that, the male and the female do become one as one agent, namely, as together performing that part of the reproductive process over which they have direct control. So, when Koppelman says that only acts which have the power to reproduce are genuinely reproductive in kind, he is mistaken. Many sexual acts are reproductive in kind which will not actually succeed in reproducing and are known to be impossible of succeeding. So these are acts in which the male and the female become a single unit.

This explains (in part) why heterosexual acts of sterile and elderly couples are reproductive in kind. But, inversely, how can we hold that homosexual acts are *not* reproductive in kind? That is, how can we answer claim (b), namely, Koppelman's claim that if sexual acts of heterosexual sterile or elderly couples are considered reproductive in kind, then it is equally plausible to say that *all* acts of seminal ejaculation are reproductive in kind? (In effect, Koppelman wants to say that heterosexual acts of sterile or elderly couples are not reproductive—but *if* they are, then so are homosexual acts.) Do not the agents in homosexual acts also exercise part of their reproductive capacities and organs?

The answer is that of course homosexual couples make use of their reproductive capacities and organs, but, unlike sterile or elderly hetero-sexual couples performing vaginal intercourse, they do not jointly per-form an act which constitutes the first part of the reproductive process. Both sets of acts (the homosexual and the heterosexual) may be *abstract-ly* described simply as "seminal ejaculation," but the homosexual act is not the joint performance by a male and a female, as a single unit, of all of the behavior under their control, which, given other conditions (for example, sufficient sperm count, ovulation) can reproduce. That is, *what the homosexual act is*, as opposed to *an extrinsic condition* of that act, makes it impossible to reproduce, and, as a consequence, if performed by two or more people, is not an act in which they become biologically one. Neither nocturnal emissions nor instances of solitary masturbation are reproductive-type acts either, and for the same reason homosexual acts are not reproductive in kind.

Koppelman could object that the infertility of the heterosexual couple is not an extrinsic condition (as we claim) but should be considered as modifying what they do—and so they are, after all, in the same boat as homosexual acts (in effect, that being reproductive in kind is not morally significant). But there are two reasons why this is not true. First, as point-ed out above, every aspect of the behavior the heterosexual couple (in a marital act) chooses to perform may be the same on two different occa-sions, and yet one act may result in procreation and the other not. This indicates that the difference—actual procreation versus not actual procre-ation—is a difference extrinsic to *what they do*. Of course, if they know that procreation is impossible, then they cannot intend or hope for pro-creation. This is all that Koppelman's analogy of the unloaded gun shows: just as one cannot intend to kill with a gun one knows is unloaded so one cannot intend or hope to procreate by an act one knows cannot in these circumstances result in procreation. But our claim is not that in a marital act one must intend to procreate, hope to procreate, or even think that procreation is in these circumstances possible. Our claim is that a marital act is an act in which the man and the woman, as complementary, become bodily and organically one, in that they jointly perform a single act, single in that it is an act that is oriented to procreation, though some other condition in the agents may prevent the completion of that orienta-tion in this act.

Second, the marital acts of a sterile or elderly married couple proclaim and bear witness to the intrinsic goodness of marriage, though marriage is the kind of community that is naturally fulfilled by the bearing and raising of children. Hence the marital acts of infertile married couples, as renewing and fostering their conjugal love and marriage, do contribute to the good of marriage in the whole community. And these marital acts, though infertile in themselves, do indirectly contribute to the aspect of the good of marriage which their own marriage does not realize, namely, the good of procreation, or the bearing and raising of children.

Objection 2

A second objection to the main argument is to claim that non-marital acts—in particular, homosexual sex acts—*do* sometimes realize a basic, common good, that they do, sometimes, somehow embody or express a personal communion. I will consider here two variations on this. The first is to say that such acts *symbolize*, or *gesture*, the personal union of the participants, perhaps as a special *gesture,* and that in this way such acts contribute to or strengthen the participants' personal union.[19] One might argue that sexual acts foster personal communion because they are a sign or expression of love. But if that is so, then why can't sexual acts between partners of the same sex symbolize love or affection? And why must a couple have a community suited for procreation (i.e., be married) in order validly to express their love sexually?

It is true that chaste sexual acts are signs or symbols of personal union. However, sexual acts are in their immediate reality much more than symbols or gestures. The question is whether the reality that is more than symbolic will involve depersonalization. When one waves at someone, or smiles at someone, or shakes her hand, the gesture is of itself rather trivial, but partly through convention and partly through natural association, it signifies a cordial act of will or emotion. The same is true of a hug or a non-passionate kiss. But insofar as these acts are symbols, the thought is moved away from the sign to the will or emotion which it signifies.[20] However, in a sexual act there is a desire directed toward the body and the desire of the other. The participants' attention is riveted on the action

[19] Cf. Gareth Matthews, OP, *The Body in Context, Sex and Catholicism* (London: SCM Press, 1992), especially 92-109.

[20] In hugging, there also seems to be an enjoyment of the simple presence or closeness of the one hugged.

itself. And the desire and attention is not just toward the physical presence of the other (as in a hug). So the action is not primarily a sign or gesture for some other reality. Indeed, sexual acts *are* symbolically powerful precisely because of what sexual intercourse between a man and woman is in reality.

Moreover, a morally right sexual act does not make present in an indeterminate way just some-union-or-other. Rather, becoming one flesh is the sort of act specifically apt to make present *marital* communion, that is, the sort of union oriented to, and fulfilled by, procreation: *that* is the kind of communion it can embody (and if it does not, then it, and the persons involved, are being *used* for extrinsic purposes). Sexual intercourse is a real, biological unity, and if it is loving and respectful sexual intercourse within marriage, it embodies or makes present marriage: not just a gesture, but a joint act in which the two become co-subjects and thus become one. Thus, it is fundamentally a real act, and a real unification, and *because of that,* it is a gesture with profound significance or meaning.[21]

It is true, however, that someone may have sex with another in order to signify something as an ulterior end. For example, an otherwise unwilling teen girl may consent to have sex with her boyfriend in order to show him how much she cares. Still, the immediate reality of the sexual act is not a mere sign or gesture. And so if there is not a real union of which the sexual act is a part—in other words if it is not a marital act—then the bodily presence of the other, and the personal presence of the other as a bodily person, is used for the sake of the experience of the sexual act, even if that experience has as an ulterior end some signification. In other words, if doing X in itself involves instrumentalizing the body, it does not cease to do so if one does X for the sake of an ulterior end, in this case, signification.

A second variation on this objection (viz., the denial that sodomitical acts lack a common good) is to claim that sex is simply a type of gift. In

---

[21] I have shown that Pope John Paul II's thought does *not* regard the sexual act as a mere gesture in: Patrick Lee, "The Human Body and Sexuality in the Teaching of Pope John Paul II," in C. Tollefsen, (ed.), *John Paul II's Contribution to Catholic Bioethics* (The Netherlands: Springer, 2004), 107-120.

sex the participants give each other pleasure, and this giving strengthens or expresses a personal communion. It is an exchange of gifts, and the gift is pleasure. Andrew Koppelman argues that it cannot be wrong to act simply for the sake of pleasure. And, as a consequence (he argues) a couple (whether heterosexual or homosexual) who "pleasure each other"— that is, aim immediately simply at pleasure, are giving each other a genuine gift and are therefore (contrary to our argument) sharing a genuine common good.[22] He presents two arguments to support this claim. First, he claims that bodily pleasure itself is a good.

> Often the pursuit of pleasure responds to a bodily need, rather than inducing one: the arousal typically precedes the act. I feel an itch before I scratch it. In scratching an itch, I am not abusing my body or regarding it as 'a lower form of life with its own dynamism,' [a reference to Germain Grisez[23]] but tending respectfully to its needs, which are my needs. And when A sexually pleasures B, by whatever means, A is tending respectfully to the needs of B's body, which are B's needs.[24]

On the next page he claims: "NNL [that is, proponents, such as ourselves, of the new natural law theory] has not refuted the alternative view (which accords with common sense much better than their view) that bodily pleasure is itself a good thing, and that when people cooperate to produce it, they are producing a common good."[25]

Koppelman is mistaken, however, when he claims that new natural lawyers have not presented arguments for their (our) claim that bodily pleasure is not of itself a good. Throughout the writings of Grisez, Boyle, Finnis and ourselves, there are several places in which such arguments have been presented.[26] In addition, in the literature in general several crit-

---

22 Andrew Koppelman, *The Gay Rights Question in Contemporary American Law* (Chicago: University of Chicago Press, 2002), 85.

23 Germain Grisez, *The Way of the Lord Jesus: Vol. 1, Christian Moral Principles* (Quincy, IL: Franciscan Press, 1983), 139.

24 Andrew Koppelman, *The Gay Rights Question, 85*

25 Ibid., 86.

26 For examples: Germain Grisez and Russell Shaw, *Beyond the New Morality, 3rd ed.* (Notre Dame Ind.: University of Notre Dame Press, 1988), chapter 3; Germain Grisez, *The Way of the Lord Jesus, Volume 1: Christian Moral Principles*, loc., cit., chapter 5;

ical discussions of hedonism have, we believe, presented serious difficulties with the idea that bodily pleasure is of itself a good. A long-standing problem is that of inappropriate pleasures—for example, sadistic pleasures. One does not wish to say that Smith's sadism was bad but at least he got pleasure from it. Rather, when one takes pleasure in an inappropriate object, the pleasure itself is bad. So, it cannot be true that bodily pleasure is *of itself* a good.

Pleasure *is* a good, for it is better, for example, to have learning with pleasure than without it; but it is not a good just by itself, it must be connected to an appropriate object in order to be a good. The question is, what must the object of a pleasure be like in order to be appropriate? Plainly, a good pleasure must not be an *illusory* one—for example, the pleasure one might obtain from believing that so and so admired one is illusory if so and so does not really admire one. Illusory pleasures take us away from reality, and from what is genuinely good.

These examples, though, suggest that there may be a basic criterion for distinguishing between good pleasures and bad ones. In general, what does make an object or activity really good and worthy of pursuit? When we act for a reason, that is when we guide our actions by reason or understanding, then the *point* of our acting is something that we understand to be really *fulfilling* or *perfective* of us and of others we care about. What makes an object or activity good and worth pursuing is that it is really *fulfilling* or *perfective*. Pleasures is not by itself, or is not always, really fulfilling—this is clear from sadistic pleasures, for example. So, pleasure is good only if it is an experience of, or an aspect of, a condition or activity that is already genuinely fulfilling. The condition or activity must first be really fulfilling, and *then* pleasure taken in it is an additional fulfillment.

What then of Koppelman's example of scratching an itch? Must we maintain that this is an instance of seeking pleasure as isolated from gen-

Germain Grisez, John Finnis, Joseph Boyle, "Practical Principles, Moral Truth, and Ultimate Ends," *American Journal of Jurisprudence* 32 (1987), 99-151; John Finnis, *Natural Law and Natural Right* (New York: Oxford University Press, 1980), 95-97; Id., *Fundamentals of Ethics* (Washington, D.C.: Georgetown University Press, 1983), chapter 2.

uine fulfillment and an instrumentalizing of the body? What is remarkably different between scratching an itch and sexual activity, of whatever sort, is the simplicity of the former and the complexity of the latter. An itch is a discomfort in some part of the body and presumably an indication of some real, though perhaps mild, bodily disorder. There (generally) is no reason whatsoever against scratching to remove that discomfort—it is a simple and direct action aimed at calming the nerve-endings at some part of the body. There is no pursuit of pleasure apart from a real fulfillment (or as isolated from the larger good of which it should be a part), as there is in the case of masturbatory sex. The same is true for eating for the pleasure of it (the activity sought is a real act of eating which is really fulfilling) or of enjoying a hot bath (the relaxation of one's muscles being a healthy function). It is not that in these cases pleasure is a side effect; pleasure *is* sought, but as part of or as connected to a genuinely fulfilling condition (though perhaps a very minor instance of fulfillment).

The claim that the provision of sexual pleasure answers a bodily need is also confused. It is true that an animal, including a human animal, finds sexual genital stimulation and orgasm pleasurable and so acquiring it has the effect of relief. But the situation with sex is similar (in this respect) to hunger and eating. Hunger involves a tension, and eating— even if what is eaten is not genuinely good for one—relieves that tension. But, understood more clearly, hunger is a desire and orientation to eating *food* or *nutrition*. In other words, the object of the *need*, as opposed to the chance object of the blind urge, is eating food, that is, a genuinely fulfilling activity—and so even if a person took pleasure in eating Styrofoam or plastic this would not show that these substances answer to a genuine need. Such desires are really aberrations in the fundamental or basic orientation or natural desire for real food.

Similarly, people have sexual desires that are in some ways similar to the way they have hunger pangs (of course the two types of desire are also in many ways very different, the desire for sex actually being much more complicated). But the question is, to what really fulfilling condition or activity are these desires really oriented? As the desire to eat plastic, for example, is really a disordered desire for real food, so the desire for orgasm isolated from bodily and personal communion is a disordered desire for what sex offers which is really fulfilling, the expression of or embodiment of a real interpersonal union. In sum, when Koppelman claims that bodily pleasure is of itself a good, which therefore can be a common good shared by an unmarried couple (hetero- or homo-sexual), he begs the question. For the issue is, not what might bring some (temporary) relief to the urge, but what really fulfilling condition or activity is this desire oriented to? Just as hunger is not oriented to pleasure but to a really fulfilling activity that is pleasurable, so sexual desire is not oriented just to stimulation and orgasm but to a really fulfilling activity that is pleasurable. So, again, pleasure is not itself the fulfillment—at least not by itself—but pleasure is fulfilling only when it is part of a condition or activity that is of itself fulfilling. Pleasure by itself cannot be the common good uniting two (or more?) in a sexual act, since to be a genuine good it must be an aspect of an activity or condition that is already intrinsically good.

In sum, only if there is a common good realized in and by the sexual act—making the couple one in this cooperative participation in that common good—do the participants treat each other and themselves as unified bodily persons, (and, thus, with respect) and embody a real, basic good. For only then is their pleasure or experience an aspect of participation in a real good, rather than individual, private gratifications making use of activities or pursuits of illusory experiences. In marriage, the couple become two-in-one-flesh, and this bodily union is an aspect of their total marital communion, actualizing (initiating or renewing) their marriage. Only if the spouses truly unite biologically, and only if this biological union is an aspect of a total personal communion, does their sexual act aim at a genuine, common good. And the sexual act can be an aspect of the total personal communion—that is, actualize or make present their personal communion—only if the personal communion is of the sort that is naturally prolonged and fulfilled in procreation, and the sexual act is a reproductive-type act making them truly two-in-one-flesh. And so, only in marriage can sexual acts realize a common good rather than induce self-alienation or an illusory experience.

ANNOTATED BIBLIOGRAPHY

A Select Listing of Works Illustrative of Natural Law Themes in this Issue

AUSTIN, John and H.L.A. Hart, *The Province of Jurisprudence Determined and The Uses of the Study of Jurisprudence* (Hackett: Indianapolis, 1998)

[This edition comprises the full text of *The Province of Jurisprudence Determined*, a classic work of moral, political, and legal philosophy, including the chapter on Utilitarianism and the detailed discussion of social contract theory, which have been excluded from previous editions. Also included is the essay "The Uses of the Study of Jurisprudence," which gives an important assessment of Austin's conception of analytical jurisprudence.] (Publisher's'abstract)

BAUR, Michael, "Natural Law and the Legislation of Virtue: Historicity, Positivity, and Circularity," *Vera Lex*. Vol. 2(1-2), 51-70 (2001)

[For Aquinas, the passage from the natural law as such to the legislation of specific acts of virtue is not immediate and direct, but must be mediated by premises derived from a people's concrete historical situation. Failure to understand this mediation is likely to lead to misunderstandings about the relation between natural law and human self-determination in history. In this paper, I argue that Aquinas's natural law theory is open to historicity and positivity, yet without being historicist or positivist. I conclude with some observations about the fundamental, nonvicious circularity that characterizes all reasoning about natural law and morality.]

——, "Reversing Rawls: Criteriology, Contractualism and the Primacy of the Practical," *Philosophy and Social Criticism*. Vol. 28(3), 251-296 (2002)

[In this paper, I offer an immanent critique of John Rawls's theory of justice which seeks to show that Rawls's understanding of his theory of justice as criteriological and contractarian is ultimately incompatible with his claim that the theory is grounded on the primacy of the practical. I agree with Michael Sandel's observation that the Rawlsian theory of justice rests on substantive metaphysical and epistemological claims, in spite of Rawls's assurances to the contrary.] (Edited.)

BIX, Brian, *Jurisprudence: Theory and Context* (Carolina Academic Press, 2004)

[*Jurisprudence: Theory and Context* is aimed at students new to the study of legal philosophy. At the same time, it offers new ideas and perspectives that will be of interest to established scholars. The first part of the book offers a brief overview of the role and method of legal philosophy. The second part introduces important individual theorists of the nature of law—H.L.A. Hart, Ronald Dworkin, Lon Fuller, John Finnis, and Hans Kelsen—while also discussing the schools of thought (e.g., legal positivism and natural law theory) they represent. Common and recurrent themes are discussed in the third part: from broad-ranging topics such as justice, punishment, and statutory interpretation, to the questions raised about the intersection of law and morality, to analytical questions regarding rights. This section also includes a novel analysis of how many legal theories can be better understood by considering their relative dependence on either "will" or "reason." The fourth section introduces the modern, critical approaches that have dominated recent jurisprudential writing: legal realism, law and economics, critical legal studies, feminism, critical race theory, law and literature, pragmatism, and postmodernism. The second edition includes many new topics (including Justice, Punishment, Common Law Reasoning and Precedent, Law and Literature, Pragmatism and Postmodernism, Game Theory, and Public Choice Theory) as well as updated and expanded material from the first edition.] (Publisher's review)

BLOCK, Walter, Reply to Frank van Dun's "Natural Law and the Jurisprudence of Freedom," *Journal of Libertarian Studies*. Vol. 18(2), 65-72 (Spring 2004)

Keywords: freedom; natural law; political philosophy; punishment.

BOYD, Craig A. and Raymond J. Van Arragon, "Is Morality Based on God's Commands?: Ethics Is Based on Natural Law," in *Contemporary Debates in Philosophy of Religion*, Michael L. Peterson (ed.) (Malden, MA: Blackwell Publishing), 299–310 (2004)

[This set of essays considers two major theistic views on the relation between God and morality. The first view, endorsed by Janine Marie Idziak, is known as the "divine command theory." It answers the above question affirmatively: an act is morally right because God commands it and morally wrong because God forbids it. Craig Boyd and Raymond Van Arragon defend a view known as the "natural law theory." It answers the question negatively: human nature determines what is right or wrong so that, roughly, an act is morally right because it helps to fulfill human nature and morally wrong because it prevents this fulfillment. Idziak, Boyd and Van Arragon draw out their theories and define them against popular objections.]

——, "Was Thomas Aquinas a Sociobiologist? Thomistic Natural Law, Rational Goods, and Sociobiology," *Zygon*, Vol. 39(3), 659-680 (2004)

[Traditional Darwinian theory presents two difficulties for Thomistic natural-law morality: relativism and essentialism. The sociobiology of E. O. Wilson seems to refute the idea of evolutionary relativism. Larry Arnhart has argued that Wilson's views on sociobiology can provide a scientific framework for Thomistic natural-law theory. However, in his attempt to reconcile Aquinas's views with Wilson's sociobiology, Arnhart fails to address a critical feature of Aquinas's ethics: the role of rational goods in natural law. I believe that Aquinas's natural-law morality is consistent with some accounts of sociobiology but not the more ontologically reductionist versions like the one presented by Wilson and defended by Arnhart. Moreover, Aquinas's normative account of rationality is successful in refuting the challenges of evolutionary relativism as well as the reductionism found in most sociobiological approaches to ethics.] (Author's abstract)

BOYLE, Joseph, "Fairness in Holdings: A Natural Law Account of Property and Welfare Rights," *Social Philosophy and Policy*. Vol. 18(1), 206-226 (Winter 2001)

Keywords: fairness; natural law; property; rights; social philosophy; welfare.

——, "Medical Ethics and Double Effect: The Case of Terminal Sedation," *Theoretical Medicine and Bioethics: Philosophy of Medical Research and Practice*, Vol. 25(1), 51-60 (2004)

[This paper explains how the doctrine of double effect can be relied on to distinguish terminal sedation from euthanasia. The doctrine of double effect is rooted in Catholic moral casuistry, but its application in law and morality need not depend on the particular framework in which it was developed. The paper further explains how the moral weight of the distinction between intended harms and merely foreseen harms in the doctrine of double effect can be justified by appeal to a limitation on the human capacity to pursue good.] (Edited.)

——, "Just War Doctrine and the Military Response to Terrorism," *Journal of Political Philosophy*, Vol. 11(2), 153-170 (June 2003)

Keywords: ethics; just war; military; political philosophy.

——, "Toward Understanding the Principle of Double Effect," *Ethics* Vol. 90, 527-538 (July 1980)

[The purpose of this paper is to articulate the principle of Double Effect, to explain its function, and to state the propositions about morality, intention and action which are permissible to voluntarily bring about a state of affairs that one does not intend if there is a serious reason to do so, even if it would be wrong to act with the intention of bringing about that state of affairs. States of affairs that are one's means or ends, are intended but causal consequences of these states of affairs need not be.]

——, "On Killing and Letting Die," *New Scholasticism* Vol. 51, 433-452 (Fall 1977)

[In this paper, I defend the moral significance of the distinction between killing and letting die. I argue that killing in euthanasia and other similar cases is always direct killing of the innocent which necessarily involves the intention of the person's death. Letting die, by contrast, need not involve such an intention. I show that the arguments which impugn the moral significance of the killing/letting die distinction systematically overlook this intentional difference. Finally, I state certain important suppositions of an ethics according to which intentional differences are normatively central, and suggest that these suppositions are what must be shown false if the killing/letting die distinction is to be shown to be morally useless.] (Author's abstract)

——, "Aquinas and Prescriptive Ethics," *Proceedings of the American Catholic Philosophical Association* Vol. 49, 82-95 (1975)

[In this paper I will attempt to situate Aquinas' ethical theory within the context of one contemporary discussion in meta-ethics. It will relate Aquinas' views on the meaning of "good" and "practical reason" to the current discussion of R. M. Hare's prescriptivism. The effort to situate Aquinas in the prescriptivist/descriptivist controversy has three parts. The first describes Hare's account of evaluative language, especially the word "good." The second states the extent to which Aquinas would agree and disagree with Hare's account. The third concludes that Aquinas' position is not vulnerable to the criticisms which Hare levies against his descriptivist critics.] (Author's abstract)

——, "The Absolute Prohibition of Lying and the Origins of the Casuistry of Mental Reservation: Augustinian Arguments and Thomistic Developments," *American Journal of Jurisprudence.* Vol. 44, 43-65 (1999)

Keywords: casuistry; ethics; law; lying.

———, "Intentions, Christian Morality, and Bioethics: Puzzles of Double Effect," *Christian Bioethics: Non-Ecumenical Studies is Medical Ethics.* Vol. 3(2), 87-88 (August 1997)

[This is an introduction to the number of *Christian Bioethics* in which it appears. It provides some background on double effect and indicates that the precise focus of the papers is the justification of the moral significance of the difference between intention and the acceptance of side effects.]

———, "Who is Entitled to Double Effect?" *Journal of Medicine and Philosophy.* 475-494 (October 1991)

[The doctrine of double effect continues to be an important tool in bioethical casuistry. Its role within the Catholic moral tradition continues, and there is considerable interest in it by contemporary moral philosophers. But problems of justification and correct application remain. I argue that if the traditional Catholic conviction that there are exceptionless norms prohibiting inflicting some kinds of harms on people is correct, then double effect is justified and necessary. The objection that double effect is superfluous is a rejection of that normative conviction, not a refutation of double effect itself. This justification suggests the correct way of applying double effect to controversial cases. But versions of double effect which dispense with the absolutism of the Catholic tradition lack justification and fall to the objection that double effect is an unnecessary complication.]

———, "Natural Law, Ownership and the World's Natural Resources," *Journal of Value Inquiry.* Vol. 23, 191-207 (September 1989)

Keywords: axiology; natural law; natural resources; ownership.

BOYLE, Joseph and Grisez, Germain, *Life and Death with Liberty and Justice: A Contribution to the Euthanasia Debate.* (University of Notre Dame Press: Notre Dame, 1979)

[This book examines issues usually grouped under the headings "Euthanasia" and "Mercy Killing," including definition of death, right to refuse treatment, suicide, voluntary and nonvoluntary euthanasia, and treatment of the legally noncompetent. These issues are considered from both jurisprudential and ethical viewpoints; the former based on liberty and justice, the latter on sanctity of life. The method is philosophical, but critical of consequentialism often assumed to be the only alternative to traditional approaches. Others' legal and ethical works on killing are critically examined; detailed proposals for legislation and medial-ethical norms are offered. Extensive bibliographies are included.]

BOYLE, Joseph (ed.), Sumner, L. W. (ed.), *Philosophical Perspectives on Bioethics*. (University of Toronto Press; Toronto, 1996)

[How should we attempt to resolve concrete bioethical problems? How are we to understand the role of bioethics in the health care system, government, and academe? This collection of original essays raises these and other questions about the nature of bioethics as a discipline. The contributors to the volume discuss various approaches to bioethical thinking and the political and institutional context of bioethics, addressing underlying concerns about the purposes of its practice. Included are extended analyses of such important issues as the conduct of clinical trials, euthanasia, justice in health care, the care of children, cosmetic surgery, and reproductive technologies.]

BRADLEY, Denis J. M., "Reason and the Natural Law: Flannery's Reconstruction of Aquinas's Moral Theory," *Thomist: A Speculative Quarterly Review*. Vol. 67(1), 119-131 (January 2003)

Keywords: ethics; moral theory; natural law; reason.

BROCK, Stephen L., *Action and Conduct: Thomas Aquinas and the Theory of Action*. (T and T Clark: Edinburgh, 1998) Reviewers: Cantu Fletes, Guadalupe. *Topicos.* Vol. 15, 213-216 (1998)

——, "The '*Ratio Omnipotentia*' in Aquinas," *Acta Philosophica*. Vol. 1 (2), 17-42 (1993)

[E una costante della tradizione ebraico- cristiana, affermare che Dio sia onnipotente. Ma come va intesa l'"onnipotenza"? San Tommaso dice che essa significa potere ogni cosa possibile, e cioe ogni cosa che non contraddica se stessa. A questa posizione si oppongono diverse obiezioni, ad alcune delle qualipare di poter rispondere piu facilmente dicendo che l'onnipotenza di Dio dia il suo poter tutto cio che non e una contraddizione "per Lui". Questa risposta, pero, e debole; inoltre, il sostegno che trova in Tommaso non e che apparente. Una soluzione piu soddisfacente si scopre alla luce di una restrizione fondamentale all'interno del concetto di "potere" da lui ammesso nel discorso su Dio. (Edited.)]

———, "St Thomas and the Eucharistic Conversion," *Thomist: A Speculative Quarterly Review.* Vol. 65(4), 529-565 (October 2001)

[Aquinas describes transubstantiation as a "conversion" of one substance into another. Yet he denies any common substrate underlying the succession of substances. Germain Grisez finds this unintelligible. The article's thesis is that Aquinas saw and resolved the basic issue contained in Grisez's objection. The key text stresses a "nature of being" common to the two substances. This nature, it is argued, is univocal. As such it constitutes a continuous object of signification that is both necessary and sufficient for the sacramental action of the words of the consecration. That action can only be understood as a supernatural kind of conversion.]

BRUGGER, Christian, "Catholic Moral Teaching and the Problem of Capital Punishment," *Thomist: A Speculative Quarterly Review.* Vol. 68910, 41-67 (January 2004)

[The purpose of the essay is to provide an interpretation of the death penalty teaching of the present Magisterium of the Catholic Church, expressed in particular in the death penalty teaching of the Catechism of the Catholic Church (1997). The essay concludes that the Catechism text, while not explicitly stating that the death penalty is in itself wrong, lays down premises which when carried to their logical conclusions, yield just such a conclusion. After criticizing common objections to this conclusion, it asks: may the church, constrained by her own doctrinal tradition, legitimately teach in a definitive way that capital punishment is per se wrong?]

BUCHANAN, Allen (ed.); Moore,-Margaret (ed.), *States, Nations, and Borders: The Ethics of Making Boundaries* (Cambridge University Press: Cambridge, 2003)

[This anthology compares the views and principles of seven prominent ethical traditions on one of the most pressing issues of modern politics—the making and unmaking of state and national boundaries. The traditions represented are Judaism, Christianity, Islam, natural law, Confucianism, liberalism and international law. The contributors, each an expert in one of these traditions, show how that tradition addresses the five dominant methods of altering state and national boundaries—conquest, settlement, purchase, inheritance, and secession. (publisher, Edited.)]

CANAVAN, Francis, "Natural Law and Judicial Review," *Public Affairs Quarterly.* Vol. 7(4), 277-286 (October 1993)

[Judicial review in the United States is the power of courts to declare acts of the other branches of government void when they conflict with the constitution. The question addressed here is not whether there is a natural law that binds governments, but whether judges are empowered to enforce it through judicial review. The answer is that they are not. The constitution includes certain natural law principles in its text, but it is itself a positive law, and the power of judges does reach beyond enforcing what is clearly in its text.]

CHAPMAN, Robert L., Review of *A Critique of the New Natural Law Theory*, Russell Hittinger (Notre Dame: Notre Dame University Press, 1987) in *Vera Lex,* Vol. XV 1995 (issued 1999), 87 – 88.

CHARLES, Daryl J., "Returning to Moral 'First Things': The Natural Law Tradition and Its Contemporary Application," *Philosophia Christi.* Series 2: Vol. 6(1), 59-76 (2004)

Keywords: christianity; ethics; natural law; personhood.

CLEARY, Denis, "Person, Natural Law, Autonomy," *Vera Lex* Vol. 15(1-2), 20-23, (1995)

[The paper examines the foundation of the sense of personal worth present in the individual, and finds it dependent upon the enlightenment springing naturally from the intelligibility of being. This enlightenment enables thought and reason, and presents people with the opportunity of acknowledging willingly what they know for what they know it to be. Such acknowledgement consolidates the ontological dignity of persons to which it adds moral dignity. The consequences for personal autonomy are twofold: ontological freedom from coercion in the choice of what is known; moral freedom to take possession of what does not already belong to another.]

COVELL, Charles, *The defence of natural law: A study of the ideas of law and justice in the writings of Lon L. Fuller, Michael Oakeshot, F.A. Hayek, Ronald Dworkin, and John Finnis* (Unknown Binding) (St. Martin's Press, 1992)

CREMASCHI, Sergio, "Two Views of Natural Law and the Shaping of Economic Science," *Croatian Journal of Philosophy*. Vol. 2(5), 181-196, (2002)

[Scottish natural jurisprudence, which tried to find a middle way between skepticism and extreme voluntarism, is less secular and more empirical than received wisdom admits. There emerged, as one of its 'accidental' outcomes, a systematic, self-contained and empirical economic theory from the search for an empirically based normative theory of social life. The basic assumption of such a theory, namely, the notion of societal laws as embedded in transindividual mechanisms, derives from the voluntarist view of natural law as 'imposed' law.] (Edited.)

DAVENPORT, John J., "A Critical Review of Natural Law and Practical Rationality," *International Philosophical Quarterly*. Vol. 43(2), 229-239 (January 2003)

[This essay argues that Mark C. Murphy's original contribution to natural law ethics succeeds in finding a way between older metaphysical and newer purely practical approaches in this genre. Murphy's reconstruction of the function argument, critique of subjectivist theories of well-being, and rigorous formulation of a flexible welfarist theory of value deserve careful attention. I defend Kant against Murphy's critique and argue that Murphy faces the problem of showing that all his basic goods are morally inviolable. Although I endorse Murphy's critique of radical virtue ethics, I raise objections to the basic moral norms he derives from his list of goods, and to the analysis of peace of mind and happiness as basic goods.]

DEN UYL, Douglas J; Rasmussen, Douglas B., "Ethical Individualism, Natural Law, and the Primacy of Natural Rights," *Social Philosophy and Policy*. Vol. 18(1), 34-69 (Winter 2001)

Keywords: ethics; individualism; natural law; natural right; social philosophy.

DEWAN, Lawrence, "Jean Porter on Natural Law: Thomistic Notes," *Thomist: A Speculative Quarterly*. Vol. 66(2), 275-309, Review (April 2002)

[Porter's book, *Natural and Divine Law*, re-examines medieval natural law theory, stressing its theological context. My paper questions the adequacy of her presentation, particularly as regards Thomas Aquinas's conception of natural law. Issues discussed include the self-evidence of natural law principles, the knowability of natural law independently of divine revelation, and her presentation of Nietzsche's views as an "alternative" ethics. Her aim to dialogue with the medievals while transforming their idea of natural law I contend actually abandons entirely what the medievals meant.]

DOLAN, Joseph V., "Relocating Justice", in *The Value of Justice: essays on the theory and practice of social virtue*, Charles Kelbley (ed.) 79-101 (New York: Fordham University Press, 1979)

DWORKIN, Ronald, *Sovereign Virtue: The Theory and Practice of Equality* (Harvard University Press: Cambridge, MA, 2002)

———, *Freedom's Law: The Moral Reading of the American Constitution* (Harvard University Press: Cambridge, MA, 1997)

[Integrity in law, says Dworkin, law professor at Oxford and NYU, must first "be a matter of principle, not compromise or strategy or political accommodation." But while Americans are increasingly hungry for political and personal morality, moral principal in interpreting the Constitution is still unfashionable. Witness Supreme Court nominees like Robert Bork and Clarence Thomas, who claimed either the seemingly neutral "original intent" reading (in Bork's case) or no constitutional philosophy at all (in Thomas's). In five chapters on those two justices, Dworkin makes a persuasive argument that these are nonetheless moral and political positions. But most of the 17 chapters (all but three of which originally appeared in the *New York Review of Books*) center on issues like abortion, affirmative action and freedom of speech. What's interesting here is to see the application of Dworkin's moral reading throughout, which in unavoidably simplistic terms is this: true democracy is not crude majoritarianism but rather a "constitutional conception" in which "collective decisions [are] made by political institutions whose structure, composition, and practices treat all members of the community, as individuals, with equal concern and respect," and that to safeguard this democracy it is necessary to protect "negative" liberties like free speech and privacy even if it curtails "positive" liberties like the ability to control or participate in public decision making. This rejection of the framers' intent and of majoritarian rule continues themes Dworkin addressed in *Life's Dominion and Taking Rights Seriously*. But this book stands on its own either as a continuation or an introduction. Complex and compelling, learned and readable, it goes to the heart of what it means to live in a democracy and, through concrete details, illuminates a very real, very admirable principle.]

(*Publisher's Weekly*, refers to hardcover edition)

———, *Life's Dominion: An Argument About Abortion, Euthanasia, and Individual Freedom* (Vintage Press, 1994)

[Today's debate over the proper place of abortion in an ethically committed society has proven every bit as divisive as was slavery in 19th-century America. Dworkin, an eminent lawyer and legal philosopher, believes that a new way of examining the central issue is now required. He argues that the key question to be resolved is how far society can go to impose a single official view upon personally held convictions of the inherent value of all life. Dworkin's analysis requires that the abstract moral principles set out in the U.S. Constitution be interpreted to insure equal concern for the dignity of all human life, and he analyzes other issues, such as euthanasia, in the same framework. Continuing the examination of moral issues raised earlier in Dworkin's *A Matter of Principle* (Harvard Univ. Pr., 1985), his new book can be favorably compared with other recent works about abortion such as Lawrence Tribe's *Abortion : A Clash of Absolutes* (LJ 2/1/91) or Roger Rosenblatt's *Life Itself* (LJ 3/15/92). While a difficult book, it is also an important one that should be read by as many concerned readers as possible. Highly recommended.] (Jerry E. Stephens, U.S. Court of Appeals Lib., Oklahoma City. Copyright 1993 Reed Business Information, Inc.—This text refers to the hardcover edition)

——, *Law's Empire* (Belknap Press: Cambridge, MA, 1988)
[In this first full-length exposition of his theory of law, Dworkin, who teaches jurisprudence at Oxford University and New York University, maintains that society should ensure for all its members a legal system that functions in a coherent and principled manner. In prose accessible to the lay reader, he discusses at length several views of American constitutional law such as "passivism" and "framers' intention." Rejecting both conventionalism and pragmatism, he advocates law as integrity which holds that propositions of law are true if they derive from justice, fairness and procedural due process in accordance with the community's legal practice. Citing examples, he further argues that law should be more than a collection of formal guidelines and that it should uphold more abstract moral principles, distinguishing between issues of policy and matters of principle affecting rights of the individual. Uniting jurisprudence with adjudication, Dworkin sees each judge as a link in a chain of law of which his or

her judgment becomes a part.] (Publishers' review, refers to the hard-cover edition)

——, *Taking Rights Seriously* (Harvard University Press: Cambridge, MA, 1977/reissued 2005)

FINNIS, John, *Aquinas: Moral, Political and Legal Theory* (Oxford University Press: Oxford, 1998)

——, *Moral Absolutes: Tradition, Revision and Truth* (Catholic University of American Press: Washington D.C., 1991)

——, (Ed.) *Natural Law* volumes 1 & 2 (New York University Press: New York, 1991)

——, *Fundamentals of Ethics* (Georgetown University Press: Washington D.C., 1983)

——, *Natural Law and Natural Rights* (Oxford University Press: Oxford, 1980)

——, "Natural Law and the Re-Making of Boundaries" in *States, Nations, and Borders: The Ethics of Making Boundaries,* Buchanan, Allen (ed.) 171-178 (Cambridge University Press: Cambridge, 2003) Keywords: boundary; natural law.

——, "Nature and Natural Law in Contemporary Philosophical and Theological Debates: Some Observations," in *The Nature and Dignity of the Human Person as the Foundation of the Right to Life: the Challenges of the Contemporary Cultural Context*, edited by Juan de Dios Vial Correa and Elio Sgreccia (Libreria Editrice Vaticana, 2003)

——, "Law and What I Truly Should Decide," *American Journal of Jurisprudence*. Vol. 48, 107-129 (2003)

Keywords: concept; decision; law; natural law; political philosophy; subject.

——, and Patrick Martin, "Caesar, Succession, and the Chastisement of Rulers" (2003) 78 *Notre Dame Law Review* 101-129

——, "Natural Law: the Classical Tradition," in Jules L. Coleman and Scott Shapiro (eds), *The Oxford Handbook of Jurisprudence and Philosophy of Law* (Oxford: Oxford University Press, 2002), 1-60

——, "Natural Law and the Ethics of Discourse," *Ratio Juris*: *An International Journal of Jurisprudence and Philosophy of Law*. Vol. 12(4), 354-373 (1999)

[This essay argues that Plato's critical analysis of the ethics of discourse is superior to Habermas's, and more generally that Habermas has no sufficient reason to propose or suppose the philosophical superiority of "modernity." The failure of Hume and Kant and much modern philosophy to understand the concept and content of reasons for action underlies Habermas's attempted distinction between ethics and morality, and Rawls's concept of public reason. A proper study of discourse also yields a metaphysics of the person and, thus, reinforces the ethics.]

——, and Anthony Fisher, O.P "Theology and the Four Principles of Bioethics: A Roman Catholic View,".in Raanan Gillon (ed.), *Principles of Health Care Ethics* (Chichester: John Wiley & Sons, 1993), 31-44.

[Morality identifies the basic reasons for human choices, and articulates principles for making those choices compatible with openness to integral human fulfillment. Many ethical approaches and many sorts of choices are incompatible with this. Faith guided by church teaching offers further and surer education for conscience, and deeper understanding of the healthcare worker's vocation. The 'four principles' have their grounding and proper meaning only within such a fully developed ethic. Beneficence requires the promotion of the life and good health of patients; non-maleficence forbids harming them, or compromising any instance of a basic human good in deceptive moral calculations and quality of life judgments. Autonomy directs respect for human dignity and responsibility; it does not justify individualism independent of God and community, or exterminative medicine. Justice and mercy enjoin solidarity, subsidiarity, fair resource allocation, and special care for the poor and helpless. This Catholic approach is shown to have implications for abortion, IVF, sterilization, euthanasia, withdrawal of treatment, and honesty in medical communication.] (Abstract)

——, "Natural Law and Legal Reasoning," in *Natural Law Theory: Contemporary Essays* ed. Robert George (Clarendon Press: Oxford, 1992)

——, "Intention and Side-Effects," in *Liability and Responsibility: Essays in Law and Morals* eds. R. Frey and C. Morris (Cambridge University Press: Cambridge, 1991)

——, "Allocating Risks and Suffering: Some Hidden Traps," *Cleveland State Law Review* (1990)

——, "Legal Enforcement of 'Duties to Oneself', Kant v. Neo-Kantians," *Columbia Law Review* (1987)

——, "On Positivism and Legal Rational Authority," *Oxford Journal of Legal Studies* (1985)

——, "The Authority of Law in the Predicament of Contemporary Social Theory," *Notre Dame Journal of Law, Ethics and Public Policy* (1984)

——, "Helping Enact Unjust Laws Without Complicity in Injustice," *American Journal of Jurisprudence* 49 11-42

FLANNERY, Kevin L., "Applying Aristotle in Contemporary Embryology," *Thomist: A Speculative Quarterly Review*. Vol. 67(2), 249-278 (April 2003)

[This article takes issue with Enrico Berti's argument that according to Aristotle human life begins at conception, proposing an alternative reading of the relevant texts, especially those contained in *Generation of Animals*. The article nonetheless makes use of ideas put forward by Berti and by Aristotle himself in order to argue that, had Aristotle known what we know today about the embryo, he would have said that life begins at conception.]

——, *Acts Amid Precepts: The Aristotelian Logical Structure of Thomas Aquinas's Moral Theory*. (Catholic University American Press: Washington D.C., 2001)

[Although most natural law ethical theories recognize moral absolutes, there is not much agreement even among natural law theorists about how to identify them. Kevin L. Flannery argues that in order to understand and determine the morality (or immorality) of a human action, it must be considered in relation to the organized system of human practices within which it is performed. Such an approach, he argues, is to be found in the natural law theory of Thomas Aquinas, especially once it is recognized that the logical structure of Aquinas's ethical theory is basically that of an Aristotelian science.] (Publishers review)

——, "Homosexuality and Types of Dualism: A Platonico-Aristotelian Approach," *Gregorianum*. Vol. 81(2), 353-372 (2000)

[L'auteur accepte la position d'auteurs comme Germain Grisez et John Finnis selon laquelle l'immoralite de l'homosexualite est connectee en quelque maniere au dualisme esprit-corps de la recherche du plaisir. Il s'efforce pourtant, par une analyse de ce que Platon et Aristote disent au sujet du plaisir dans le Philebus et l'Ethique de

Nicomaque, de decrire le genre—ou, plutot, les genres—de dualisme dont il s'agit. Le resultat, il pense, est une analyse qui evite la position insoutenable selon laquelle le plaisir n'est en aucune maniere a etre poursuivi pour lui-meme.]

———, "Practical Reason and Concrete Acts" in *Natural Law and Moral Inquiry.* Robert George (ed.), 107-134 (Georgetown University Press: Washington D.C., 1998)

[In "Metaphysics IV", Aristotle performs an "elenchic" demonstration of the first principle of theoretical reason, the principle of noncontradiction. Both Aristotle and Thomas Aquinas recognize, besides theoretical reason, the sphere of practical reason and Aquinas explicitly recognizes a first principle in practical reason. This article offers, therefore, an elenchic demonstration of this principle (i.e., that "good is to be done and pursued and evil avoided"). The upshot of the article is that, as in the theoretical sphere, concrete significations are an essential part of the demonstration itself and, therefore, an essential part of practical reason.]

———, "The Aristotelian First Principle of Practical Reason," *Thomist: A Speculative Quarterly Review.* Vol. 59(3), 441-464 (July 1995)

[The article seeks to demonstrate that the Thomistic first principle of practical reason, "good is to be done and pursued, and evil is to be avoided," understood as the analogue in the practical sphere of the principle of noncontradiction, is present also in Aristotle's ethical writings. To this end, it offers an exegesis of especially *Nicomachean Ethics* v, 9, 1136a10-b14. It examines also other texts (e.g., *Eudemian Ethics* vii, 6 1240b21-28) which discuss the way in which the soul of the person subject to weakness of will (*akrasia*) might be analyzed.]

———, "A rationale for Aristotle's Notion of Perfect Syllogisms," *Notre Dame Journal of Formal Logic.* Vol. 28, 455-471 (July 1987)

Keywords: logic; perfection; syllogism.

FORTE, David F. (ed.), *Natural Law and Contemporary Public Policy*. (Georgetown University Press: Washington D.C., 1998)

[Prominent thinkers in the natural law tradition apply the principles of natural law to contemporary political and social problems in this volume, the first to explore the practical uses of this philosophy. Contributors demonstrate how natural law can be used to resolve a wide range of complex social, political, and constitutional issues by addressing controversial subjects that include the family, taxation, war, racial discrimination, medical technology, and sexuality. Revealing the wide impact of the natural law revival, this volume brings together authors from across the political spectrum. It also includes a critique of the natural law position by a respected commentator.] (Publisher's review)

FOSTER, John. *The Divine Lawmaker: Lectures on Induction, Laws of Nature, and the Existence of God* (Clarendon Press: Oxford, 2004)

[John Foster presents a clear and powerful discussion of a range of topics relating to our understanding of the universe: induction, laws of nature, and the existence of God. He begins by developing a solution to the problem of induction—a solution whose key idea is that the regularities in the workings of nature that have held in our experience hitherto are to be explained by appeal to the controlling influence of laws, as forms of natural necessity. His second line of argument focuses on the issue of what we should take such necessitational laws to be, and whether we can even make sense of them at all. With this causal account of laws in place, he is now equipped to offer an argument for theism. His claim is that natural regularities call for explanation, and that, whatever explanatory role we may initially assign to laws, the only plausible ultimate explanation is in terms of the agency of God. Finally, he argues that, once we accept the existence of God, we need to think of him as creating the universe by a method which imposes regularities on it in the relevant law-yielding way.]

FOSTER, Susanne, "Unnatural Foods and the Natural Law," *Philosophical Inquiry: International Quarterly*. Vol. 26(3), 41-49 (Summer 2004)

[The purpose of the article is to explore the methods whereby natural law classifies activities as natural or unnatural. By applying the distinction to a new class of actions, the article considers whether the distinction can be reduced to absurdity or whether it is helpful in revealing a vice inherent in a consumer-based society.]

FULLER, Lon, L., *The Morality of Law,* Revised Edition (The Storrs Lectures Series) (Yale University Press: New Haven, 1965)

GAHL, Jr. Robert A., "From the Virtue of a Fragile Good to a Narrative Account of Natural Law," *International Philosophical Quarterly.*Vol. 37(4), 457-472 (December 1997)

[After describing claims against the compatibility of virtue and natural law theories, I draw from Pamela Hall's *Narrative and Natural Law* to argue for a reading of Aquinas capable of reconciling virtues and natural law. Martha Nussbaum's insightful virtue-theory fails to explain moral experience insofar as it emphasizes the tragic character of life. The narrative moral epistemology embedded in Aquinas's thought shows the interdependency of law and virtues. A narrative account of natural law can be used to overcome tragic complexity and to tell a rationally defensible, comic story about the moral agent's ecstatic quest for the transcendent.]

GAUTHIER, David, "Hobbes: The Laws of Nature," *Pacific Philosophical Quarterly.* Vol. 82(3-4), 258-284 (September 2001)

[Are Hobbes's laws of nature to be understood primarily as theorems of reason, or as commands of God, or as commands of the civil sovereign? Each of these accounts can be given textual support; each identifies a role that the laws may be thought to play. Examining the full range of textual references, discussing the place of the laws of nature in Hobbes's argument, and considering how the laws may be known, give strongest support to the first of the three accounts, that the laws are primarily rational precepts and only secondarily civil and divine commands.]

GEORGE, Robert P., "Human Cloning and Embryo Research," The 2003 John J. Conley Lecture on Medical Ethics," *Theoretical Medicine and Bioethics.* Vol. 25(1), 3-20 (2004)

[The author, a member of the U.S. President's Council on Bioethics, discusses ethical issues raised by human cloning, whether for purposes of bringing babies to birth or for research purposes. He first argues that every cloned human embryo is a new, distinct, and enduring organism, belonging to the species Homo sapiens, and directing its own development toward maturity. He then distinguishes between two types of capacities belonging to individual organisms belonging to this species, an immediately exercisable capacity and a basic natural capacity that develops over time. He argues that it is the second type of capacity that is the ground for full moral respect, and that this capacity (and its concomitant degree of respect) belongs to cloned human embryos no less than to adult human beings.]

———, "Holmes on Natural Law" in *Nature in American Philosophy* (Studies in Philosophy and the History of Philosophy, Vol. 42), Jean De Groot (ed.) 127 –137 (Catholic University Press Washington D.C., 2004)

———, *Clash Of Orthodoxies: Law, Religion & Morality In Crisis* (ISI Books: Wilmington: DE, 2001)

———, *In Defense of Natural Law* (Georgetown University Press: Washington D.C., 2001)

In *Making Men Moral*, his 1995 book, George questioned the central doctrines of liberal jurisprudence and political theory. In his new work he extends his critique of liberalism, and also goes beyond it to show how contemporary natural law theory provides a superior way of thinking about basic problems of justice and political morality. Students as well as scholars in law, political science, and philosophy will find George's arguments stimulating, challenging, and compelling.] *This text refers to the hardcover version* (Editor's review)

——, and Christopher Wolfe (Ed.) *Natural Law and Public Reason* (Georgetown University Press, Washington, D.C. 2000)

——, "The Concept of Public Morality," *American Journal of Jurisprudence.* Vol. 45, 17-31 (2000)
Keywords: common good; environment; ethics; morality; public.

——, (ed.) *The Anatomy of Law: Essays on Legal Positivism* (Oxford University Press: Oxford, 1999)

——, (ed.) *Natural Law and Moral Inquiry: Ethics, Metaphysics, and Politics in the Work of Germain Grisez.* (Georgetown University Press: Washington D.C., 1998)

——, (ed.) *Natural Law Theory: Contemporary Essays* (Oxford University Press: Oxford 1994)
[Natural law theory is enjoying a revival of interest in a variety of scholarly disciplines including law, philosophy, political science, and theology and religious studies. This volume presents twelve original essays by leading natural law theorists and their critics. The contributors discuss natural law theories of morality, law and legal reasoning, politics, and the rule of law. Readers get a clear sense of the wide diversity of viewpoints represented among contemporary theorists, and an opportunity to evaluate the arguments and counterarguments exchanged in the current debates between natural law theorists and their critics. Contributors include Hadley Arkes, Joseph M. Boyle, Jr., John Finnis, Robert P. George, Russell Hittinger, Neil MacCormick, Michael Moore, Jeffrey Stout, Joseph Raz, Jeremy Waldron, Lloyd Weinreb, and Ernest Weinrib.] (Publisher's review)

——, "Liberty Under the Moral Law: On B. Hoose's Critique of the Grisez-Finnis Theory of Human Good," *Heythrop Journal.* Vol. 34(2), 175-182 (April 1993)

Keywords: catholicism; freedom; good; human; liberty; moral; religion.

———, "Moral Particularism, Thomism, and Traditions," *Review of Metaphysics.* Vol 42, 593-605 (March 1989)

[The author criticizes Alasdair MacIntyre's claim that there can be no tradition-independent standards of practical rationality, and argues that MacIntyre's position is, in any event, inconsistent with the Thomistic tradition to which MacIntyre now proclaims allegiance. He argues that MacIntyre's strong moral particularism cannot escape a decisive (and decidedly un-Thomistic) relativism. Still, he gives MacIntyre credit for a devastating critique of those forms of (antiperfectionist) liberalism which treat wants as reasons for action. He points out, however, that MacIntyre's critique does not tell against perfectionist liberal political theories like the one recently set forth and defended by Joseph Raz.]

———, "Individual Rights, Collective Interests, Public Law, and American Politics," *Law and Philosophy.* Vol. 8(2), 245-261 (August 1989)

[This article criticizes an influential liberal conception of individual rights and collective interests and proposes, as an alternative, a conception drawn from the tradition of natural law theory. It also criticizes Ronald Dworkin's attempt to derive a right to pornography from a general right to be treated by one's government with equal concern and respect.]

GODART Van der Kroon, Annette, "Schopenhauer's Theory of Justice and Its Implication to Natural Law," *Schopenhauer Jahrbuch.* Vol. 84, 121-145 (2003)

[In this article arguments will be given to demonstrate the weakness of Schopenhauer's position towards natural law. The aim was to show that Schopenhauer thought that he was a classical natural law thinker, but in fact was not. The elements of his natural law theory differ from those of the classical natural law theory: (1) eternal, unchangeable law: Schopenhauer does not accept abstract right in a constitution; (2)

reason: Schopenhauer demoted reason from its predominance in human life and placed will in its stead; (3) freedom: If natural law concerns subjects of individual will and those subjects are determined and they possess natural rights all the same, then natural law is compatible with determinism. When Schopenhauer's determinism does not contradict natural law that would be a new kind of natural law position.]

GOGGANS, P., "Ethical Individualism and the Natural Law," *Ratio: An International Journal of Analytic Philosophy*. Vol. 13(1), 28-36 (March 2000)

["Generic qualities" are qualities typical of a kind because of the nature of that kind. It is commonly thought that generic qualities are morally irrelevant. I argue that generic qualities are relevant in certain instances. First, we need to believe that this is so in order to be morally competent. Second, there is no other way to account for the rationality of the universal response to *Oedipus the King*.] (Edited)

GOSSIAUX, Mark D., Review of *Common Truths: New Perspectives on Natural Law*, Edward B. McLean (Wilmington, DE: ISI Books, 2000) in *Vera Lex*, Vol. 2 (new series) Winter 2001, 191–199

GRANT, W. Matthews, "The Naturalistic Fallacy and Natural Law Methodology," in *Truth Matters: Essays in Honor of Jacques Maritain*, John G. Trapani Jr, (ed.), 168-181 (Catholic University of America Press: Washington D.C., 2004)

Keywords: natural law; ought.

GRISEZ, Germain and Russell Shaw, *Beyond the New Morality: The Responsibilities of Freedom* 3rd edition (University of Notre Dame Press: Notre Dame, 1988)

——, and Boyle, Joseph, "Response to Our Critics and Our Collaborators" in *Natural Law and Moral Inquiry*, Robert P. George, (ed.), 213-237 (Georgetown University Press: Washington D.C., 1998)

——, *Life and Death With Liberty and Justice: A Contribution to the Euthanasia Debate* (University of Notre Dame Press: Notre Dame, 1980)

——, *Abortion: The myths, the realities, and the arguments* (World Publishing Co.: NewYork, 1970)

——, *A new formulation of a natural-law argument against contraception* (Unknown Binding, 1966)

HART, H. T. A., *The Concept of Law* 2nd edition (Oxford University Press: Oxford, 1997)

[First published in 1961, *The Concept of Law* is the most important and original work of legal philosophy written this century. It is considered the masterpiece of H.L.A. Hart's enormous contribution to the study of jurisprudence and legal philosophy. Its elegant language and balanced arguments have sparked wide debate and unprecedented growth in the quantity and quality of scholarship in this area— much of it devoted to attacking or defending Hart's theories. Principal among Hart's critics is renowned lawyer and political philosopher Ronald Dworkin who in the 1970s and 1980s mounted a series of challenges to Hart's *The Concept of Law*. It seemed that Hart let these challenges go unanswered. However, after his death in 1992, his answer to Dworkin's criticism was discovered among his papers. In this valuable and long-awaited new edition Hart presents an Epilogue in which he answers Dworkin and some of his other most influential critics including Fuller and Finnis. Written with the same clarity and candor for which the first edition is famous, the Epilogue offers a sharper interpretation of Hart's own views, rebuffs the arguments of critics like Dworkin, and powerfully asserts that they have based their criticisms on a faulty understanding of Hart's work. Hart demonstrates that Dworkin's views are in fact strikingly similar to his own and in a final analysis, Hart's response leaves Dworkin's criticisms considerably weakened and his positions largely in question. Containing Hart's final and powerful response to Dworkin in addition to the revised text of the original *The Concept of Law*, this thought-provoking and persuasively argued volume is essential reading for lawyers and philosophers throughout the world.] (Publishers' review)

—— and Tony Honore, *Causation in the Law* (Oxford University Press: Oxford, 1985)

——, *Essays on Bentham: Studies in Jurisprudence and Political Theory* (Clarendon Press: Oxford, 1982)

——, *Law, Liberty, and Morality* (Stanford University Press: Palo Alto, 1972)

——, "Prolegomenon to the Principles of Punishment," *Proceedings of the Aristotelian Society* 1960; 60: 1-26
Key terms: Distribution, Excuses, Justification, Punishment, Reform, Retributivism, Social Philosophy, Utilitarianism.

——, "Decision, Intention and Certainty," *Mind: A Quarterly Review of Philosophy*, JA 58; 67: 1-12

——, "Are There any Natural Rights?" *Philosophical Review* AP 55; 64: 175-191

HASHMI, Sohail H. and Steven P. Lee (eds.) *Ethics and Weapons of Mass Destruction: Religious and Secular Perspectives* (Cambridge: Cambridge University Press, 2004)
[This volume offers a unique perspective on the discussion of weapons of mass destruction (WMD) by broadening the terms of the debate to include both secular and religious viewpoints not normally considered. Contributors represent the following diverse ethical traditions: Buddhism, Christianity, Confucianism, feminism, Hinduism, Islam,

Judaism, liberalism, natural law, pacifism, and realism. The two introductory chapters outline the technical aspects of WMD and international agreements for controlling WMD. A concluding essay compares the different ethical traditions.] (Publisher, Edited.)

HELD, Jacob M., "Assisted Suicide and Problems of Natural Law in Light of Political Liberalism and Pluralism," *Vera Lex*. Vol. 3(1-2), 91-104 (Winter 2002)

[The purpose of this article is not simply an analysis of assisted suicide as a political and legal issue. The overlying concern is the applicability of natural law, as exemplified in metaphysical conceptions of personhood, within a political dialogue founded on liberal ideals, for example those of John Rawls. The case for euthanasia highlights the fact that opponents often times ground their positions in metaphysical worldviews which fall outside the limit of acceptable, political discourse. The political answer to this question must be based on a political conception of the person, not on particular, exclusionary metaphysical worldviews.]

HERDT, Jennifer A., "Free Choice, Self-Referential Arguments, and the New Natural Law," *American Catholic Philosophical Quarterly*. Vol. 72(4), 581-600 (Fall 1998)

[The self-referential form of argumentation used by Joseph Boyle, Germain Grisez, and Olaf Tollefsen in Free Choice is promising for natural law thinking, as it offers certainty without appealing to external foundations, but their argument in defense of free choice is unsuccessful. The authors argue that the very denial of free choice presupposes the existence of free choice, but all that is required is rationality and subjective uncertainty during deliberation. Moreover, the "free choice" which they defend is arbitrary and criterionless; an alternative understanding of freedom is suggested which would be substantial and would also be compatible with a hierarchy of basic goods.]

HINTON, Beverly, "A Critical Look at Finnis's Natural Law Ethics and the Role of Human Choice," *Journal of Value Inquiry*. Vol. 37(1), 69-81 (2003)

[Traditionally, the justification of the objectivity of natural law values appeals to factors independent of the subject. Finnis proposes a justification of values by appeal to an intuitive ground internal to the subject. I argue that Finnis isolates the subject's internal experience of values from the subject's experience of desires and choices, and in so doing he undermines the viability of his internalist project.]

HITTINGER, Russell, *The First Grace: Rediscovering the Natural Law in a Post-Christian World* (ISI Books, Wilmington: DE, 2003)

[The last two decades or so have seen a marked resurgence of interest in natural law thought. Russell Hittinger has been a major figure in this movement. *The First Grace: Rediscovering the Natural Law in a Post-Christian World* reveals the power and subtlety of Hittinger's philosophical work and cultural criticism. Hittinger first defines the natural law, considers its relationship to the positive law, and explains how and when judges are to be guided by natural law considerations. Then, in the book's second section, he contends with a number of controversial legal and cultural issues from a natural law perspective. Among other things, he shows how the modern propensity to make all sorts of "rights claims" undermines the idea of limited government; how the liberal legal culture's idea of privacy elevates the individual to the status of a sovereign; and how the Supreme Court has come to see religion as a potentially dangerous phenomenon from which children must be protected. Throughout, Hittinger convincingly demonstrates that to oppose freedom and law is to misunderstand the nature of both.] (Publishers review)

——, "Natural Law as Law," *American Journal of Jurisprudence* 1 (1994)

——, "John Rawls, Political Liberalism: A Critical Study," *The Review of Metaphysics* 47 (March 1994)

——, "Natural Law in the Positive Laws: A Legislative or Adjudicative Issue?" *The Review of Politics* 5 (January 1993)

——, "Liberalism and the American Natural Law Tradition," *Wake Forest Law Review* 3 (1990)

——, "Theology and Natural Law," *Communio* (Fall 1990)

——, "Natural Law Theory, Virtue Ethics, and Eudaimonia," *International Philosophical Quarterly* (December 1989)

——, "Varieties of Minimalist Natural Law," *American Journal of Jurisprudence* (Fall 1989)

——, "Review of Finnis, Boyle, Grisez, *Nuclear Deterrence, Morality and Realism* in *International Philosophical Quarterly* (June 1989)

——, "Review of John Finnis's, *Fundamentals of Ethics* in *The Modern Schoolman* (May 1986)

——, *A Critique of the New Natural Law Theory*, Notre Dame University Press (1987)

HURD, Heidi M., "Moral Rights and Legal Rules: A Natural Law Theory," *Legal Theory*. Vol. 6(4), 423-455 (December 2000)
Keywords: ethics; legal; moral theory; natural law; rights.

IGLESIAS Rozas, Teresa, "Reasons for Action: *Aquinas: Moral, Political and Legal Theory* by John Finnis, Oxford University Press, 1998," *International Journal of Philosophical Studies*. Vol. 8(2), 238-246 (January 2000)

[Critical notice acknowledging this work in the natural law tradition, as an outstanding contribution to the field in the discursive context of analytic philosophy. The moral grounds of law and social life are unfolded and argued for not through polemical contrast. A novel view of the notion of the common good is presented. The most original contribution of the work is to identity the principle 'your-neighbor-as-yourself' as the 'highest', 'first', 'architectonic', most primary binding', 'master principle of morality'—now also located at the centre of legal and social theory.]

IKUENOBE, Polycarp, "A Natural Law Critique of Liberal Approaches to a Multicultural Consequence of Globalism," *Vera Lex*. Vol. 3(1-2), 1-39 (Winter 2002)

[One consequence of globalism is the migration of different peoples to Western democracies. This has created the problem of multiculturalism, in terms of how a state with a dominant cultural majority can accommodate diversity of minority cultures. I examine some liberal views and I argue that they cannot address this problem. A plausible liberal view that can, in a way that gives credence to cultural rights, must be grounded in the precepts of natural law. These precepts are substantively and procedurally good moral principles derived from human nature and reason, which specify how to maintain an acceptable society.]

——, "Natural Law, Liberal Principles, and the Moral Acceptance of Rules," *Vera Lex*. Vol. 2(1-2), 133-162 (Winter 2001)

[I argue that Hart's rule of recognition is not only semantically and epistemically adequate, but is also morally adequate, in that it includes or specifies some moral principles of social justice as a set of procedural constraints for identifying a law, such that the constraints shape the substantive content of the law. I argue for this thesis against the backdrop that Hart's theory captures a paradigm case of legal system. I argue that such a legal system cannot exist or be conceptually adequate without some moral content that satisfies liberal principles of formal and substantive justice.] (Author's abstract)

KACZOR, Christopher, *Proportionalism and the Natural Law Tradition* (Catholic University Press: Washington D.C., 2002)

[In this book, Christopher Kaczor argues against the plausibility of proportionalism and its first proponents, namely Peter Knauer, Joseph Fuchs, Bruno Schuller, Louis Janssens, and Richard McCormick. Examining the genealogy of the movement, he disputes a received history that depicts proportionalism as a recovery of Thomas Aquinas. Instead, contends Kaczor, proportionalism is best seen as the organic successor to the moral manuals of the pre-Vatican II era. Proportionalism arises not from Thomas but rather extends many of the tendencies and presuppositions of the manuals.] (Publisher, edited)

KLOSKO, George, "The Natural Basis of Political Obligation," *Social Philosophy and Policy*. Vol. 18(1), 93-114 (Winter 2001)

[Because individuals require essential benefits from the state, the baseline position on questions of political obligation should not be an absence of political bonds—the state of nature—but individuals as members of communities, while the need for such benefits generates obligations to fellow community members, under the principle of fairness. This analysis is defended against different claims concerning the possibility of alternative supply of public goods, advanced by A. John Simmons and Michael Taylor. In order to free individuals of political obligations they would otherwise have, alternative mechanisms must satisfy a standard of reasonable plausibility, which they are not likely to do.]

KOLAKOWSKI, Leszek, "Reviving Natural Law," *Critical Review*: *An Interdisciplinary Journal of Politics-and-Society*. Vol. 15(1-2), 195-202 (Winter-Spring 2003)

[Despite numerous attempts to invalidate the concept of natural law as presupposing the belief in God or in universal rules of human reason, this concept is no less valid now than it was in the thirteenth or seventeenth centuries. All that is required to uphold the belief in natural law is a kind of metaphysical faith in the notion of human dignity, which provides us with the surest barriers against both unjust positive legislation and totalitarian political systems.]

LEE, Patrick, "The Pro-Life Argument from Substantial Identity: A Defence," *Bioethics.* Vol. 18(3), 249-263 (June 2004)

[This article defends the following argument: what makes you and I valuable so that it is wrong to kill us now is what we are (essentially). But we are essentially physical organisms, who, embryology reveals, came to be at conception/fertilization. I reply to the objection to this argument (as found in Dean Stretton, Judith Thomson, and Jeffrey Reiman), which holds that we came to be at one time, but became valuable as a subject of rights only some time later, in virtue of an acquired characteristic. I argue against this position that the difference between a basic, natural capacity and some degree of development of such a capacity is a mere difference in degree, that this position logically implies the denial of equal personal dignity, and that the selection of the required degree of development of a capacity is necessarily arbitrary.]

——, "Justifications for Our Free Speech: Examining the Role of Autonomous Agency in Scanlon's Moral Theory," *International Journal of Applied Philosophy.* Vol. 17(2), 211-224 (Fall 2003)

[In two influential articles setting forth his arguments against restrictions on free expression in the 1970s, Harvard philosopher T. M. Scanlon suggested and later rejected the notion that autonomous agency ought to be a primary constraint on most justifications used to restrict speech. The concept of autonomy, he said, was "notoriously vague and slippery" as a basis for judging free-speech restrictions. Instead, Scanlon argued that free expression—and proposed restrictions on it—should be justified in terms of our various "interests" in speech as participants and as audience members. Reliance on autonomy does not provide the justificatory force for a theory of free expression, he said.

——, "Human Beings Are Animals," *International Philosophical Quarterly.* Vol. 37(3), 291-303 (September 1997)

Keywords: animal; biology; body; ethics; human being.

——, "The Relationship Between Intellect and Will in Free Choice According to Aquinas and Scotus," *Thomist: A Speculative Quarterly Review.* Vol. 49, 321-342 (July 1985)

Keywords: free choice; intellect; metaphysics.

——, "Aquinas and Scotus on Liberty and Natural Law," *Proceedings of the American Catholic Philosophical Association.* Vol. 56, 70-78 (1982)

Keywords: ethics; liberty; natural law.

LINDGREN, J. Ralph (ed.), *Horizons of Justice* (Lang: New York, 1996)

[Since classical Greece the term "justice" has been used to denote those properties that distinguish practices and institutions that deserve the support and loyalty of peoples they affect from those in which that support is optional. Traditionally, legitimacy was accorded to practices and institutions that support values systems that are compatible with one's own. The recent trend toward recognizing a diversity of cultures blocks that move. This change has profound implications for the role of "justice" in our multicultural world. The essays in this volume explore different aspects of this changed role of "justice."]

LLOYD, S. A., "Hobbes's Self-Effacing Natural Law Theory," *Pacific Philosophical Quarterly.* Vol. 82(3-4), 285-308 (September 2001)

[This paper investigates the structure of Hobbes's normative theory and argues that he developed a "self-effacing" natural law theory that diverges in interesting ways from both positivist and natural law conceptions of law. In the process, it proposes and defends a new way of understanding how it is that Hobbes's laws of nature require civil obedience, as well as a new understanding of the relationship between natural law and the right of nature in Hobbes.]

MACDONALD, Sara, "Problems with Principles: Montesquieu's Theory of Natural Justice," *History of Political Thought.* Vol. 24(1), 109-130 (Spring 2003)
Keywords: history; justice; natural law.

MCLEAN, Edward B., *Common Truths: New Perspectives on Natural Law* (ISI Books, Wilmington, DE: 2000)

MATTHEWS, Gareth B., "Saint Thomas and the Principle of Double Effect" in *Aquinas's Moral Theory*, MacDonald, Scott (ed.), 63-78 (Cornell University Press: Ithaca, 1998)
[To many ethicists the Principle of Double Effect seems clearly Thomistic, even if they are unable to say why this is so. I try to show that, although *ST* IIaeIIae.64.7 might seem promising as a Thomistic basis for this principle, it is insufficient. There is, however, an indirect way to get from what Thomas says about self-defense to a modern formulation of the principle. Perhaps modern medical ethicists are thus justified in considering the principle at least broadly Thomistic. Finally, I suggest that the principle can be thought to derive its force from the "Pauline Principle" that we should not do evil that good may come of it.]

MAY, William E., "Germain Grisez on Moral Principles and Moral Norms: Natural and Christian" in *Natural Law and Moral Inquiry: Ethics, Metaphysics, and Politics in the Work of Germain Grisez*, Robert P. George (ed.), 3-35 (Georgetown University Press: Washington D.C., 1998)

MCDONOUGH, William, "Alasdair MacIntyre As Help for Rethinking Catholic Natural Law Estimates of Same-Sex Life Partnerships," *Annual of the Society of Christian Ethics.* Vol. 21, 191-213 (2001)

[Christian ethics struggles to articulate a method for thinking about homosexuality and the sexual acts of same-sex oriented persons. In 1988, Hanigan suggested a promising "social import" approach and then judged homosexual acts deficient. MacIntyre's *Dependent Rational Animals* (1999) articulates a fuller social import approach to morality. Although he does not address homosexuality, MacIntyre rejects narrow understandings of family and of "disinterested friendship": we need "communal relations that engage our affections" to grow in "the virtues of acknowledged dependence." How do gay people grow in these virtues? What if Hanigan got the method right, but the evaluation wrong?]

MUMFORD, Stephen, "Normative and Natural Laws," *Philosophy*: The *Journal of the Royal Institute of Philosophy*. Vol. 75(292), 265-282 (April 2000)

[A theory of laws is developed that takes from E. J. Lowe the notion of natural laws being consistent with certain classes of exceptions. Neither abnormal cases, such as albino ravens, nor miracles falsify covering laws. This suggests that law statements cannot have the form of a universally quantified conditional. Lowe takes it that this is best explained by natural laws having normative force. I argue that there is a non-normative, descriptivist account that also explains the exception cases and which is preferable. I also suggest an improved account of miracles within the descriptivist account.]

MURPHY, Mark C., "Natural Law Jurisprudence," *Legal Theory*. Vol. 9(4), 241-267 (December 2003)

Keywords: jurisprudence; natural law; political philosophy; positivism; rights.

———, "Natural Law, Consent, and Political Obligation," *Social Philosophy and Policy*. Vol. 18(1), 70-92 (Winter 2001)

[Recent accounts of political obligation offered by natural law theorists have eschewed any appeal to consent theory. In this paper, I provide an account of the generic form of natural law accounts of political obligation; I show that recent natural law accounts of political obligation fail because of their refusal to appeal to consent; and I argue that there is a way for natural law theory to appeal to consent without embroiling itself in the objections that have plagued consent theories as a class.]

———, "Natural Law, Impartialism, and Others' Good," *Thomist: A Speculative Quarterly Review.* Vol. 60(1), 53-80 (January 1996)

[Henry Veatch and Joseph Rautenberg recently argued that the moral theory defended by Germain Grisez, John Finnis, and Joseph Boyle is more akin to utilitarian impartialism than to Aristotelian or Thomistic eudaimonism. I argue that although Veatch and Rautenberg are correct to label the Grisez-Finnis-Boyle view a type of impartialism, they misunderstand both the character of its impartialism and the mistake on which it rests. A clearer understanding of what is at issue between impartialist and eudaimonist natural law theories brings into focus the severity of the problem faced in trying to decide between these accounts.]

———, "Self-Evidence, Human Nature, and Natural Law," *American Catholic Philosophical Quarterly.* Vol. 69(3), 471-484 (Summer 1995)

[John Finnis has argued both (NL1) that the principles of natural law are self-evident and underivable and (NL2) that the principles of the natural law are grounded in human nature. I argue, however, that on Finnis's understandings of (NL1) and (NL2), these claims could not both be justifiably asserted. I then turn to the task of providing an account on which we can assert sufficiently strong interpretations of both (NL1) and (NL2). The central thesis of this account is that the principles of the natural law can be self-evident qua judgments of practical reason yet not self-evident qua judgments of theoretical reason.]

MURPHY, Jr. William, "Martin Rhonheimer's Natural Law and
  Practical Reason," *Sapientia*. Vol.56(210), 517-548 (2001)
  Keywords: autonomy; ethics; natural law; practical reason; reason.

NEMETH, Charles P., *Aquinas in the Courtroom: Lawyers, Judges, and
  Judicial Conduct*. (Praeger: Westport, 2001)

  [Using St. Thomas Aquinas's natural law philosophy and Divine
  Exemplar argument to prompt new discussion of ethical questions
  that lawyers and judges should confront, the author delivers a complete occupational profile for the professional conduct of judges and
  lawyers. St. Thomas's discourse on such topics as procedural law,
  judicial and advocate conduct and character, criminal and civil practice standards, and sentencing guidelines provides a blueprint for the
  Christian lawyer and judge by laying out the professional and ethical
  parameters that make the actor operate in accordance with reason and
  morality.]

  (Publisher's review)

NOWLIN, Jack Wade, "Natural Law, the Constitution, and Judicial
  Moral Expertise: An Epistemic Analysis," *Vera Lex*. Vol. 2(1-2), 71-
  113 (Winter 2001)

  [The purpose of this article is to explore one facet of the moral arguments often asserted in favor of expansive judicial power in
  American constitutional law. The facet explored is the epistemic
  problems surrounding the assertion that the judicial process promotes
  greater moral insight than does the legislative process, that judges
  possess some special power of "moral expertise," given the features
  of their training and institutional setting. This article concludes that
  such arguments fail on epistemic grounds related to the meaning of
  the concept of "moral expertise," which either has a "thin" meaning
  hard to link to particular moral conclusions or "thick(er)" meanings
  that are highly controversial and hard to link to the judicial process.]

ORREGO, Cristobal, "H. L. A. Hart's Arguments against Classical Natural Law Theory," *American Journal of Jurisprudence.* Vol. 48, 297-323 (2003)

[The article examines H. L. A. Hart's most important arguments against classical natural law theory as expounded by, among others, Thomas Aquinas. The author analyzes first the arguments against the teleological view of natural law, then those against the union of law and morals, and finally the theoretical and practical shortcomings that, according to Hart, affect natural law theory. The author refutes in detail every argument, acknowledging that Hart was right only on some points of some rationalist theories of natural law.]

RAZ, Joseph, *Practical Reason and Norms* (Oxford University Press: Oxford, 1999)

[In what way are rules normative, and how do they differ from ordinary reasons? What makes normative systems systematic? What distinguishes legal systems, and in what consists their normativity? Joseph Raz answers these three questions by taking reasons as the basic normative concept, and showing the distinctive role reasons have in every case, thus paving the way to a unified account of normativity.] (Publisher's review)

——, *Morality of Freedom* (Oxford University Press: Oxford, 1988)

[Ranging over central issues of morals and politics and the nature of freedom and authority, this study examines the role of value-neutrality, rights, equality, and the prevention of harm in the liberal tradition, and relates them to fundamental moral questions such as the relation of values to social forms, the comparability of values, and the significance of personal commitments.] (Publisher's review)

——, *The Authority of Law: Essays on Law and Morality* (Oxford University Press: Oxford, 1983)

["He is a remarkably skillful interpreter of the positivist legal philosophers and probably the most stimulating current contributor to discussion of the issues they raised."—Thomas Morawetz in *Ethics.*

Joseph Raz examines here the nature of law and its relations to morality, concentrating on the issue of the proper moral attitude of a citizen towards the law of his country. A discussion of the concept of legitimate authority is followed by a detailed explanation and defense of the legal positivist's approach to law. Within this framework the author examines several areas where legal analysis is often thought to be penetrated by moral values, particularly the social functions of the law, judicial creativity, and the ideals of the rule of law.] (Publishers' review)

REDPATH, Peter A., "Are There Non-Natural Law Views of Rights and Responsibilities?" *Contemporary Philosophy*. Vol. 17(4), 5-10 (July-August 1995)

[In discussions of issues related to human rights and responsibilities, it is not uncommon to find contemporary thinkers distinguishing among various types of such views—such as, for example, among natural law, social contract, normative, and so on. When such distinctions are made, especially by people who think of themselves as philosophers, the presumption seems to be that it is possible to have not only a view of human rights and responsibilities but also a philosophical view of such rights and responsibilities which is devoid of a natural law foundation. As far as I can determine, such a presumption is without rational foundation, for the presumption itself rests upon an impossibility. That is to say, as far as I can determine, all views of human rights and responsibilities (whether they be philosophical, or theological, or rhetorical, or of some other point of origin) are founded upon some natural law view. Furthermore, as far as I can determine, not all views of natural law which are appealed to as grounds for human rights and responsibilities (either because of content of the view or of the way in which the view is derived.) can be properly called "philosophical".]

RHONHEIMER, Martin, "The Cognitive Structure of the Natural Law and the Truth of Subjectivity," *Thomist: A Speculative Quarterly Review*. Vol. 67(1), 1-44 (January 2003)

[Natural law is not simply a conjunction of norms to be read in a natural order "that is in front of our eyes." Instead, according to Thomas Aquinas, the natural law is something constituted in the natural judgments of the natural reason of each human person. This is why the natural law is an expression of human nature and the moral order rooted in this nature. To conceive of the natural law as the natural principles of practical reason opens up the road to understanding the connection between the precepts of the natural law and the moral virtues.]

——, "The Moral Significance of Pre-Rational Nature in Aquinas: A Reply to Jean Porter (and Stanley Hauerwas)," *American Journal of Jurisprudence*. Vol. 48, 253-280 (2003)

Keywords: ethics; moral theory; natural law; nature; reason.

ROBINSON, Daniel N., "Review Essay: In Defense of Natural Law: Robert George's Jurisprudence," *American Journal of Jurisprudence*. Vol. 45, 117-131 (2000)

[Among the most influential of the new school of natural law theorists, Robert George has refined and enlarged the jurisprudence of John Finnis, Germain Grisez and Joseph Boyle. He has advanced detailed criticisms of the neoliberal jurisprudence associated variously with Joel Feinberg, John Rawls and Ronald Dworkin. The controversial elements in the contesting schools are examined and found to be in important respects based on different and defective understandings of such basic concepts as truths per se nota, of the indemonstrabilia, and goods at once basic and incommensurable. Through an analysis of these and related concepts, it becomes evident that the alleged problems with natural law theory are based chiefly on systematic misunderstandings, and on alternatives precepts largely incapable of rendering intelligible the rule of law itself.]

RUSSELL, J. S., "Trial by Slogan: Natural Law and *Lex Iniusta Non Est Lex*," *Law and Philosophy*: *An International Journal for Jurisprudence and Legal Philosophy.* Vol. 19(4), 433-449

[Norman Kretzmann's recent analysis of the natural law slogan *"lex iniusta non est lex"* (an unjust law is not a law) demonstrates the coherence of the slogan and makes a case for its practical value, but I shall argue that it also ends up showing that the slogan fails to mark any interesting conceptual or practical division between natural law and legal positivist views about the nature of law. I argue that this is a happy result.] (Abstract)

SULMASY, Daniel P., and Jansen, Lynn A., "Proportionality, Terminal Suffering and the Restorative Goals of Medicine," *Theoretical Medicine and Bioethics.* Vol. 23(4-5), 321-337 (2002)

[While the importance of treating suffering has generally been acknowledged, insufficient attention has been paid to the question of whether different types of terminal suffering require different responses from health care professionals. In this paper we introduce a distinction between two types of suffering likely to be present at the end of life, and we argue that physicians must distinguish between these types if they are to respond appropriately to the suffering of their terminally ill patients. After introducing this distinction and explaining its basis, we further argue that the distinction informs a (novel) principle of proportionality, one that should guide physicians in balancing their competing obligations in responding to terminal suffering.]

——, "What Is An Oath and Why Should a Physician Swear One?," *Theoretical Medicine and Bioethics.* Vol. 20(4), 329-346 (August 1999)

[Oaths are distinct from codes. Codes are collections of specific moral rules. Codes are not performative utterances. They do not commit future intentions and do not involve the personhood of the one enjoined by the code. Recent attacks on oath-taking by physicians are discussed. Two arguments in favor of oath-taking are presented: one on the basis of the nature of medicine as a profession and the other on the basis of rule-utilitarian considerations. No attempt is made to define which oath a physician should swear.] (Edited.)

——, "Futility and the Varieties of Medical Judgment," *Theoretical Medicine: An International Journal for the Philosophy and Methodology of Medical Research and Practice.* Vol. 18(1-2), 63-78 (March-June 1997)

[Pellegrino has argued that end-of-life decisions should be based upon the physician's assessment of the effectiveness of the treatment and the patient's assessment of its benefits and burdens. This would seem to imply that conditions for medical futility could be met either if there were a judgment of ineffectiveness, or if the patient were in a state in which he or she were incapable of a subjective judgment of the benefits and burdens of the treatment. I argue that a theory of futility according to Pellegrino would deny that latter but would permit some cases of the former. I call this the "circumspect" view. I defend the circumspect view on the basis of a previously neglected aspect of the philosophy of medicine—an examination of varieties of medical judgment. I then offer some practical applications of this theory in clinical practice.] (Edited.)

——, "What's So Special About Medicine?" *Theoretical Medicine.* Vol. 14(1), 27-42 (March 1993)

[Health care has increasingly come to be understood as a commodity. The ethical implications of such an understanding are significant. The author argues that health care is not a commodity because health care (1) is non-proprietary, (2) serves the needs of persons who, as patients, are uniquely vulnerable, (3) essentially involves a special human relationship which ought not be bought or sold, (4) helps to define what is meant by 'necessity' and cannot be considered a commodity when subjected to rigorous conceptual analysis. The Oslerin conception that medicine is a calling and not a business ought to be reaffirmed by both the professional and the public. Such a conception would have significant ramifications for patient care and health care policy.]

SCHULTZ, Aldrich, Janice L., "Revisiting Aquinas on 'Naturalism': A Response to Patrick Lee," *American Catholic Philosophical Quarterly.* Vol. 77(1), 114-131 (Winter 2003)

[This article defends as correct and as faithful to Aquinas's thought the tenets of "descriptivism" (sometimes called "naturalism") in the context of criticisms that Patrick Lee has made in "Is Thomas's Natural Law Theory Naturalist?" (*American Catholic Philosophical Quarterly* 71:4 (1997): 567-87). "Revisiting Aquinas" argues that evaluative utterances are descriptive; so even if human goods were immediately known by practical reason (a position nonetheless rejected.), their understanding would be a descriptive one, which moral objectivity requires.] (Edited.)

SULLIVAN, Denis, "Disagreement and Objectivity in Ethics: Aquinas on the Common Precepts of the Natural Law," *Proceedings of the American Catholic Philosophical Association.* Vol. 74, 231-244 (2000)

[In his only essay devoted to ethics, Willard Quine concludes that ethics lacks the kind of objectivity he is willing to ascribe to science. This is because, he claims, in science, but not in ethics, it is always, in principle, possible to resolve disagreements by appealing to observation. More recently Crispen Wright has argued in roughly the same way. In this paper I argue that Thomas Aquinas, in his theory of the natural law, and especially in his use of the concept of the common precepts of the natural law, provides a plausible response to this challenge to the objectivity of ethics.]

TUMULTY, Peter, "Natural Law Theory, Liberalism and the Fact-Value," in *Philosophy and Culture*, Vol. 3, Venant Cauchy (ed.), (Montreal: Ed. Montmorency) 486-492

Keywords: ethics; natural law.

VAN-DUN, Frank, "Natural Law and the Jurisprudence of Freedom," *Journal of Libertarian Studies.* Vol. 18(2), 31-54 (Spring 2004)

Keywords: freedom; harm; natural law; political philosophy; punishment.

WEITHMAN, Paul J., "Natural Law, Morality, and Sexual Complementarity" in *Sex, Preference, and Family: Essays on Law and Nature*. Martha C. Nussbaum (ed.), 227-246 (Oxford University Press: New York, 1997)

[The author attempts to refute John Finnis's argument that homosexual activity is morally wrong and that its moral wrongness gives government good (though perhaps not conclusive) reason to discourage it.]

WIDULSKI, Peter, "Liberalism and Natural Law," *Vera Lex* Vol. 2(1-2), 25-50 (Winter 2001) Keywords: ethics; legal theory; liberalism; natural law.

WILLIAMS, A. N., "Argument to Bliss: The Epistemology of the *Summa Theologiae*," *Modern Theology*. Vol. 20(4), 505-526 (October 2004)

[The essay examines intellectual virtue in the *Summa theologiae*, taking it as an interpretative key to the epistemology of the *Summa theologiae* as a whole. Because Aquinas blurs the line between the acquired and the theological virtues, and between virtues and the gifts of the Spirit, it becomes impossible to maintain the distinction between the realms of nature and grace, or between natural reason and revealed truth: grace permeates the most ordinary activities of human reasoning. This reading of the *Summa theologiae* raises questions about many contemporary debates, particularly those concerning natural law.] (Abstract)

ZUCKERT, Michael, "Natural Law, Natural Rights, and Classical Liberalism: On Montesquieu's Critique of Hobbes," *Social Philosophy and Policy*. Vol. 18(1), 227-251 (Winter 2001) Keywords: liberalism; natural law; natural right; social philosophy.

REPORT

REPORT ON THE 28TH ANNUAL INTERNATIONAL MEETING
OF THE AMERICAN MARITAIN ASSOCIATION

"The Renewal of Civilization: Toward Justice and Peace"
Emory University and at the Sheraton Midtown Atlanta hotel at
Colony Square, October 21-24, 2004
Sponsored by: Emory University and chaired by Christopher
M. Cullen, S.J., of Fordham University

When one chooses to give or hear a presentation one simultaneously chooses not to hear any of the others running concurrently. As there were well over fifty presentations, I will not make any pretense of a complete survey here, but will rather mention only some of the featured speakers as well as comment on what were, for me, special moments in this very well-attended conference.

We began with the featured presentations of President Alice Ramos's (St. John's University) welcoming address entitled, "Toward a Recovery of the Moral Sense,"and Ralph McInerny's (University of Notre Dame) "The Philosopher in the City." In the latter, McInerny described the characteristics and activities of the individual Thomist philosopher. Responding to this paper, Jude Dougherty said, "Would that I could decree that every undergraduate could get a copy of this. This was one of his best!" And when Peter Simpson questioned, "Shouldn't we go beyond St. Thomas?" McInerny responded, "Of course we can go beyond St. Thomas, provided we have caught up with him first! The truth is the central thing. Nothing philosophical is alien to us."

The plenary papers continued with Elizabeth Fox-Genovese's (Emory University) "Prudence and Grace: Craft and Genius in an Age of Individualism according to Maritain and T.S. Eliot," Peter Simpson's (City University of New York) "'We are Wounded Souls': Maritain's America Fifty Years On," Thomas Flynn's (Emory University) "Is Marcel an Existentialist?," Jorge L. A. Garcia's (Boston College) "White Nights of the Soul: Moral Reflection in Nolan's Film *Insomnia*," Paul Griffiths' (University of Illinois at Chicago) "Curiosity as a Philosophical Problem: An Augustinian Analysis," Robert Sokolowski's (The Catholic University of America) "Art and Christian Intelligence" and Paul Weithman's (University of Notre Dame) defense of his book, *Religion and the Obligations of Citizenship* (Cambridge University Press, 2002).

At the banquet the Humanitarian Award was presented to Francis Slade of St. Francis College, Brooklyn, New York. The Maritain Medal for Scholarly Excellence was awarded to Robert Sokolowski of The Catholic University of America.

Most striking about many of the presentations was the recurring idea of the public nature and accessibility of ordinary human knowledge. Consonant with one of the AMA's vocations of promoting realism in its varying forms, this conference highlighted the public and non-private nature of knowledge.

Paul Griffiths' talk on "Curiosity as a Philosophical Problem: An Augustinian Analysis" was particularly arresting in this regard. According to Griffiths, and for Augustine, curiosity, not to be confused with genuine studiousness, is the appetite for the ownership for new knowledge (*De Trinitate* X). The curious man is rapid by his desire for what he does not know. Curiosity is a burdensome and unsatisfiable appetite. It is the lust for novelty that misses the genuine value in things themselves. The curious man never stays very long on any one thing and this precludes any form of genuine contemplation. What the novelty seekers see are idols. Their eyes are turned towards less. Concomitant with this is chattiness. It is like the hunger over a sort of Manichean "dream food." It is the attempt to own knowledge. The curious person wants to *make* knowledge, to make it proper to himself, to privatize it, to see it for himself alone. Curiosity involves the lust for dominance! The curious gaze reverses the movement of creation back to the "nihil." For Augustine, the public is better than the private; and this is exactly the reverse of the ideal held today said Griffiths. Modern scholarship seems to praise what Augustine condemns. Private things are those things the access to which is controlled. Griffiths asks us to notice how we talk about what we do as scholars. We will talk about our new and unique contributions. For Augustine, however, the eternal knowables must partake of the being of God and no person can have private sequestered knowledge of God's eternal nature. In the end, the curious lose. The curious in their curiosity lose what they seek to know and what they get is not what they see. All they end up with is simulacra! In this regard, I can't help but think about Simon and Garfunkel's popular song "The Dangling Conversation."

Ralph Nelson (University of Windsor) in his "The Conflict Over Humanism," talked about how the freedom of choice is confused with the freedom of autonomy and about how Kant mistakenly says that autonomy is not won but is part of the nature of the mind. Nelson spoke of three ways philosophers have conceived of the unity between all human beings. There is the nominalist unity of humanity which consists in just a word. Second, is the idealist's notion of unity, that of a subsisting idea, and third, there is the realist notion of human nature. It is only in this last notion that humans can actually be perceived to share a foundation of a common human nature and possess actual rights.

After John G. Trapani, Jr. (Walsh University) had parsed out a theory of linguistic communication in his "We [Well, at least Ostensibly] Hold These Truths: Objective Truth, Reasoned Conviction, and the Survival of Democracy," he claimed that it is important to note that the founding fathers did not say we hold these "values"or "ideals, " where there might be some ambiguity and disagreement, but that they used the word "truths" thus implying that opinions contrary to these are false. Trapani went on to argue that there are some certain metaphysical principles about which society presupposes a general informed and reasoned consent, and without which consent it cannot survive!

When Pamela Proietti (University of Memphis) criticized John Locke in her "The High Price of Tolerance: The Fundamental Flaws in Liberalism's Founding," it was because of Locke's denial of the accessibility of knowledge, his skepticism. Her paper caused us to question whether skepticism was as necessary to a view of tolerance as Locke thought it was, in, for example, his "Letter Concerning Toleration."

Jorge L.A. Garcia (Boston College) in his "White Nights of the Soul: Moral Reflection in Nolan's Film *Insomnia*," gave a multimedia presentation on a movie that highlighted in a fascinating way the objective and ever-present nature of moral conscience and guilt in the context of the ever-present and everlasting day of Alaska. I was inspired to go home to rent the DVD!

Anne M. Wiles (James Madison University) in her "Maritain on Connatural Knowledge" and in the context of the poetry and life of Dante, spoke of Maritain's notion of intuition and how it was receptive to *esse*, that dynamic and energizing act of being; and how intuition was a genuine intellectual activity that plunged deeply into a being. "All objects murmur being to those who can hear." The most interesting idea was that, according to Wiles, poetic knowledge involves your whole self and all your experiences! This, it seems to me, is quite provocative, for it means that every experience we pick up in our lives adds to our, if you can forgive my phrase, "aesthetic antennae," our ability to take in the world, and to know the depths of reality.

Important announcements were made. Ralph McInerny is the new president of the association, John Hittinger is the vice-president. Gavin Colbert will edit the upcoming volume on this conference.

The next conference, the 29th Annual Meeting, is entitled "Philosophy and Vocation: Intellectual and Spiritual Conditions for Renewal" and it is from October 13-16, 2005, in Washington at the Phoenix Park Hotel and at The Catholic University of America. Plenary speakers will be Richard Schenk, O.P., Joseph Koterski, S.J., Msgr. John Wippel, Lawrence Dewan, O.P., Sr. Prudence Allen, R.S.M., Thomas Hibbs, Bradley Lewis, Thomas Rourke, Michael Novak, Edmund Pelligrino, and Tracey Rowland, author of *Culture and the Thomist Tradition after Vatican II.*

For further information about the conference or about the American Maritain Association please contact The American Maritain Association at the Jacques Maritain Center, 714 Hesburgh Library, Notre Dame, IN 46556. Tel: (574) 631-5825; E-mail: Alice. F.osberger.1@nd.edu

Gregory J. Kerr, PhD
DeSales University

CONTRIBUTORS

Michael Baur is Associate Professor in the Philosophy Department at Fordham University, and Director of Fordham's Natural Law Colloquium. He holds a PhD in philosophy from the University of Toronto and a J.D. from Harvard Law School, and has published articles on Kant, Fichte, Hegel, Aquinas, Lonergan, Adorno, Rawls, Heidegger, and Gadamer.

Joseph Boyle is a professor in the Department of Philosophy at the University of Toronto. He is a fellow of St. Michael's College where he served as Principal for a decade. He studied with Germain Grisez and has contributed to the development of the natural law theory associated with Grisez and John Finnis, by articles and by three co-authored books.

Stephen L. Brock teaches Medieval Philosophy at the Pontifical University of the Holy Cross in Rome. He has written a book on human action in the philosophy of Thomas Aquinas, and articles on various aspects of Thomas's thought.

E. Christian Brugger is an Assistant Professor at the Institute for the Psychological Sciences in Arlington, VA. He earned a D.Phil. in Christian Ethics from the University of Oxford. He also holds a Masters in moral philosophy from Harvard Divinity School and a Masters in moral theology from Seton Hall University. He is the author of *Capital Punishment and Roman Catholic Moral Tradition* (Notre Dame Press, 2003) and has published widely on topics in ethics and natural law in journals like *The Thomist*, *National Catholic Bioethics Quarterly*, and *Notre Dame Journal of Law, Ethics and Public Policy*.

Fr. Kevin L. Flannery, SJ, is Ordinary Professor of the History of Ancient Philosophy at the Pontifical Gregorian University (Rome); he is the author of *Ways into the Logic of Alexander of Aphrodisias* (Brill, 1995) and *Acts Amid Precepts: The Aristotelian logical structure of Thomas Aquinas's moral theory* (Catholic University of America Press, 2001), plus a number of articles on ethical issues and on ancient and medieval philosophy.

Robert P. George, McCormick Professor of Jurisprudence and Director of the James Madison Program in American Ideals and Institutions at Princeton University

Patrick Lee, professor at Franciscan University of Steubenville, received his PhD at Marquette University in 1980. Lee's book, *Abortion and Unborn Human Life*, was published in 1996, and he has written various articles in scholarly and popular journals, on St. Thomas and on ethical issues.

Daniel P. Sulmasy, OFM, MD, PhD, a Franciscan friar, internist, and philosopher, is Sisters of Charity Chair in Ethics at St. Vincent's Hospital—Manhattan, and Professor of Medicine and Director of the Bioethics Institute of New York Medical College. He is Editor-in-Chief of the journal *Theoretical Medicine and Bioethics*. His latest books are *The Rebirth of the Clinic* and *A Balm for Gilead: Meditations on Spirituality and the Healing Arts,* both forthcoming from Georgetown University Press in 2006.

A small number of back copies of VERA LEX remain at a cost of USD $10.00 a copy.* A complete back set of VERA LEX is $115.00 (see list below). Those who order will receive, without charge, all five previous *graphically reproduced* issues neatly bound: Vol. 1, No. 1 (1979) through Vol. III, No. 1 (1982). [Vol. II No. 2 was not issued.] For more information on Pace titles, please visit the website: *http://www.pace.edu/press*

1982 Vol. III,	No. 2	**Reason in the Natural Law**
1986 Vol. VI,	No. 1	**Edmund Burke and the Natural Law: Theory and Practice**
	No. 2	**Is There a Natural Law in Hebrew Tradition?**
1987 Vol. VII,	No. 1	**Natural Law and Constitutionalism**
	No. 2	**Natural Law and Constitutionalism II**
1988 Vol. VIII,	No. 1	**Rights I**
	No. 2	**Rights II**
1989 Vol. IX,	No. 1	**(General Interest)**
	No. 2	**The Spanish Tradition** (Index: Yves R. Simon)
1990 Vol. X,	No. 1	**Thomas Aquinas**
	No. 2	**(General Interest)**
1991 Vol. XI,	No. 1	**Equity as Natural Law**
	No. 2	**Sacred and Secular Natural Law**
1992 Vol. XII,	No. 1	**Jurisprudence and the Natural Law**
	No. 2	**Legal Positivism, Pragmatism**

1993 Vol. XIII,   **Dignity as Natural Law**
Nos. 1&2 (double issue) (Rosmini, Trigeaud)

1994 Vol. XIV,   **Empirical Natural Law, Human Nature, Science**
Nos. 1&2 (double issue)

1995 Vol. XV,   **Autonomy, Independence, Liberty**
Nos. 1&2 (double issue) (Includes 6-year cumulative index: 1990-1995)

2000 New Series Vol I   **Natural Law and Natural Environment**
Nos. 1&2 (double issue)   (available direct from Pace UP)

2001 New Series Vol. II   **Liberalism and Natural Law**
Nos. 1&2 (double issue)   (available direct from Pace UP)

2002 New Series Vol. III   **Globalism and Natural Law**
Nos. 1&2 (double issue)   (available direct from Pace UP)

2003 New Series Vol. IV   **Feminism and Natural Law**
Nos. 1&2 (double issue)   (available direct from Pace UP)

2004 New Series Vol. V   **Medieval Natural Law Theories**
Nos. 1&2 (double issue)   (available direct from Pace UP)

*Two back issues of VERA LEX are out of print. However, the originals are available in <u>xeroxed</u> form for USD $5.00.

1983-84 Vol. IV, **Hugo Grotius** (index)
Nos. 1&2 (double issue)

1985 Vol. V No. 1 **Giambattista Vico**
(No. 2 was not issued.)

Environmental Values

EDITOR:
Alan Holland
Dept. of Philosophy, Furness Coll.,
Lancaster University, LA1 1YG, UK

ASSOCIATED EDITORS:
Michael Hammond
Lancaster University
Robin Grove-White
Lancaster University
John Proops
University of Keele

REVIEWS EDITORS:
Clive Spash
University of Cambridge
Jeremy Roxbee-Cox
Lancaster University

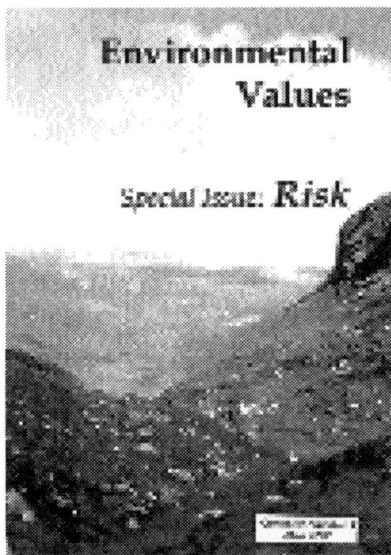

Environmental Values

Special Issue: *Risk*

ENVIRONMENTAL VALUES is concerned with the basis and justification of environmental policy. It aims to bring together contributions from philosophy, law, economics and other disciplines, which relate to the present and future environment of humans and other species; and to clarify the relationship between practical policy issues and more-fundamental underlying principles or assumptions.

The White Horse Press, 10 High Street, Knapwell, Cambridge CB3 8NR, UK
ISSN: 0963-2719 Quarterly (February, May, August, November)
Vol. 9, 2000, 144 pages per issue. Includes annual index.

Institutions: (1 year) £96 ($155 US)

(Institutional Rate Includes ELECTRONIC ACCESS)

Individual (1 year) £40 ($65 US)

Student/unwaged (1year) £30 ($50 US)

Official Journal of the International Association for
Environmental Philosophy

Environmental Philosophy

$40 ($25 for students) annually with membership to International
Association for Environmental Philosophy

$25 individual non-membership subscription

Send payment to:
Kenneth Maly
Department of Philosophy
University of Wisconsin-LaCrosse,
LaCrosse, WI 54601

Published by the International Association for Environmental Philosophy, the University
of Wisconsin-LaCrosse and the Division of the Environment, University of Toronto

www.ingramcontent.com/pod-product-compliance
Lightning Source LLC
Chambersburg PA
CBHW021554210326
41599CB00010B/445